Lecture Notes in Computer Science   7644

Commenced Publication in 1973
Founding and Former Series Editors:
Gerhard Goos, Juris Hartmanis, and Jan van Leeuwen

Andrey Bogdanov   Somitra Sanadhya (Eds.)

Security, Privacy, and Applied Cryptography Engineering

Second International Conference, SPACE 2012
Chennai, India, November 3-4, 2012
Proceedings

 Springer

Volume Editors

Andrey Bogdanov
KU Leuven
ESAT/SCD/COSIC
Kasteelpart Arenberg 10
3001 Leuven-Heverlee, Belgium
E-mail: andrey.bogdanov@esat.kuleuven.be

Somitra Sanadhya
IIIT Delhi
Okhla Industrial Area, Phase III
New Delhi, India 110020
E-mail: somitra@iiitd.ac.in

ISSN 0302-9743   e-ISSN 1611-3349
ISBN 978-3-642-34415-2   e-ISBN 978-3-642-34416-9
DOI 10.1007/978-3-642-34416-9
Springer Heidelberg Dordrecht London New York

Library of Congress Control Number: 2012949648

CR Subject Classification (1998): E.3, C.2, K.6.5, D.4.6, J.1, G.2.1

LNCS Sublibrary: SL 4 – Security and Cryptology

Typesetting: Camera-ready by author, data conversion by Scientific Publishing Services, Chennai, India

Printed on acid-free paper

Springer is part of Springer Science+Business Media (www.springer.com)

Preface

This volume contains the papers presented at SPACE 2012: the International Conference on Security, Privacy and Applied Cryptography Engineering held during November 2–3, 2012, in Chennai, India. This year's conference had a focus on the latter aspect—applied cryptography and cryptographic engineering. We believe that cryptology is an applied science in its essence which makes the areas in question most impactful.

We received 61 submissions. The Program Committee completed 203 reviews. Eleven papers were accepted for publication. We had four keynote talks on top of that, delivered by Thomas Peyrin, Bart Preneel, Pierangela Samarati and Berk Sunar, being top notch researchers in their respective domains.

The two core days of the conference were accompanied by four days of special-purpose tutorials. There were two days of pre-conference and two days of post-conference workshops. The workshops covered a wide array of topics ranging from mobile platform security, side channel attacks in cryptography to the provable security of cryptographic protocols. The speakers were eminent researchers from the world of industry and academia.

This was the second conference in the SPACE series. The first conference was named InfoSecHiComNet 2011 and its proceedings were published as LNCS volume 7011 in 2011. The Program Chairs of that conference—Marc Joye, Michael Tunstall, and Debdeep Mukhopadhyay—worked hard to start this series of conference. We are extremely thankful to these founders of the conference for establishing a solid platform for us, building on which has been easy.

SPACE 2012 was held in cooperation with the International Association for Cryptologic Research (IACR). We are extremely thankful to its current President, Bart Preneel, for awarding this status. This without doubt helped considerably to make this year's conference a success.

We would like to acknowledge the General Chairs Sanjay Burman and V. Kamakoti for the successful organization of the conference. They not only took pains to ensure the smooth running of the workshops and the conference, but also worked hard to get all the funding for the events. This event could not have been held without the energy and effort put in by the General Chairs. Special thanks go to Swarup Bhunia, who worked tirelessly as the Publicity Chair of the conference. Debdeep Mukhopadhyay was helpful at every stage of the conference organization. We would have found it hard to make it a successful event without the timely help of all of them.

The administration of IIT Madras was extremely positive and helpful in the organization of the conference. They warmly agreed to extend all support and facilities for SPACE 2012. Most of the speakers and guests of SPACE were housed in the excellent guest house of IIT Madras. The Society for Electronic Transactions and Security (SETS), Chennai, kindly provided their space and resources for organizing the workshops. We are especially thankful to the director of SETS, R. Balasubramaniam, for all the help extended. SETS also provided us the formal legal umbrella under which we could apply to the IACR to hold this event.

We were lucky to find generous funding support from various agencies. We are particularly thankful to the Ministry of Information Technology, who funded us under the Information Security Education and Awareness (ISEA) scheme. We take this opportunity to warmly appreciate the funding support from the Defense Research and Development Organization (DRDO), Government of India and Center of Excellence in Cryptology (CoEC), Kolkata. Besides these, we also received industry funds. We would like to thank all our sponsors for the support they provided.

We thank all authors of submitted papers for considering SPACE 2012 to publish their work. Last but by no means least, we would like to thank the Program Committee members of SPACE 2012 for their numerous reviews and enlightening discussions that were a tremendous help in the challenging task of selecting papers for presentation.

September 2012   Andrey Bogdanov
                                                        Somitra Sanadhya

Organization

Program Committee

Rafael Accorsi	University of Freiburg, Germany
Toru Akishita	Sony Corporation, Japan
Elena Andreeva	COSIC, Katholieke Universiteit Leuven, Belgium
Andrey Bogdanov	COSIC, Katholieke Universiteit Leuven, Belgium
Rajat Subhra Chakraborty	IIT Kharagpur, India
Donghoon Chang	IIIT Delhi, India
Carlos Cid	Information Security Group, Royal Holloway, University of London, UK
Abhijit Das	IIT Kharagpur, India
Kris Gaj	George Mason University, USA
Craig Gentry	IBM, USA
Dieter Gollmann	Hamburg University of Technology, Germany
Johann Johann Großschädl	University of Luxembourg, Luxembourg
Tim Gueneysu	Horst Görtz Institute for IT-Security, Ruhr-University Bochum, Germany
Tibor Jager	Karlsruhe Institute of Technology, Germany
Marc Joye	Technicolor, France
Stefan Katzenbeisser	Technische Universität Darmstadt, Germany
Çetin Kaya Koç	University of California Santa Barbara, USA
Ilya Kizhvatov	Riscure, The Netherlands
Tanja Lange	Technische Universiteit Eindhoven, The Netherlands
Gregor Leander	Technical University of Denmark, Denmark
Kerstin Lemke-Rust	Hochschule Bonn-Rhein-Sieg, Germany
Dongdai Lin	State Key Laboratory of Information Security, Institute of Information Engineering, Chinese Academy of Sciences, China
Keith Martin	Information Security Group, Royal Holloway, University of London, UK
Debdeep Mukhopadhyay	IIT Kharagpur, India
David Naccache	Ecole normale supérieure, France
Arpita Patra	ETH Zurich, Switzerland
Joachim Posegga	Institute for IT Security and Security Law (ISL) University of Passau, Germany
Bart Preneel	COSIC, Katholieke Universiteit Leuven, Belgium

Francesco Regazzoni	ALaRI Institute, University of Lugano, Switzerland
Vincent Rijmen	COSIC, Katholieke Universiteit Leuven, Belgium
Matt Robshaw	Orange Labs, France
Bimal Roy	Indian Statistical Institute, Kolkata, India
Pierangela Samarati	Università degli Studi di Milano, Italy
Somitra Sanadhya	IIIT Delhi, India
Sumanta Sarkar	University of Calgary, Canada
Martijn Stam	University of Bristol, UK
François-Xavier Standaert	UCL Crypto Group, Belgium
Berk Sunar	Worcester Polytechnic Institute (WPI), USA
Michael Tunstall	University of Bristol, UK
Gilles Van Assche	STMicroelectronics, Belgium
Bo-Yin Yang	Academia Sinica, Taiwan
Jianying Zhou	Institute for Infocomm Research, Singapore

Additional Reviewers

Aagren, Martin
Akdemir, Kahraman
Ali, Sk. Subidh
Ardagna, Claudio Agostino
Arnold, Michael
Bard, Gregory
Barenghi, Alessandro
Bartkewitz, Timo
Bernhard, David
Bilal, Zeeshan
Braun, Bastian
Buhan-Dulman, Ileana
Böhl, Florian
C. Ramanna, Somindu
Chen, Yu
Choudhury, Ashish
Chu, Cheng-Kang
Daemen, Joan
Delerablée, Cécile
Durvaux, David
El Aimani, Laila
Foresti, Sara
Gonzales Cerveron, Maria Teresa
Grosso, Vincent
Habib, Bilal
Hammouri, Ghaith

Hanley, Neil
Herrmann, Mathias
Herrmann, Michael
Hiwatari, Harunaga
Homsirikamol, Ekawat
Jacob, Nisha
Kamel, Dina
Karakoyunlu, Deniz
Kasem-Madani, Saffija
Kohlweiss, Markulf
Kusakawa, Masafumi
Lepoint, Tancrède
Liu, Peng
Maes, Roel
May, Alex
Mischke, Oliver
Naya-Plasencia, María
Nitaj, Abderrahmane
Oswald, David
Pandit, Tapas
Pashalidis, Andreas
Peeters, Michaël
Peters, Thomas
Poeppelmann, Thomas
Rebeiro, Chester
Ren, Kui

Rial, Alfredo
Rogawski, Marcin
Ruj, Sushmita
Schreckling, Daniel
Sen Gupta, Sourav
Shahid, Rabia
Sharif, Malik Umar
Striecks, Christoph
Tumeo, Antonino

Velegalati, Rajesh
Vercauteren, Frederik
von Maurich, Ingo
Witteman, Marc
Wojcik, Marcin
Xu, Jia
Xu, Zhiqian
Zhou, Yongbin

Table of Contents

A Novel Circuit Design Methodology to Reduce Side Channel Leakage

Andreas Gornik, Ivan Stoychev, and Jürgen Oehm

Ruhr-Universität Bochum, Analogue Integrated Circuits Research Group,
Universitätsstraße 150, 44780 Bochum, Germany
http://www.ais.ruhr-uni-bochum.de

Abstract. To estimate the probable information leakage of a logic circuit through a side channel is a major problem for circuit designers. In this paper a novel circuit design methodology is presented to estimate and reduce the side channel leakage of logic gates. The focus lies on the investigation of side channel leakage during circuit design. With this novel methodology three different logic circuit families are compared. Additionally, the process of improving a logic circuit using this methodology is shown in detail.

Keywords: circuit design, DPA countermeasures, side channel leakage.

1 Introduction

Beside the classical cryptanalysis, side channel attacks can be used to break cryptographic systems. These side channel attacks use the information that is presented by the physical implementation of the system. This information can be e.g. the execution time of an operation, the electromagnetic radiation or the current consumption of the cryptographic system. The latter became very popular for attackers since the publication of differential power analysis (DPA) attacks [1], because only low cost equipment is needed for this kind of attack.

As a consequence, circuit designers developed countermeasures to reduce the information leakage through the power consumption. But the effectiveness of these countermeasures can only be checked after the whole system is implemented. This leads to extreme costs for the development, if the circuit designer does not have a possibility to check the probable information leakage of the circuit during the design process.

Therefore a design tool is needed which helps to predict the effectiveness of a side channel countermeasure during the circuit design. Such a design tool for circuit design on the transistor level is not known to the authors, until now. Thus a new methodology to reduce the possible information leakage during the design of logic gates on the transistor level is presented in this paper.

The remainder of this article is structured as follows: in Sect. 2 a categorization of countermeasures is done and the actual work is arranged according to this categorization. In the next section the mathematical concept for the analysis of the circuits is explained, which is implemented in an analysis methodology

A. Bogdanov and S. Sanadhya (Eds.): SPACE 2012, LNCS 7644, pp. 1–15, 2012.

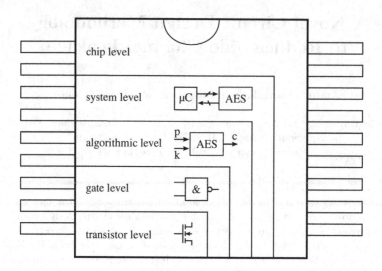

Fig. 1. Design levels

described in Sect. 4. The results of the analysis of three logic styles are presented in Sect. 5. These results are used to improve a logic gate with the analysis methodology which is presented in Sect. 6. The article closes with a conclusion and an outlook in Sect. 7.

2   Categorization of DPA-Countermeasures

The countermeasures against DPA attacks can be divided by their level of integration, like in a top to bottom design. Therefore there is a chip level, a system level, an algorithmic level, a gate level and finally a transistor level as depicted in Fig. 1.

On the chip level several countermeasures were proposed like e.g. introducing noise on the supply voltage lines by randomly switching loads [2], or buffering the supply voltage with capacitors [3]. These measures are often implemented in one circuitry which protects the whole chip. Because of this, less circuit area is used as with other protection on gate or transistor level. The weakness of such circuits is, if they can be overridden, the whole chip is unprotected. Additionally they only try to hide the information leakage from lower levels, without the prevention of leakage where it occurs e.g. at the gate or transistor level.

The next level of protection is the system level. In contrast to the chip level, the protection against leakage is included in the system architecture. One concept is introduced in [4], where a session key is generated from a main key, and each key function is separately protected against DPA. Using FPGAs there is the possibility to take unused circuitry for generating noise on the supply lines, randomize the clock or prevent clock frequency manipulations [5].

On the algorithmic level the encryption algorithm is modified to complicate DPA attacks. This can be done e.g. by masking the bits which are operated [6], randomization of the processed data [7], a combination of masking and randomization [8] or by randomly inserted delays [9].

The next level from top to bottom is the gate level. On this level new logic gates with less information leakage are created by using standard cells (logic gates provided by a chip manufacturer). This is quite popular, because it is cheaper and needs less circuit design knowledge than a full custom design of new standard cells. To complicate DPA some circuit designers try to make the current consumption more symmetric or invariant [10], insert random delays [11] or mask the data [12,13].

At the bottom is the transistor level. To get a protection against leakage on this level, there has to be a full custom design for all logic gates which will be used in a design. Hence this kind of protection needs more time and effort than the levels discussed before and additionally an experienced circuit designer to avoid information leakages. Because of this the levels above, especially the system and algorithmic level, are more popular for developing DPA countermeasures. Nonetheless there have been several proposals to build up logic gates with reduced information leakage. This is justified by the possibility to reduce the information leakage where it occurs, in the transistor switching. All other levels can only try to hide this leakage, but cannot prevent it.

Most of the proposed circuits focus on equal power consumption for each transition and are therefore differential (dual rail) circuits. These circuits can be divided into static [14,15] and dynamic respectively pre-charged circuits [16]. There are also circuits which use random switching to protect against DPA [17,18].

The main problem designing logic circuits with a resistance against DPA attacks, is to measure the information leakage. On levels above the transistor level, there is a relatively quick possibility to synthesize the circuit by a digital design flow, and to simulate the current consumption of the system. These simulation can be used for an DPA attack to get a rough estimation of its resistance.

On the transistor level, everything has to be designed manually, and every gate has to be checked by itself. The first proposals for checking the side channel leakage of a logic gate was to calculate the normalized standard deviation (NSD) of the current or the normalized energy deviation (NED) of the energy consumption [19]. These measures could be used for classifying differential logic gates. Due to the nature of the standard deviation, the NSD gives only a very rough estimation if a gate has equal power consumption as discussed in Sect. 3. The NED cannot be used generally, because it is tailored for the use with dynamic logic circuits which is also discussed in the next section of this paper.

Another proposed measure is based on the information theoretic evaluation of information leaking from logic gates [20,21]. But this method still does not deliver information that can be used for circuit design. Thus a new analytical concept is introduced in the next section.

3   Analytical Concept

To get a measure for a probable information leakage, it has to be explored where the leakage comes from. Most implementations of logic styles with a resistance against DPA use differential circuits. For these circuits each transition of the input and output signals should generate the same amount of current which flows through the logic gate. Therefore it has to be checked, if the current is always the same for each transition.

One way to get a measure for the current I_{dyn}, that is generated by a transition from state X to state Y, is to calculate the integral of the absolute value:

$$flow(X \rightarrow Y) = \int_{t_0}^{t_0+T} |I_{\text{dyn}}| \, dt \; . \tag{1}$$

The absolute value is used to take the negative part of the current trace into account, which would normally reduce the value of the integral. For the comparison of the current flow for each transition, a transition matrix $\mathbf{T}$ can be built by using the calculated *flow*. Equation (2) shows such a transition matrix for a logic gate with two input signals. In this matrix each state is represented by its decimal value. For example $3 \rightarrow 2$ stands for $\binom{A}{B} = \binom{1}{1} \rightarrow \binom{1}{0}$, where $\binom{A}{B}$ is the combination of the input signals A and B.

The transitions and with this the *flow* are time invariant, which means that it does not matter at which time they occur. Thus propagation times do not play a role for this metric when a signal change happens after the output signal of the circuit under test is stable. A change of the input signals during the change of the output signal is not predictable and can have a unmanageable amount of possibilities of occurrence. Because of that, the signal changes for the transitions $1 \rightarrow 2$ and respectively $2 \rightarrow 1$ are assumed to happen at the same time.

$$\mathbf{T} = \begin{pmatrix} 0 \rightarrow 0 & 0 \rightarrow 1 & 0 \rightarrow 2 & 0 \rightarrow 3 \\ 1 \rightarrow 0 & 1 \rightarrow 1 & 1 \rightarrow 2 & 1 \rightarrow 3 \\ 2 \rightarrow 0 & 2 \rightarrow 1 & 2 \rightarrow 2 & 2 \rightarrow 3 \\ 3 \rightarrow 0 & 3 \rightarrow 1 & 3 \rightarrow 2 & 3 \rightarrow 3 \end{pmatrix} \tag{2}$$

The values in this matrix give an overview how the *flow* differs between the transitions and can be used by a circuit designer to improve a logic gate at the transistor level, as shown in Sect. 6. But this is not sufficient to characterize the overall leakage of a logic gate. To gain a more detailed measure, the difference between the current of two transitions $I_{\text{dyn},1}$ and $I_{\text{dyn},2}$ over a time T is examined. For this (1) is extended and called *verbosity*, because this is the information that leaks to the attacker.

$$verbosity = \frac{1}{T} \cdot \int_{t_0}^{t_0+T} ||I_{\text{dyn},1}| - |I_{\text{dyn},2}|| \, dt \tag{3}$$

In this equation the absolute value is used to take account of all parts of the current being positive or negative, or the current $I_{dyn,2}$ greater than $I_{dyn,1}$.

To get a *verbosity* which is independent from the amplitude of the current, the current is set into relation to the sum of the two currents as shown in (4). This value is called *relative verbosity*, short *RV*.

$$RV = \frac{\frac{1}{T} \cdot \int\limits_{t_0}^{t_0+T} ||I_{dyn,1}| - |I_{dyn,2}|| \, dt}{\frac{1}{T} \cdot \int\limits_{t_0}^{t_0+T} |I_{dyn,1}| + |I_{dyn,2}| \, dt} = \frac{\int\limits_{t_0}^{t_0+T} ||I_{dyn,1}| - |I_{dyn,2}|| \, dt}{\int\limits_{t_0}^{t_0+T} |I_{dyn,1}| + |I_{dyn,2}| \, dt} \qquad (4)$$

With this measure the current of two transitions can be compared. This example is extended to all possible combinations of the transitions. The result is the *total relative verbosity*, short *TRV*:

$$TRV = \frac{1}{N} \cdot \sum_{i=1}^{n-1} \sum_{k=i}^{n-1} \frac{\int\limits_{t_0}^{t_0+T} ||I_{dyn,i}| - |I_{dyn,k+1}|| \, dt}{\int\limits_{t_0}^{t_0+T} |I_{dyn,i}| + |I_{dyn,k+1}| \, dt} . \qquad (5)$$

Where N denotes the number of all possible combinations of the transitions and n stands for the number of all possible transitions of the logic gate under test. N can be calculated with the help of n:

$$N = \sum_{m=1}^{n-1} m = \frac{n(n-1)}{2} . \qquad (6)$$

The *TRV* can be used by a circuit designer to compare logic gates within one logic family or to compare logic families with each other as shown in Sect. 5.

The former proposed measures NSD and NED [19] base on the standard deviation of the measured/simulated current trace respectively the minimum and maximum values of the energy per cycle:

$$NSD = \frac{\sigma}{\mu} \qquad (7)$$

$$NED = \frac{\max(energy/cycle) - \min(energy/cycle)}{\max(energy/cycle)} . \qquad (8)$$

Where σ stands for the standard deviation and μ for the mean of the trace under investigation. The NSD can be used to analyze several clock cycles, or complete transition schemes. Because it is based on the standard deviation, it cannot show the absolute difference between transitions. In addition the standard deviation depends on the switching activity of the analyzed circuit. If the switching activity is not equal for all circuits under test, it is not a meaningful measure. Another drawback of the NSD is that the standard deviation is divided by the mean of the analyzed trace. A large value of the mean, which can be generated easily by a large DC power consumption, can falsify this measure, too. Hence the NSD is only a rough measure for the difference between transitions or the resistance against side channel attacks.

When the cycle for the NED is interpreted as one clock cycle, this measure can only be used for dynamic logic circuits, because only these circuits have two separate current/energy peaks per cycle. Static logic circuits only have one significant energy peak per cycle and therefore they cannot be compared with this measure. A possible extension could be to regard several transitions as one cycle. But then the NED has still the drawback, that only the maximum and the minimum energy is compared and all values in between are ignored.

In addition, the NED is based on the energy which is drawn by the circuit as its name says. To calculate the energy the following equations are used:

$$E = \int_{t_0}^{t_0+T} u(t) \cdot i(t) dt \tag{9}$$

In a simulation environment the voltage $u(t)$ is normally constant. Hence only the integral over the current $i(t)$ is calculated, where negative parts of the current compensate positive parts and thus some information is lost.

Compared to NSD the *verbosity* measures are more accurate, because all transitions are compared exactly with each other and it is independent from the DC power consumption. Regarding the NED we get more information about the traces with the *verbosity*, because the absolute values are calculated here. Additionally we get an overall measure for all transition (TRV), as well as information about each transition through the transition matrix $\mathbf{T}$.

4 Methodology

A proposal for a methodology that uses the presented analytical concept is shown in Fig. 2. A circuit designer creates a logic gate with a program for schematic entry and generates a netlist for the test circuit. This netlist is simulated with an analog circuit simulator and the resulting current traces are evaluated with a script, which generates the values for the TRV and the transition matrix. In the remainder of this section these parts are described in detail.

4.1 Circuit Netlist

The netlists for the examined logic gates were built with a design kit for a 90 nm process. Then these gate netlists were placed in a test circuit which fits to the amount of input signals of the logic gate. A test circuit for a gate with two input signals is depicted in Fig. 3.

The logic gate in this test circuit is driven by two input signals A and B. These signals are combined in such a way, that each transition of the input signal, e.g. $\binom{A}{B} = \binom{1}{0} \rightarrow \binom{0}{1}$, occurs only once. In this way unnecessary transitions are avoided and the simulation time is minimized. To represent the use in a

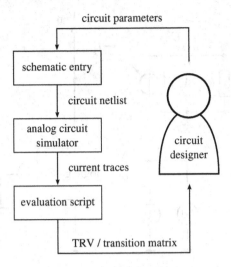

Fig. 2. Methodology

digital circuit, the logic gate drives a capacitive load C_L. In order to obtain information about the current consumption for each transition, only the dynamic current which is generated by each transition is investigated. This is necessary to compare logic gates with high static current consumption with those that have a low leakage current.

To separate the dynamic part of the current from the static part, a first order RC-filter with a cutoff frequency of:

$$\omega_g = \frac{1}{RC} = 1\,\frac{1}{s} \tag{10}$$

$$\Rightarrow f_g = \frac{\omega_g}{2\pi} \approx 0,16\,\text{Hz} \tag{11}$$

is used. This filter only works for an input voltage, therefore the current I_{gate} is transformed to a voltage V_{gate} with a conversion factor of 1. This is done by a current controlled voltage source. The output voltage of the filter V_{dyn} is equivalent to the dynamic current generated by the logic gate. This kind of filtering can be accepted, because the dynamic behavior of the current is negligible altered. The resulting netlist is then simulated with an analog circuit simulator.

4.2 Analog Circuit Simulator

A numerical correct subtraction is only achieved if minuend and subtrahend are vectors with the same length, which are in this case the simulated current traces. Therefore an analog circuit simulator is needed which generates data only with equally spaced time steps. Some of the simulators generate additional time steps at times when special events occur and break this equal spacing. Such simulators cannot be used for this kind of operation.

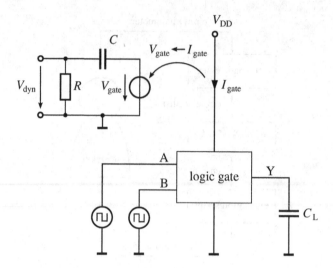

Fig. 3. Test circuit for logic gates with two input signals

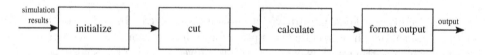

Fig. 4. Structure of the used evaluation script

4.3 Evaluation Script

The results of the analog circuit simulator have to be further processed. This is done by an evaluation script (cf. Fig. 4).

The simulation results are imported into the script and all used variables are set, like the period of the transitions and the number of input signals of the analyzed gate. Then the amount of points per current trace is calculated from the start and end point of the measured current. According to this data the trace is cut into pieces to get one current trace for each transition. These traces, which are vectors with an equal amount of points, are afterwards used for the calculation of the verbosity and to generate the transition matrix $\mathbf{T}$ as described in Sect. 3. To minimize the error which is introduced by cutting the current traces, a mathematical extension of the trace is done as follows. Normally a capacitor needs an infinite amount of time to completely discharge because of:

$$V_C(t) = V_0 \cdot e^{-\frac{t}{\tau}}; \quad \tau = R \cdot C \ . \tag{12}$$

Thus the voltage V_{dyn} would need an infinite amount of time to reach zero. This creates an error in the calculation of the TRV, because a part of the trace is cut off. To compensate this error the value of the following analytical integral has to be solved:

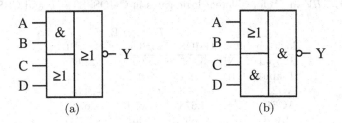

Fig. 5. (a) MAOI gate, (b) MOAI gate

$$\int_{t_0}^{\infty} |||I_{\text{dyn},1}| - |I_{\text{dyn},2}||\, dt \ = \int_{t_0}^{\infty} |||V_{\text{dyn},1} \cdot e^{-\frac{t}{\tau}}| - |V_{\text{dyn},2} \cdot e^{-\frac{t}{\tau}}||\, dt \qquad (13)$$

$$= (|||V_{\text{dyn},1}| - |V_{\text{dyn},2}|||) \cdot \int_{t_0}^{\infty} e^{-\frac{t}{\tau}}\, dt \ = |||V_{\text{dyn},1}| - |V_{\text{dyn},2}||| \cdot \tau \qquad (14)$$

For the used cutoff frequency of $\omega_g = 1\,\frac{1}{s}$ follows that $\tau = 1\,s$. Therefore only the difference of the last points of the cut traces have to be added to the numerical integration for the *TRV*. With this method, the traces can be reduced in length and hence the calculation time and data storage can be reduced also without loosing accuracy.

5   Results

As described in Sect. 2 the methodology is developed for symmetric differential logic styles. Thus we compare two symmetric and differential logic styles, *Charge Recycling Sense Amplifier Based Logic* (CRSABL) with feedback circuit [16] and a subthreshold implementation of *Source Coupled Logic* (SCL) [22], with standard CMOS logic. The special variant of SCL is used (also known as MCML), because of the lower power consumption compared to standard implementations. To distinguish between the SCL flavors we call the SCL logic gates which work in subthreshold region STSCL. It was shown, that SCL gates in general leak less information than standard CMOS gates [14,15].

A VHDL description for a PRESENT S-Box [23] was written and synthesized. The logic gates, that are needed to build the gate netlists, were designed for each logic style and with them the S-Box circuit. MAOI and MOAI gates shown in Fig. 5 are not as common as AO or AOI gates, but are needed to minimize the gate netlist of the S-Box implementation.

All logic gates and S-Box implementations were analyzed with the presented methodology. For CRSABL the pre-charge phase and the evaluate phase are taken into account for the analysis.

In Tab. 1 the results for the *TRV* are shown. The *TRV* is a measure for the difference between current traces, therefore values near to zero are better than

Table 1. *TRV* in dB for different logic gates in CMOS, STSCL and CRSABL

logic circuit	CMOS	*TRV* / dB STSCL	CRSABL
2 input NAND	-5.255	-8.992	-22.655
2 input NOR	-5.031	-8.995	-23.129
AO21	-6.730	-7.780	-24.374
AO31	-7.678	-7.394	-26.495
MAOI	-7.896	-8.461	-25.047
MOAI	-7.785	-8.484	-25.894
S-Box	-7.956	-10.167	-27.014

greater ones. To see the differences between the values more clearly, the *TRV* is given in decibel, hence large negative values are better than small ones.

The results show that all S-Box circuits have a better *TRV* than each of the single gates. The reason might be the simultaneously switching of all involved gates, which possibly equals out differences between the transitions of single logic gates. It can be seen, that both differential logic styles have better results than CMOS, as expected. But it is also noticeable, that CRSABL is much better than STSCL. The reason for this is explored in the next section.

6   Improvement of a Logic Gate

Regarding the transition matrix $\mathbf{T}_{\text{CRSABL}}$ of the CRSABL NAND gate, it can be seen, that all values are nearly in the same range, which is clear because of the *TRV* in dB (TRV_{dB}) of $-22.66\,$dB. These low values derive from the structure of CRSABL, because it uses a pre-charge an an evaluation phase to achieve an equal current flow for each transition.

$$\mathbf{T}_{\text{CRSABL}} = \begin{pmatrix} 5.83 & 5.91 & 5.89 & 5.89 \\ 5.77 & 5.81 & 5.85 & 5.84 \\ 5.81 & 5.82 & 5.77 & 5.90 \\ 6.28 & 6.28 & 6.28 & 6.29 \end{pmatrix} \cdot 10^{-3} \tag{15}$$

In comparison, a non optimized standard implementation of a STSCL NAND gate, depicted in Fig. 6(a), is examined. This 2 input STSCL NAND is chosen as example, because the optimization can be followed more easily. This circuit was not used for calculating the results in Sect. 5, but the improved one presented later in this section.

The PMOS transistors are used as a resistive load for the gate to generate the output voltage. The corresponding transition matrix $\mathbf{T}_{\text{STSCL,asym}}$ is shown in (16). It depicts that single transition values vary a lot from each other which can also be seen in the low TRV_{dB} of $-6.81\,$dB.

$$\mathbf{T}_{\text{STSCL,asym}} = \begin{pmatrix} 0 & 0.59 & 2.34 & 3.57 \\ 0.54 & 0 & 2.58 & 3.25 \\ 2.15 & 3.93 & 0 & 3.22 \\ 3.69 & 2.20 & 2.98 & 0 \end{pmatrix} \cdot 10^{-7} \tag{16}$$

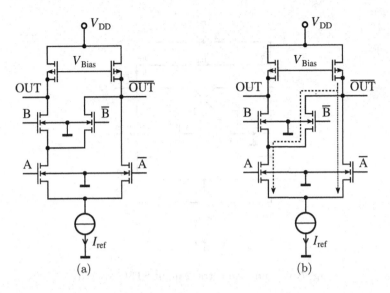

Fig. 6. (a) Asymmetric 2 input STSCL NAND, (b) same with current paths

Regarding the complementary transitions $2 \to 1 \,/\, 1 \to 2$ and $3 \to 1 \,/\, 1 \to 3$, the values have a bigger difference than other complementary transitions such as $0 \to 1 \,/\, 1 \to 0$. This can be explained by the structure of the circuit. For the state $\binom{A}{B} = \binom{1}{0} = 2$ the left current path in Fig. 6(b) is active. If this state changes to $\binom{A}{B} = \binom{0}{1} = 1$, then the right current path is active. These two paths are not the same, because in the left path the capacitances of an additional transistor have to be charged and thus a different amount of current is flowing. This is the same with the complementary transitions $3 \to 1 \,/\, 1 \to 3$, but with different current paths. On the other hand, we get lower values for the transitions $0 \to 1 \,/\, 1 \to 0$, because the current flows through almost equal paths.

For an improvement of these values, the logic gate is modified as depicted in Fig. 7. The right current path is extended with a differential pair of NMOS transistors, so that it is equal to the left current path. With this the logic gates becomes symmetric regarding the output. Hence this gate is called output-symmetric.

The transition matrix $\mathbf{T}_{\text{STSCL,outsym}}$ of this gate shows an improvement in the complementary transitions that have been discussed. This is also displayed by the lower TRV_{dB} of $-7.13\,\text{dB}$. Although the complementary transitions have improved, there is still a big difference between the single transitions, e.g. if we compare $1 \to 0$ and $0 \to 3$. Because of this, the symmetry of the NAND gate has to be further improved.

$$\mathbf{T}_{\text{STSCL,outsym}} = \begin{pmatrix} 0 & 0.56 & 2.81 & 3.39 \\ 0.51 & 0 & 2.81 & 3.08 \\ 2.20 & 2.76 & 0 & 2.90 \\ 3.30 & 2.86 & 2.90 & 0 \end{pmatrix} \cdot 10^{-7} \qquad (17)$$

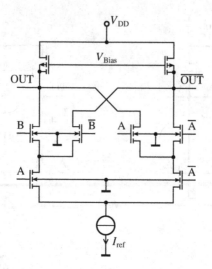

Fig. 7. Output-symmetric 2 input STSCL NAND

In Fig. 8 an input and output symmetric variant of the NAND gate is shown. The symmetry is achieved by adding the complementary paths for the signal B to the output-symmetric circuit.

As can be seen in $\mathbf{T}_{\text{STSCL,sym}}$, the values of the single transitions have been improved, as well as the TRV_{dB} value of $-8.99\,\text{dB}$. The symmetric implementation of the STSCL NAND gate was used for the overall comparison in Sect. 5.

$$\mathbf{T}_{\text{STSCL,sym}} = \begin{pmatrix} 0 & 1.04 & 1.02 & 3.11 \\ 0.97 & 0 & 2.31 & 2.67 \\ 0.97 & 2.32 & 0 & 2.67 \\ 3.10 & 2.23 & 2.21 & 0 \end{pmatrix} \cdot 10^{-7} \qquad (18)$$

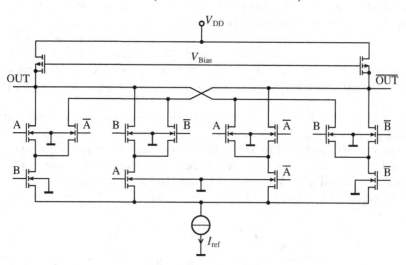

Fig. 8. Input and output symmetric 2 input STSCL NAND

In comparison to $\mathbf{T}_{CRSABL}$ the values for complementary transitions of the transition matrix $\mathbf{T}_{STSCL,sym}$ are quite close together, with the result, that these might be difficult to distinguish for an attacker. This is a result of the symmetry of the circuit. But the complementary transitions differ a lot from other complementary transitions and thus the overall leakage of the symmetric STSCL NAND gate is higher than the overall leakage of the CRSABL NAND gate, whose values for the complementary transitions are not that close together.

7   Conclusion and Outlook

In this paper a novel and unique design methodology to reduce the information leakage of differential logic gates has been presented. A comparison of three logic families using this methodology shows that STSCL gates and CRSABL gates leak less information than standard CMOS logic gates.

Furthermore the weaknesses of an asymmetric STSCL NAND gate were analyzed with the proposed design methodology. It was demonstrated how a circuit designer can reduce the information leakage of this gate by using the *TRV* and the transition matrix $\mathbf{T}$.

Although the methodology can be successfully used to reduce the probable information leakage of differential logic gates, there are still some open issues. For example mismatch through fabrication tolerances is not considered. Mismatch can lead to different results, because symmetric gates can be sensitive to mismatch in the transistor geometries and threshold voltages. Therefore a methodology to design gates with less influence from mismatch would be a great improvement. Another extension for this methodology would be the analysis of non differential logic gates or logic gates with a random or masked power consumption.

References

1. Kocher, P.C., Jaffe, J., Jun, B.: Differential Power Analysis. In: Wiener, M. (ed.) CRYPTO 1999. LNCS, vol. 1666, pp. 388–397. Springer, Heidelberg (1999)
2. Schneider, O., Uffmann, D.: Circuit Configuration for Generating Current Pulses in the Supply Current of Integrated Circuits. US Patent US 7, 017, 048 B2 (March 2006)
3. Shamir, A.: Protecting Smart Cards from Passive Power Analysis with Detached Power Supplies. In: Paar, C., Koç, Ç.K. (eds.) CHES 2000. LNCS, vol. 1965, pp. 71–77. Springer, Heidelberg (2000)
4. Medwed, M., Standaert, F.-X., Großschädl, J., Regazzoni, F.: Fresh Re-keying: Security against Side-Channel and Fault Attacks for Low-Cost Devices. In: Bernstein, D.J., Lange, T. (eds.) AFRICACRYPT 2010. LNCS, vol. 6055, pp. 279–296. Springer, Heidelberg (2010)
5. Güneysu, T., Moradi, A.: Generic Side-Channel Countermeasures for Reconfigurable Devices. In: Preneel, B., Takagi, T. (eds.) CHES 2011. LNCS, vol. 6917, pp. 33–48. Springer, Heidelberg (2011)
6. Oswald, E., Mangard, S., Pramstaller, N., Rijmen, V.: A Side-Channel Analysis Resistant Description of the AES S-Box. In: Gilbert, H., Handschuh, H. (eds.) FSE 2005. LNCS, vol. 3557, pp. 413–423. Springer, Heidelberg (2005)

7. Itoh, K., Yajima, J., Takenaka, M., Torii, N.: DPA Countermeasures by Improving the Window Method. In: Kaliski, B.S., Koç, Ç.K., Paar, C. (eds.) CHES 2002. LNCS, vol. 2523, pp. 303–317. Springer, Heidelberg (2003)
8. Herbst, C., Oswald, E., Mangard, S.: An AES Smart Card Implementation Resistant to Power Analysis Attacks. In: Zhou, J., Yung, M., Bao, F. (eds.) ACNS 2006. LNCS, vol. 3989, pp. 239–252. Springer, Heidelberg (2006)
9. Coron, J.S., Kizhvatov, I.: Analysis and Improvement of the Random Delay Countermeasure of CHES 2009. In: Mangard, S., Standaert, F.-X. (eds.) CHES 2010. LNCS, vol. 6225, pp. 95–109. Springer, Heidelberg (2010)
10. Tiri, K., Verbauwhede, I.: A Logic Level Design Methodology for a Secure DPA Resistant ASIC or FPGA Implementation. In: Proceedings on Design, Automation and Test in Europe Conference and Exhibition 2004, vol. 1, pp. 246–251. IEEE Computer Society (February 2004)
11. Bucci, M., Luzzi, R., Guglielmo, M., Trifiletti, A.: A Countermeasure against Differential Power Analysis based on Random Delay Insertion. In: IEEE International Symposium on Circuits and Systems, ISCAS 2005, vol. 4, pp. 3547–3550. IEEE (May 2005)
12. Popp, T., Mangard, S.: Masked Dual-Rail Pre-charge Logic: DPA-Resistance Without Routing Constraints. In: Rao, J.R., Sunar, B. (eds.) CHES 2005. LNCS, vol. 3659, pp. 172–186. Springer, Heidelberg (2005)
13. Fischer, W., Gammel, B.M.: Masking at Gate Level in the Presence of Glitches. In: Rao, J.R., Sunar, B. (eds.) CHES 2005. LNCS, vol. 3659, pp. 187–200. Springer, Heidelberg (2005)
14. Toprak, Z., Ienne, P., Paar, C.: Design of Low-Power DPA-Resistant Cryptographic Functional Units. In: Proceedings of the 1st ECRYPT Workshop on Cryptographic Advances in Secure Hardware, CRASH 2005 (2005)
15. Regazzoni, F., Badel, S., Eisenbarth, T., Groschdl, J., Poschmann, A., Toprak, Z., Macchetti, M., Pozzi, L., Paar, C., Leblebici, Y., Ienne, P.: Simulation-based Methodology for Evaluating DPA-Resistance of Cryptographic Functional Units with Application to CMOS and MCML Technologies. In: Proceedings of International Conference on Embedded Computer Systems: Architectures, Modeling, and Simulation (SAMOS IC 2007) (July 2007)
16. Tiri, K., Verbauwhede, I.: Charge Recycling Sense Amplifier Based Logic: Securing Low Power Security IC's against Differential Power Analysis. In: Proceeding of the 30th European Solid-State Circuits Conference, ESSCIRC 2004, pp. 179–182. IEEE (September 2004)
17. Suzuki, D., Saeki, M., Ichikawa, T.: Random Switching Logic: A Countermeasure against DPA based on Transition Probability. Techreport, Mitsubishi Electric Corporation, Mitsubishi Electric Engineering Company Limited, IACR ePrint (2004), eprint.iacr.org/2004/346.pdf
18. Chen, Z., Zhou, Y.: Dual-Rail Random Switching Logic: A Countermeasure to Reduce Side Channel Leakage. In: Goubin, L., Matsui, M. (eds.) CHES 2006. LNCS, vol. 4249, pp. 242–254. Springer, Heidelberg (2006)
19. Tiri, K., Akmal, M., Verbauwhede, I.: A Dynamic and Differential CMOS Logic with Signal Independent Power Consumption to Withstand Differential Power Analysis on Smart Cards. In: Proceedings of the 29th European Solid-State Circuits Conference, ESSCIRC 2002, pp. 403–406 (2002)

20. Standaert, F.-X., Malkin, T.G., Yung, M.: A Unified Framework for the Analysis of Side-Channel Key Recovery Attacks (extended version). Cryptology ePrint Archive, Report 2006/139 (2006)
21. Macé, F., Standaert, F.-X., Quisquater, J.-J.: Information Theoretic Evaluation of Side-Channel Resistant Logic Styles. In: Paillier, P., Verbauwhede, I. (eds.) CHES 2007. LNCS, vol. 4727, pp. 427–442. Springer, Heidelberg (2007)
22. Tajalli, A., Vittoz, E., Leblebici, Y., Brauer, E.: Ultra low Power Subthreshold MOS Current Mode Logic Circuits Using a Novel Load Device Concept. In: 33rd European on Solid State Circuits Conference, ESSCIRC 2007, pp. 304–307 (2007)
23. Poschmann, A.Y.: Lightweight Cryptography: Cryptographic Engineering for a Pervasive World. Europäischer Universitäts-Verlag (2009)

The Schedulability of AES as a Countermeasure against Side Channel Attacks

Stephane Fernandes Medeiros

Université libre de Bruxelles, Bruxelles, Belgium
stfernan@ulb.ac.be

Abstract. Side Channel Attacks are a major concern in modern security. Two main countermeasure techniques have been studied in order to counteract them: hiding and masking. Hiding techniques try to randomize the obtained traces by adding noise or by swapping instructions of the performed algorithm. In this work, we present a randomization of AES where AES operations can be executed even if previous operations, in the corresponding non-randomized execution of AES, are not finished. We present theoretical and practical results about the distribution of the execution times and show interesting results in comparison to existing techniques. An implementation is available on the author's website[1].

Keywords: Side Channel Attacks, Power Analysis Attacks, hiding, randomized execution, AES.

1 Introduction

Side Channel Attacks (SCA) exploit information leakage from cryptographic devices such as execution times [10], electromagnetic emanations [7] and power consumption [11].

Since their introduction by Kocher [11], Power Analysis Attacks have been widely studied in the literature [15–18] not only in order to improve these attacks but also to propose corresponding countermeasures. Power Analysis Attacks take advantage of the data-dependent power consumption of cryptographic devices to retrieve secret information such as a secret key. An attacker needs to measure several times the power consumption of a device performing cryptographic operations. Each of these measures is called a power trace, or simply a trace, and represents the power consumption of a single execution of the device. In most cases, Power Analysis Attacks exploit the fact that the device always performs the same operations at the same time for different traces. Therefore, for each moment of time, the instantaneous power consumption in all of the traces, collected on the same device for the same algorithm, will be linked to the same operation. Alignment of power traces hugely helps the attack to succeed but is not mandatory since alignment techniques exist. The attacker just needs to collect more traces if they are not aligned [13].

---

[1] http://homepages.ulb.ac.be/~stfernan/

A. Bogdanov and S. Sanadhya (Eds.): SPACE 2012, LNCS 7644, pp. 16–31, 2012.

Countermeasures against Power Analysis Attacks consist in breaking the dependency between used data and power consumption. To achieve this objective, those countermeasures can add secret masked values to the algorithm, and must therefore modify the algorithm to deal with these masks (masking countermeasures), so the power consumption will not only be linked to one secret value. Another possibility is to change the moment of time where an operation will take place by randomizing the sequence of operations (hiding countermeasures). Main approaches in hiding countermeasures are the reduction of the signal-to-noise ratio (SNR) and the randomized ordering of instructions [12].

A broad overview of SCA countermeasures can be found in [13] where Mangard et al. present, among other things related to Power Analysis Attacks, hiding and masking countermeasures at the software level, the hardware level and the logical level.

Daemen and Rijmen [4] already suggest, in 1999, some countermeasures against Power Analysis such as desynchronisation of power traces by adding dummy instructions, software balancing and power consumption randomization by using noisy hardware modules.

Clavier et al. [3] mention Random Process Interrupts as a countermeasure against Power Analysis. It consists in interleaving the code's execution with dummy instructions so that power traces are not aligned. Authors also show how to apply Power Analysis Attacks when such a countermeasure is implemented.

In [14], May et al. propose a new processor design that randomizes the instruction stream executed by the processor. Authors focus on DES [6] and integer multiplication used in RSA and EC-DSA. It is a general technique that can be applied to any cryptographic algorithm and which does not require changing the original algorithm.

Irwin et al. [9] also propose the modification of the instruction stream on non-deterministic processors as a countermeasure against Power Analysis Attacks. It identifies independent instructions in order to allow crossing their execution with the help of a mutation unit added to the conventional processor pipeline. It does not modify the executed algorithm since it is a general approach. Authors work in the context of AES [5].

In [19], Tillich et al. proposed a combination of hiding and masking countermeasures for AES where the hiding part consists in randomizing the execution of some rounds. When performing the AddRoundKey operation, it can operate on each byte in a non-deterministic way. The same holds for SubBytes and Mix-Columns operations. But each operation has to be finished in order to perform the next one and thus, each round has to be finished before starting the next one. Two consecutive AES executions will not produce the same power traces since it is possible for each operation, in the first and last rounds, to start from different STATE indexes.

1.1 Our Contribution

In this paper, we analyze the AES algorithm to allow permutation of operations at the algorithm level, e.g. to allow a SubBytes (SB) operation to be performed[2] on a byte before performing an AddRoundKey (ARK) operation on another byte. While our proposition suits AES by design, it can be adapted to other cryptographic primitives by analyzing the dependencies of their operations.

In Tillich's proposition [19], ARK operations have to be completely performed, no matter the order, before performing SB operations. Our contribution allows to perform an ARK on one byte directly followed by a SB on the same byte and then to execute another ARK on another byte, possibly followed by a MixColumns (MC) operation. Another difference is the fact that a masking countermeasure is used in Tillich's scheme. In this paper, we focus on the randomization of the execution. However, masking can be added to our proposition in order to improve the security of the scheme.

Our proposition consists in adding another program, a scheduler, that will ensure the correctness of the algorithm execution, i.e. ensure that each operation can be performed and is performed with correct inputs following the logic of the original algorithm. The original algorithm (AES in our case) has to be modified in order to be applied at byte level instead of being applied to 16 bytes at a time. SubBytes and AddRoundKey operations will be applied to one byte at a time while ShiftRows and MixColumns will be applied to four bytes at a time since these operations operate on a complete line or column. We do not modify the AES algorithm, we adapt it in such a way it can be applied at byte level, nevertheless all intermediate values computed are the same than in the original AES, except that these values are not necessarily computed at the same time than in the original version of AES.

The results of our theoretical analysis can be reused in any other scheduling research regarding AES's operations, as we provide their possible minimum and maximum execution time.

This paper is organized as follows: in Section 2, we discuss SCA and hiding countermeasures. Section 3 presents our proposition of schedulable AES. In Section 4, we analyze our scheduler proposition in a theoretical (4.1) and a practical (4.2) way. In Section 5, we experimentally compare our proposition to an unprotected scheme and to Tillich's scheme. We finally conclude our paper in Section 6.

2   Side Channel Countermeasures

SCA countermeasures are divided into two families: hiding countermeasures and masking countermeasures.

2.1   Hiding

Hiding countermeasures cover two domains: amplitude dimension and time dimension [13]. The first one changes the instantaneous power consumption by adding more noise and/or by reducing the signal. The second one tries to randomize the execution of the algorithm in order to obtain unaligned power traces.

---

[2] If certains pre-conditions are met as we explain in section 3.

Amplitude Dimension

To change the instantaneous power consumption, one has to modify the signal-to-noise ratio (SNR). Each instruction that does not belong to the cryptographic algorithm, performed in parallel with those of the cryptographic algorithm, will decrease the SNR by increasing the power consumption and thus adding more noise to the power traces. It is possible to use "noise engines" [2, 13] that will perform parallel instructions in order to increase the power consumption. Another countermeasure consists in trying to have a constant power consumption, but such a countermeasure is very difficult to achieve [13].

Time Dimension

Techniques to modify the time dimension of a trace, i.e. to change the instant where an instruction will be performed, are more numerous: skipping clock pulses, randomly changing the clock frequency, having multiple clock domains, inserting dummy instructions, inserting dummy clock cycles [1, 3, 4, 13], etc. All these techniques will modify the outline of the trace.

Shuffling [19] is another possibility to randomize the execution of an algorithm by swapping the order of its instructions' execution when allowed.

2.2   Masking

Masking [1, 13] intends to decorrelate the power consumption from the manipulated data by adding other secrets to the cryptographic process called the mask values. Key and Plaintext are masked at the start of the process. Masks can be arithmetic or boolean. The encryption algorithm has to be modified in order to deal with the masks. For instance, in AES, the Sbox has to be modified in order to respect the following constraint: $S'(m \oplus x) = S(x) \oplus m$, where m denotes the mask value and S the Sbox function, meaning that the output of the modified Sbox applied to a masked value has to be the same than the masked output of the original Sbox.

3   SchedAES

3.1   Notations

In the rest of the paper, we will use the following abbreviations and concepts. AES operations AddRoundKey, SubBytes, ShiftRows and MixColumns will be respectively denoted by the following abbreviations: ARK, SB, SR and MC. To identify the rounds and the bytes of STATE on which an operation is performed, indexes will be used in addition to the abbreviations, e.g. $ARK_{k,i,j}$ denotes the AddRoundKey operation of round k applied to the j-th byte of the i-th line of STATE[3]. SR and MC operations will only have two indexes: the round index and the line or column index. Finally, note that when a MC operation will be performed, all of the SR operations may not have been performed. This means

---

[3] For ease of coding, we assume STATE indexes start at 0.

that the bytes needed to perform the MC operation will not be aligned. The column index will thus denote a "virtual" column corresponding to the column of STATE as if all SR operations had been performed. Operations will be applied to one byte at a time for ARK and SB or to four bytes when performing SR or MC, and will not be applied on all the bytes of STATE at the same time.

3.2 Preconditions

As we mentioned above, it is possible to randomize some parts of AES such as the SubBytes operation by not performing it line by line and column by column but in a random order. It is also possible to use non-deterministic processors that will check for instructions' dependencies and allow swapping the order of non-dependent instructions.

Our proposition is to implement a scheduler that will control the execution of AES. The scheduler will manage a set of allowed operations Θ. After the execution of an operation (ARK, SB, SR or MC), it will check if further operations are allowed and add them to Θ. An operation can be added by the scheduler to Θ if all of its predecessors have been performed.

Initially, the set of allowed operations, Θ, will contain the 16 initial ARK operations:

$$\Theta = \{ARK_{0,i,j} \mid 0 \le i, j \le 3\}.$$

It corresponds to the initial AddRoundKey of AES. Note that in this first version of the scheduler, we assume that the Key Scheduling has already been done.

Other operations will be added[4] to Θ when the following preconditions are met:

SubBytes
$SB_{k,i,j}$ can be added to Θ when $ARK_{k-1,i,j}$ has been performed.

ShiftRows
ShiftRows is a particular operation because it is not mandatory to physically perform it. In our implementation we impose the following rule: $SR_{k,i}$ can be performed when all of the $ARK_{k-1,i,j}$, with $0 \le j \le 3$, have been done. When a SR operation has been performed on line i, SB and ARK operations, linked to line i, in Θ have to updated consecutively, e.g. if $ARK_{5,1,2}$ is in Θ and $SR_{5,1}$ has been executed then $ARK_{5,1,2}$ will be replaced by $ARK_{5,1,1}$. Furthermore, $SR_{k,i}$ can be executed only if $SR_{k-1,i}$ has already been done.

MixColumns
$MC_{k,j}$ can be added to Θ once all the SB_k corresponding to the j-th virtual column have been performed. Since all SR have not necessarily been performed,

---

[4] These operations are allowed to be performed once they are inserted in Θ the set of allowed operations.

the bytes MC will use will be located at physical column j if the SR operation has already been done for that line, or at physical column $(i + j) \bmod 4$ if there is still one SR operation to perform for line i. We do not take into account cases where more than one SR operation has to be performed for the same line due to the conditions we imposed above to the SR operations. Therefore, when we execute MC operations, we know that bytes are located at the correct column in STATE or are one SR late.

AddRoundKey
ARK_k operations will be added four at a time, one per line, after performing the corresponding $MC_{k-1,j}$ operation. Depending on the SR operations, $ARK_{k,i,j}$ or $ARK_{k,i,(i+j)mod4}$ will be added to Θ. For the ARK_{10} operation, the precondition has to be modified since there are no MC_{10} operations. $ARK_{10,i,j}$ will be added to Θ after the execution of $SB_{10,i,j}$.

3.3   Implementation Issues

We made several implementations of the scheduler. Code updates were always done in order to improve the overhead of the control structure. The first solution used 824 booleans[5], a set of all possible actions and one STATE matrix per round. Our second solution used 412 booleans[6], a set of possible actions and one STATE matrix. Our last implementation required only 40 8-bit integers[7], a set of possible actions and one STATE matrix. Note that the use of one STATE matrix per round has the drawback of hugely increasing the memory overhead but has the advantage that all operations can be performed on a single byte at a time, even MC and SR operations.

The Key Scheduling operation has not been taken into account in our scheduler because we wanted to focus on the main part of the algorithm. Therefore, we made the assumption that the Key Scheduling had already been performed. Note that it is possible to include the Key Scheduling by adding some preconditions: an ARK operation can be performed with the same precondition we already mentioned and if the subkey byte it will use is already computed.

The AES scheduler pseudo-code can be found in Appendix A. Algorithm 1 represents the main body of the scheduler with the initialization and the execution loop where the scheduler randomly picks an operation in Θ before performing it and updating Θ. Algorithm 2 is the main body of the update process of Θ, which consists in identifying the processed action α and calling the appropriate update fonction. Algorithms 3, 4, 5 and 6 show the update process to accomplish after performing each operation.

---

[5] Two booleans for each operation: one to know if the action can be performed and the second to know if the operation has been performed.
[6] To know if an action has been performed.
[7] To know for each action the last round index performed. 16 integers for ARK, 16 integers for SB, 4 integers for MC and 4 integers for SR.

3.4 Simulation Verification

In order to stochastically validate our scheme, we have performed 1,000,000 encryptions, with randomly chosen plaintexts and keys. These inputs were used with the normal AES scheme and with our SchedAES scheme. We have compared the outputs and obtained 100% matches.

4 Scheduler Analysis

4.1 Theoretical Analysis of SchedAES

In this section, we discuss some theoretical results such as the relative minimum and maximum instants of time where an operation can take place. By instant of time we mean the index of the instruction during the algorithm, e.g. an operation performed at time 0 will be the first operation executed. Since there are 412 operations in the algorithm, indexes will go from 0 to 411. To compute this information we recursively enumerate predecessors and successors of an operation. For instance, $ARK_{0,0,0}$ has no predecessor so its minimum execution time is 0 and 351 operations depend on it[8], so its maximum execution time is 60. Table 1 summarizes all the information about minimum and maximum execution time. Note that operations have been grouped by round since they have the same minimum and maximum values independently from the bytes indexes. These are theoretical results since they are based on precedence constraints and not on experimental observations.

Table 1. Minimum and maximum execution instant times

operation	min	max	operation	min	max	operation	min	max	operation	min	max
									ARK0	0	60
SB1	1	62	SR1	4	74	MC1	8	63	ARK1	9	100
SB2	10	102	SR2	41	114	MC2	48	103	ARK2	49	140
SB3	50	142	SR3	81	154	MC3	88	143	ARK3	89	180
SB4	90	182	SR4	121	194	MC4	128	183	ARK4	129	220
SB5	130	222	SR5	161	234	MC5	168	223	ARK5	169	260
SB6	170	262	SR6	201	274	MC6	208	263	ARK6	209	300
SB7	210	302	SR7	241	314	MC7	248	303	ARK7	249	340
SB8	250	342	SR8	281	354	MC8	288	343	ARK8	289	392
SB9	290	394	SR9	321	410	MC9	328	408	ARK9	329	408
SB10	330	410	SR10	361	411				ARK10	331	411

As we can see, the difference between minimum and maximum execution instant of time is quite large. The smallest difference is observed for MC1 to MC8 with 56 different moments of time where the operations can take place. The highest value is 104 for the SB9 operation. In comparison with Tillich's scheme,

---

[8] In other words, there are 60 operations that do not depend on it.

an initial AddRoundKey operation can take place at 61 different moments of time in our scheme instead of 16 moments of time in Tillich's scheme. While this number stays the same for all ARK operations in Tillich's scheme for each round, it varies from 61 to 102 (depending on the round) in ours.

4.2   Practical Analysis of SchedAES

Theoretical analysis, from the previous section, shows that there exist a lot of possibilities for an action to be performed at different instants of time. However, all these possibilities are not equiprobable: this means that for an initial $ARK_{0,i,j}$ operation to be executed at instant 60, all the operations independent of it have to be performed before. This scenario will, of course, happen less often than having a part of those operations to be performed before an $ARK_{0,i,j}$ operation. Minimum and maximum execution times are representative of *best case scenario* (each operation is executed as soon as possible) and *worst case scenario* (each operation is executed as late as possible). In order to collect practical information, we performed $1,000,000$ full AES encryptions with our scheduler. During each encryption we observed the instant of time when each operation is performed. Table 2 summarizes the results. For each operation, Table 2 gives the average moment of execution, its standard deviation and the moment of time when 75% and 90% of the operations have been performed. We grouped this empirical data information by operation for the same round without looking at indexes.

As we can see, it is theoretically possible to execute operations in a large time domain. Practically, due to randomization, the majority of operations are concentrated in a smaller part of their execution time domain. We observe that for the inner rounds (3 to 8) the standard deviation of each operation is almost the same. The standard deviation is smaller for the beginning operations due to the *lack* of possibilities when choosing operations. The standard deviation is greater for final operations than in inner rounds, except for the SR_{10} operation[9], taking advantage of the randomization of the entire scheme.

Despite the fact that a large range of execution times is available in theory, a smaller range arises in practice. This is due to the fact that for some operations to be performed at some later instants of time, it is necessary to execute almost all of the other operations. It is possible to try to get a larger range of execution times during the practical experiments by balancing the executions and trying to distribute the operations over time. However, this solution would require more computations and would thus leak more information about the decisions during these computations.

The first operation of our scheme is the weakest point of it because it offers the same randomness as in Tillich's scheme (16 possible ARK_0 operations in both cases). For the second operation to perform we still have 16 operations (15 ARK and 1 SB) that can be executed due to the fact that an SB operation has been added to Θ instead of 15 operations (15 ARK) in Tillich's scheme. In

---

[9] SR_{10} also has a smaller execution time domain (Table 1).

Table 2. Average and standard deviation of execution times

operation	avg	dev	75%	90%	operation	avg	dev	75%	90%
SB1	22.41	11.66	30	39	SR1	32.44	11.67	40	50
SB2	58.9	13.89	69	78	SR2	74.33	10.77	81	91
SB3	98.99	13.8	109	118	SR3	114.3	10.78	121	131
SB4	138.99	13.8	149	158	SR4	154.29	10.78	161	171
SB5	178.99	13.8	189	198	SR5	194.3	10.78	201	211
SB6	218.99	13.8	229	238	SR6	234.3	10.78	241	251
SB7	258.99	13.8	269	278	SR7	274.3	10.78	281	291
SB8	298.99	13.8	309	318	SR8	314.29	10.77	321	331
SB9	339.20	14.32	349	358	SR9	355.07	12.36	361	374
SB10	383.12	15.58	397	405	SR10	399.91	7.57	407	410
					ARK0	11.92	9.86	19	27
MC1	41.87	10.6	51	59	ARK1	50.68	12.47	61	67
MC2	81.86	10.34	91	99	ARK2	90.72	12.34	101	107
MC3	121.86	10.34	131	139	ARK3	130.72	12.33	141	147
MC4	161.86	10.34	171	179	ARK4	170.72	12.33	181	187
MC5	201.86	10.34	211	219	ARK5	210.72	12.33	221	227
MC6	241.86	10.34	251	259	ARK6	250.72	12.33	261	267
MC7	281.86	10.34	291	299	ARK7	290.72	12.33	301	307
MC8	321.86	10.34	331	339	ARK8	330.76	12.46	341	347
MC9	363.64	12.72	373	384	ARK9	373.82	14.96	386	396
					ARK10	391.04	14.85	405	410

Tillich's proposition, we are sure that the first 16 operations will all be ARK_0 operations: over $1,000,000$ executions, the $16,000,000$ ARK_0 will all be randomly distributed over the 16 first instants, whereas in our proposition, we observe that $10,997,161$ ARK_0 operations are distributed over the same period. Our scheme offers more randomization, except for the first instant of time, and this applies to all operations of all rounds.

Adding dummy AES rounds on dummy STATES in parallel to the beginning of our AES computation will increase the randomization of the execution and improve the security of the first instants of time.

5   Performance Analysis

5.1   Attack Results

In this section we present the results of a DPA attack we performed on three different schemes: an unprotected AES scheme, Tillich's proposition scheme where operations on bytes were randomly executed inside the 4 main AES operations, and finally our SchedAES scheme.

The attack has been performed with different number of traces (100, 200, 500, 1000, 2000, 5000 and 10000) in order to compare the effectiveness of the countermeasure and using a fixed key. The traces were generated based on the simulated power consumption of the manipulated data with randomly chosen plaintexts and the fixed key. We use the Hamming weight model in order to simulate our traces: after each byte modification of the STATE matrix we write the Hamming weight of the new value. We also add noise, of mean 0 and standard deviation of 0.3, to the simulated values.

We then apply, for each byte of the key, the "general DPA attack strategy", described by Mangard *et al.* in [13], using the exact Hamming weight model as hypothetical power consumption.

Attacks using power traces alignment methods were not feasible because we used simulated power traces, where each operation corresponds to one value, and pattern matching techniques were impossible to use on our power traces.

Table 3. Correct guessed bytes of the key based on the number of traces allowed for the attack when attacking ARK_0 and SB_1 operations

Number of traces	ARK			SB		
	Unprotected	Tillich	SchedAES	Unprotected	Tillich	SchedAES
100	16	1	0	16	8	0
200	16	0	0	16	14	1
500	16	1	1	16	16	1
1000	16	3	1	16	16	3
2000	16	5	5	16	16	4
5000	16	11	9	16	16	12
10000	16	16	16	16	16	16

Table 3 summarizes the results of the attack on the three different AES implementations. The results express the number of correctly guessed bytes of the key based on 2 parameters: the number of used power traces and the targeted operation. We decided to attack the initial AddRoundKey operation and the first round SubBytes operation. Therefore, based on Table 1, we limited the power traces to the 64 first points (representing the 64 first operations). For the AES implementation without countermeasure, full key recovery was made possible with only 100 power traces, for the ARK operations as well as for the SB operation. The Tillich implementation allowed a full key recovery with 10,000 power traces when attacking the ARK operation and only 500 for the SB operation. Finally, our proposition achieved the same results as the Tillich implementation when attacking ARK but needed ten times more power traces when attacking SB.

5.2   Execution Times

In order to perform the attack described in Section 5.1, we performed 10,000 encryptions for each of the schemes. Table 4 summarizes the execution times of the three schemes for 10,000 encryptions[10] .

---

[10] 2.4 GHz Intel Core 2 Duo with 4 GB RAM.

Table 4. Time in seconds for performing 10, 000 encryptions and the number of traces required to fully recover the key

	Unprotected	Tillich	SchedAES
time	26.87	32.75	188.82
# traces	100	500	10000

Table 4 shows that our scheme is approximately 6 to 7 times slower than the two other implementations. The execution time was not our main focus for this work. However, the optimization of our proposition has to be researched.

Finally, our implementation is two times bigger, in terms of source code size, than the two other implementations we used.

6   Conclusion

We show in this paper that shuffling can do more than just swapping two instructions and allows many possible execution paths. In comparison to Tillich's technique [19], our technique allows more possibilities even if this number is in practice smaller than what theory predicts.

Our technique requires a greater overhead (our source code is twice as large as basic AES) and is on average 6 to 7 times slower in comparison to Tillich's one due to the fact that a scheduler is needed to schedule the operations. However, according to our experiments, our technique requires 10 times more traces to fully recover the key.

This solution seems interesting in the context of side channel attacks and particularly against power analysis attacks where power traces need to be aligned in order for the attack to succeed more easily. The number of different possible executions takes a prohibitively long time to compute due to preconditions between operations.

Other countermeasures can be added to our proposition in order to strengthen it against SCA: masking, execution of dummy AES at the same time so the action that is performed at a moment of time will be related to the desired AES computation or to one of the dummy computations. The computing of all of the dummy AES should not necessarily start at the same time than the desired one but some of them should start earlier. It is interesting to notice that in the context of multiple block encryptions a countermeasure like Inter-Block Shuffling [8] could also be applied in conjunction with our scheme.

Since all the intermediate values computed in SchedAES are the same than in a normal AES, classical cryptanalysis like linear and differential cryptanalysis seem, at first look, having no different effect on SchedAES. However, this issue can be explored in a futur work.

In our proposition, we make the assumption that the Key Expansion has already been performed. Adding the Key Expansion to the scheme will add more randomness and will allow more different executions. Our goal was to focus on the four main (ARK, SB, SR, MC) AES operations, but future works will take Key Expansion into account.

Other future works are (1) the physical implementation and the attack of the proposition with real measurement power traces and considering attacking schemes that take into account power traces misalignment, (2) to be more permissive with SR operations by allowing them to be skipped in order to have different length of traces, (3) to consider other selection policies for the scheduler. Finally, we should investigate how this technique could be applied to other algorithms.

References

1. Ambrose, J., Ignjatovic, A., Parameswaran, S.: Power Analysis Side Channel Attacks. VDM Verlag (2010)
2. Benini, L., Macii, A., Macii, E., Omerbegovic, E., Pro, F., Poncino, M.: Energy-Aware Design Techniques for Differential Power Analysis Protection. In: DAC, pp. 36–41. ACM (2003)
3. Clavier, C., Coron, J.-S., Dabbous, N.: Differential Power Analysis in the Presence of Hardware Countermeasures. In: Koç, Ç.K., Paar, C. (eds.) CHES 2000. LNCS, vol. 1965, pp. 252–263. Springer, Heidelberg (2000)
4. Daemen, J., Rijmen, V.: Resistance Against Implementation Attacks: A Comparative Study of the AES Proposals. In: Second Advanced Encryption Standard (AES) Candidate Conference (1999)
5. Daemen, J., Rijmen, V.: The Design of Rijndael: AES - The Advanced Encryption Standard. Springer (2002)
6. DES. Data Encryption Standard. In: FIPS PUB 46, Federal Information Processing Standards Publication, pp. 46–52 (1977)
7. Gandolfi, K., Mourtel, C., Olivier, F.: Electromagnetic analysis: Concrete results. In: Koç, Ç.K., Naccache, D., Paar, C. (eds.) CHES 2001. LNCS, vol. 2162, pp. 251–261. Springer, Heidelberg (2001)
8. Großschädl, J., Kizhvatov, I.: Performance and Security Aspects of Client-Side SSL/TLS Processing on Mobile Devices. In: Heng, S.-H., Wright, R.N., Goi, B.-M. (eds.) CANS 2010. LNCS, vol. 6467, pp. 44–61. Springer, Heidelberg (2010)
9. Irwin, J., Page, D., Smart, N.P.: Instruction Stream Mutation for Non-Deterministic Processors. In: Shulte, M., Bhattacharyya, S., Burgess, N., Schreiber, R. (eds.) 13th International Conference on Application-specific Systems, Architectures and Processors (ASAP), pp. 286–295. IEEE Computer Society Press (July 2002)
10. Kocher, P.C.: Timing Attacks on Implementations of Diffie-Hellman, RSA, DSS, and Other Systems. In: Koblitz, N. (ed.) CRYPTO 1996. LNCS, vol. 1109, pp. 104–113. Springer, Heidelberg (1996)
11. Kocher, P.C., Jaffe, J., Jun, B.: Differential Power Analysis. In: Wiener, M.J. (ed.) CRYPTO 1999. LNCS, vol. 1666, pp. 388–397. Springer, Heidelberg (1999)
12. Mangard, S.: Hardware Countermeasures against DPA – A Statistical Analysis of Their Effectiveness. In: Okamoto, T. (ed.) CT-RSA 2004. LNCS, vol. 2964, pp. 222–235. Springer, Heidelberg (2004)
13. Mangard, S., Oswald, E., Popp, T.: Power Analysis Attacks: Revealing the Secrets of Smart Cards. Advances in Information Security. Springer-Verlag New York, Inc., Secaucus (2007)
14. May, D., Muller, H.L., Smart, N.P.: Non-deterministic Processors. In: Varadharajan, V., Mu, Y. (eds.) ACISP 2001. LNCS, vol. 2119, pp. 115–129. Springer, Heidelberg (2001)

15. Messerges, T.S., Dabbish, E.A., Sloan, R.H.: Investigations of Power Analysis Attacks on Smartcards. In: Proceedings of the USENIX Workshop on Smartcard Technology on USENIX Workshop on Smartcard Technology, pp. 151–162. USENIX Association, Berkeley (1999)
16. Örs, S.B., Gürkaynak, F.K., Oswald, E., Preneel, B.: Power-Analysis Attack on an ASIC AES implementation. In: ITCC (2), pp. 546–552. IEEE Computer Society (2004)
17. Örs, S.B., Oswald, E., Preneel, B.: Power-Analysis Attacks on an FPGA – First Experimental Results. In: Walter, C.D., Koç, Ç.K., Paar, C. (eds.) CHES 2003. LNCS, vol. 2779, pp. 35–50. Springer, Heidelberg (2003)
18. Standaert, F.-X., van Oldeneel tot Oldenzeel, L., Samyde, D., Quisquater, J.-J.: Power Analysis of FPGAs: How Practical is the Attack? In: Y. K. Cheung, P., Constantinides, G.A. (eds.) FPL 2003. LNCS, vol. 2778, pp. 701–711. Springer, Heidelberg (2003)
19. Tillich, S., Herbst, C., Mangard, S.: Protecting AES Software Implementations on 32-Bit Processors Against Power Analysis. In: Katz, J., Yung, M. (eds.) ACNS 2007. LNCS, vol. 4521, pp. 141–157. Springer, Heidelberg (2007)

A   Algorithms

Algorithm 1. AES SCHEDULER: PSEUDO-CODE

1: {Initialization}
2: $\Theta = \{$ $ARK_{0,0,0}$, $ARK_{0,0,1}$, $ARK_{0,0,2}$, $ARK_{0,0,3}$, $ARK_{0,1,0}$, $ARK_{0,1,1}$, $ARK_{0,1,2}$, $ARK_{0,1,3}$, $ARK_{0,2,0}$, $ARK_{0,2,1}$, $ARK_{0,2,2}$, $ARK_{0,2,3}$, $ARK_{0,3,0}$, $ARK_{0,3,1}$, $ARK_{0,3,2}$, $ARK_{0,3,3}$ $\}$

3: {Execution loop}
4: **while** not finished **do**
5:    α = randomly pick operation in Θ
6:    perform α
7:    Θ = updateTheta(α)
8: **end while**

Algorithm 2. UPDATETHETA: PSEUDO-CODE

Require: operation α , set of possible operations Θ
Ensure: set of possible operations Θ updated

1: remove α from Θ
2: *operation_name* = operation part of α
3: k = round index of α
4: i = line index of α
5: j = column index of α

6: **if** *operation_name* is ARK **then**
7:     arkUpdate(k,i,j)
8: **else if** *operation_name* is SB **then**
9:     sbUpdate(k,i,j)
10: **else if** *operation_name* is SR **then**
11:     srUpdate(k,i)
12: **else if** *operation_name* is MC **then**
13:     mcUpdate(k,j)
14: **end if**

Algorithm 3. ARKUPDATE: PSEUDO-CODE

Require: indexes k, i and j, set of possible operations Θ
Ensure: set of possible operations Θ updated

1: {Nothing to update after ARK_{10}}
2: **if** k $\leq$ 9 **then**
3:     add $SB_{k+1,i,j}$ to Θ

4:     {if all the $ARK_{k,i}$ are done for line i}
5:     **if** $ARK_{k,i,0}$ and $ARK_{k,i,1}$ and $ARK_{k,i,2}$ and $ARK_{k,i,3}$ and $SR_{k,i}$ done **then**
6:         add $SR_{k+1,i}$ to Θ
7:     **end if**
8: **end if**

Algorithm 4. SBUPDATE: PSEUDO-CODE

Require: indexes k, i and j, set of possible operations Θ
Ensure: set of possible operations Θ updated

1: **if** k $\leq$ 9 **then**
2:     vj = determine the virtual column's index based on i and j

3:     {if all SB_k corresponding to vj are done}
4:     **if** $SB_{k,0,vj}$ and $SR_{k,0}$ done OR $SB_{k,0,vj}$ and $SR_{k-1,0}$ done **then**
5:       **if** $SB_{k,1,vj}$ and $SR_{k,1}$ done OR $SB_{k,1,(vj+1)mod4}$ and $SR_{k-1,1}$ done **then**
6:         **if** $SB_{k,2,vj}$ and $SR_{k,2}$ done OR $SB_{k,2,(vj+2)mod4}$ and $SR_{k-1,2}$ done **then**
7:           **if** $SB_{k,3,vj}$ and $SR_{k,3}$ done OR $SB_{k,3,(vj+3)mod4}$ and $SR_{k-1,3}$ done **then**
8:             add $MC_{k,vj}$ to Θ
9:           **end if**
10:         **end if**
11:       **end if**
12:     **end if**
13: **else**
14:     add $ARK_{k,i,j}$ to Θ
15: **end if**

Algorithm 5. SRUPDATE: PSEUDO-CODE

Require: indexes k and i, set of possible operations Θ
Ensure: set of possible operations Θ updated

1: apply SR operation to all ARK operations, concerning line i, in Θ
2: apply SR operation to all SB operations, concerning line i, in Θ
3: apply SR operation to line i in the control structure

4: {Check if MC operations can be allowed}
5: **if** k < 9 **then**
6:     **for** $vj = 0 \rightarrow 3$ **do**
7:       **if** $SB_{k+1,0,vj}$ and $SR_{k+1,0}$ done OR $SB_{k+1,0,vj}$ and $SR_{k,0}$ done **then**
8:         **if** $SB_{k+1,1,vj}$ and $SR_{k+1,1}$ done OR $SB_{k+1,1,(vj+1)mod4}$ and $SR_{k,1}$ done **then**
9:           **if** $SB_{k+1,2,vj}$ and $SR_{k+1,2}$ done OR $SB_{k+1,2,(vj+2)mod4}$ and $SR_{k,2}$ done **then**
10:             **if** $SB_{k+1,3,vj}$ and $SR_{k+1,3}$ done OR $SB_{k+1,3,(vj+3)mod4}$ and $SR_{k,3}$ done **then**
11:               add $MC_{k+1,vj}$ to Θ
12:             **end if**
13:           **end if**
14:         **end if**
15:       **end if**
16:     **end for**
17: **end if**

18: {Check if next SR for line i can be allowed}
19: **if** $ARK_{k,i,0}$ and $ARK_{k,i,1}$ and $ARK_{k,i,2}$ and $ARK_{k,i,3}$ done and $k \neq 10$ **then**
20:     add $SR_{k+1,i}$ to Θ
21: **end if**

Algorithm 6. MCUPDATE: PSEUDO-CODE

Require: indexes k and j, set of possible operations Θ
Ensure: set of possible operations Θ updated

1: **for** $i = 0 \to 3$ **do**
2:     **if** $SR_{k,i}$ done **then**
3:         add $ARK_{k,i,j}$ to Θ
4:     **else**
5:         add $ARK_{k,i,(j+i) \bmod 4}$ to Θ
6:     **end if**
7: **end for**

Impact of Extending Side Channel Attack on Cipher Variants: A Case Study with the HC Series of Stream Ciphers*

Goutam Paul[1] and Shashwat Raizada[2]

[1] Department of Computer Science and Engineering,
Jadavpur University, Kolkata 700 032, India
goutam.paul@ieee.org
[2] Applied Statistics Unit,
Indian Statistical Institute, Kolkata 700 108, India
shashwat.raizada@gmail.com

Abstract. Side channel attacks are extremely implementation specific. An attack is tailor-made for a specific cipher algorithm implemented in a specific model. A natural question is: what is the effect of a side channel technique on a variant of the cipher algorithm implemented in a similar model? The motivation for such an investigation is to study the feasibility of using a cipher variant as a mode of recovering from a successful side channels attack. As a case study, we consider the HC series of stream ciphers, viz., HC-128 and HC-256. We extend the HC-128 fault attack and the HC-256 cache analysis onto the HC-256 and HC-128 ciphers respectively under similar models. The techniques applied on one variant is not trivially translatable to the other and the issue was left open until the current work. We propose a technique to recover half the state of HC-128 using cache analysis, which can be cascaded with the differential attack towards a full state recovery and hence key recovery. Similarly, we analyze the state leakage of HC-256 under differential fault attack model to achieve partial state recovery.

Keywords: Cache Analysis, Cryptography, eSTREAM, Fault Attack, Side Chanel Cryptanalysis, Stream Cipher.

1 Introduction

The software profile of the eSTREAM [3] final portfolio contains the stream cipher HC-128 [16] which is a lighter version of HC-256 [17] stream cipher born as an outcome of 128-bit key limitation imposed in the competition. Several research works exist on the cryptanalysis of HC-128 [8,9,4,11,13]. However, HC-256 has been undergone only a few cryptanalytic attempts [18,12].

Side channel cryptanalysis attacks are targeted to a specific implementation of a cipher. In a commercially popular device with large user-base, the immediate

---

* This work was done in part while the first author was visiting RWTH Aachen, Germany as an Alexander von Humboldt Fellow.

A. Bogdanov and S. Sanadhya (Eds.): SPACE 2012, LNCS 7644, pp. 32–44, 2012.

reaction to an attack is to change the underlying crypto algorithm, but with a low replacement cost. Variants of the original algorithm form a preferential choice because of the structural similarity with the original cipher. For example, in Wi-Fi networks, when the RC4 implementation in WEP [5] protocol suffered several attacks, a natural choice in the subsequent WPA [6] protocol was a variant of RC4 implementation (with different key and IV size and different form of key and IV mixing), before the longterm change-over to the block cipher AES in WPA2 [7].

In this paper, we examine the security of using a variant algorithm to thwart a side channel vulnerability. The HC series of stream ciphers have been used for this purpose. Both HC-128 and HC-256 have been exposed to distinct side channel cryptanalytic attacks, as follows:

- a differential fault attack on HC-128 [4],
- a cache timing analysis analysis on HC-256 [18].

For both the above works, extending the attack on one HC variant to the other is not straight-forward. In [4], there is no mention about the extendibility of the attack to HC-256. On the other hand, the author of [18] mentions the following point in a subsequent work [19] that studied the cache timing analysis of all the eSTREAM finalists.

> HC-128 ... has a slightly smaller inner state ... and surprisingly big changes of the internal workings. Most state update equations are modified, and this has a profound impact on the above cache timing attack. It turns out that the attack can not be transferred to HC-128 in a straightforward way. Thus, further analysis of HC-128 is necessary to determine its resistance against cache timing attacks.

We like to point out here that one of the key difference in the structure of HC-128 and HC-256 is that in the former the two state tables are updated independently, whereas in the latter they are inter-dependant. This makes extending the differential fault analysis of HC-128 [4] to HC-256 a challenging task.

In this work, we analyze the effect of the attacks on one HC variant to the other for the first time. We specifically analyze how much state information can be leaked when the HC-256 variant is chosen against the fault attack on HC-128, and the latter is chosen against the cache timing analysis of the former. We consider the same implementations that are considered in [4,18]. For details of the implementation issues, one may refer to [16, Section 5] and [17, Section 5].

1.1 Overview of Cache Analysis and Differential Fault Attacks

Cache analysis is a side channel cryptanalysis technique that has been introduced independently by Bernstein [1] and Osvik et al. [10], primarily for the AES block cipher. We give a simple description of the cache analysis adapted from [18]. *Cache* is a temporary storage area that is closer to the CPU compared to the RAM and is used to replicate frequently accessed data for enabling faster access. Data once stored in the cache, can be further used by accessing the cached copy rather than by re-fetching from the RAM. If the CPU finds the data it needs in the cache, a *cache hit* is said to occur. Otherwise a *cache miss* occurs and the cache must be immediately loaded with the requisite data from the RAM. Cache management in modern processors divides the available cache memory into blocks of b bytes. For a given block, all the b bytes must be loaded together. To ensure consistency between the data in the RAM and the cache, a record of cache blocks being loaded into the cache is maintained. This record serves as the initial raw-data for commencing the cache analysis. The adversary first fills the entire cache with his own data. Next, during normal computation, user's data replaces some data of the adversary. When adversary tries to reload his own data from the cache. If it takes longer time, then he knows the address of the user's data from the cache record. This method can be considered as a *cache access attack*. However, since the time to load the data plays a crucial role in leaking the address of the data, we follow the same nomenclature as in [18] and call this as *cache timing attack*. In this paper, we extend the cache timing analysis of HC-256 [18] to its reduced version HC-128 using a similar framework. Though cache-analysis attacks may not be constituted as an concrete attack on HC-128, we believe these findings will assist further exposure towards analysis of the cipher.

Fault attacks [2] are an invasive side channel cryptanalytic technique in which faults are inserted into the cryptographic device. The goal may be to corrupt the value of an internal state register or memory location or to make a small change in the execution flow, such as skipping an instruction or changing a memory address etc. The corresponding change in the cipher output obtained are used to extrapolate the internal state. A differential fault attack against a stream cipher resets the cipher with the same key, but injecting different faults. The resulting keystreams have small differences and the attack exploits these differentials. In this paper, we extend the differential fault attack on HC-128 [4] to HC-256 and study the resulting state leakage.

1.2   Layout of the Paper

In Section 2 and Section 4 we discuss the internal structures of HC-128 and HC-256 stream cipher respectively. In Section 3 the description of the cache analysis model as applied to HC-128 along with the inferences have been presented. This issue had been left as an open problem in [18]. In Section 5 we analyze the fault attack on HC-256. We conclude the paper and discuss possible future works in Section 6.

2   Description of HC-128

We summarize the key points of the structure and the keystream generation of the cipher below. The following operators are used in HC-128.

$+$: addition modulo 2^{32}.

$\boxminus$: subtraction modulo 512.

$\oplus$: bit-wise exclusive OR.

$\|$: bit-string concatenation.

$\gg$: right shift operator (defined on 32-bit numbers).

$\ll$: left shift operator (defined on 32-bit numbers).

$\ggg$: right rotation operator (defined on 32-bit numbers).

$\lll$: left rotation operator (defined on 32-bit numbers).

Two internal state arrays P and Q are used in HC-128, each with 512 many 32-bit elements. A 128-bit key array $K[0,\ldots,3]$ and a 128-bit initialization vector $IV[0,\ldots,3]$ are used, each entry being a 32-bit element. Let s_t denote the keystream word generated at the t-th step, $t = 0, 1, 2, \ldots$.

The following six functions are used in HC-128.

$$f_1(x) = (x \ggg 7) \oplus (x \ggg 18) \oplus (x \gg 3),$$
$$f_2(x) = (x \ggg 17) \oplus (x \ggg 19) \oplus (x \gg 10),$$
$$g_1(x, y, z) = ((x \ggg 10) \oplus (z \ggg 23)) + (y \ggg 8),$$
$$g_2(x, y, z) = ((x \lll 10) \oplus (z \lll 23)) + (y \lll 8),$$
$$h_1(x) = Q[x^{(0)}] + Q[256 + x^{(2)}],$$
$$h_2(x) = P[x^{(0)}] + P[256 + x^{(2)}],$$

where $x = x^{(3)} \| x^{(2)} \| x^{(1)} \| x^{(0)}$ is a 32-bit word, with $x^{(0)}, x^{(1)}, x^{(2)}$ and $x^{(3)}$ being the four bytes from right to left.

The key and IV setup of HC-128 recursively loads the P and Q array from expanded key and IV and run the cipher for 1024 steps to use the outputs to replace the table elements. It happens in four steps as follows.

Let $K[i + 4] = K[i]$ and $IV[i + 4] = IV[i]$ for $0 \leq i \leq 3$.

The key and IV are expanded into an array $W[0, \ldots, 1279]$ as follows:
$$\begin{aligned} W[i] &= K[i], &&\text{for } 0 \leq i \leq 7; \\ &= IV[i - 8], &&\text{for } 8 \leq i \leq 15; \\ &= f_2(W[i - 2]) + W[i - 7] \\ &\quad + f_1(W[i - 15]) + W[i - 16] + i, &&\text{for } 16 \leq i \leq 1279. \end{aligned}$$

Update the tables P and Q with the array W as follows:
$$P[i] = W[i + 256], \text{ for } 0 \leq i \leq 511,$$
$$Q[i] = W[i + 768], \text{ for } 0 \leq i \leq 511.$$

Run the cipher 1024 steps to replace the table elements as follows:
For $i = 0$ to 511, do
$$P[i] = (P[i] + g_1(P[i \boxminus 3], P[i \boxminus 10], P[i \boxminus 511])) \oplus h_1(P[i \boxminus 12]);$$
For $i = 0$ to 511, do
$$Q[i] = (Q[i] + g_2(Q[i \boxminus 3], Q[i \boxminus 10], Q[i \boxminus 511])) \oplus h_2(Q[i \boxminus 12]);$$

The keystream is generated using the following algorithm.

```
i = 0;
repeat until enough keystream bits are generated
{
    j = i mod 512;
    if (i mod 1024) < 512
    {
        P[j] = P[j] + g₁(P[j ⊟ 3], P[j ⊟ 10], P[j ⊟ 511]);
        sᵢ = h₁(P[j ⊟ 12]) ⊕ P[j];
    }
    else
    {
        Q[j] = Q[j] + g₂(Q[j ⊟ 3], Q[j ⊟ 10], Q[j ⊟ 511]);
        sᵢ = h₂(Q[j ⊟ 12]) ⊕ Q[j];
    }
    end-if
    i = i + 1;
}
end-repeat
```

3   Cache Analysis of HC-128

In the attack model, we assume that the adversary is running a special process in the CPU in which the cipher is executing. The adversary's process executes calls so as to fill the entire cache with his own data, causing the HC-128 cached data to be evicted. When the HC-128 process gains control of the CPU it must reload data into the cache pertinent to current instruction. The cache block size b in present day processors range from 16 bytes to 128 bytes. The arrays P and Q have 512 many word entries. As four bytes make a word, $b/4$ array elements will be mapped to a single cache block size. If the cache block is aligned with the index of the array, we will have the elements from indices 0 to $(b/4) - 1$ in the first cache block and the elements from indices $(b/4)$ to $(b/2) - 1$ in the second block and so on, till the elements from indices $511 - (b/4)$ to 511 in the final cache block.

3.1   Bits Obtainable from Cache Information

The keystream words are generated using both the arrays P and Q, each consisting of 512 many words. However, the updates of P and Q arrays are independent. For 512 many iterations, the array P is updated with the older values from P itself and during this time the array Q is accessed but not updated. For the next 512 many iterations the array Q is updated with the older values of Q and during this time the array P is accessed for keyword generation but not updated. This access and update pattern continues alternatively. At this phase, the key-stream is generated using two functions h_1, h_2 of similar kind. The equations used are as follows.

$$s_j = h_1(P[j \boxminus 12]) \oplus P[j] \quad \text{(keystream when } P \text{ is updated)},$$
$$s_j = h_2(Q[j \boxminus 12]) \oplus Q[j] \quad \text{(keystream when } Q \text{ is updated)}.$$

Every time the h_1 (or h_2) function is called, it uses bytes 0 and 2 of $P[j \boxminus 12]$ (or $Q[j \boxminus 12]$) to access the elements of Q (or P) array. Since a cache with block size b holds $b/4$ array elements, the cache blocks can be numbered using the first $8 - \log_2(b/4)$ bits. For each call, two elements of the array are accessed. This gives $16 - 2\log_2(b/4)$ bits of each element of the arrays P and Q corresponding to the cache fill sought at the time h_1 or h_2 is called. Thus, the number of bits obtained depends on b and is given in the table.

Table 1. Cache block size vs. number of bits learnt

Cache Block Size b:	16	32	64	128
No. of bits obtained:	12	10	8	6

Using the above, we can form an array with the known elements of P and Q. Let P_k and Q_k denote the array corresponding to the k-th iteration of the update. On completion of the KSA, we will get the fist array denoted by P_0 and Q_0. On generation of the first 512 keystream words, we get another array denoted by P_1 and for the next 512 words we get the Q_1 array, and so on.

3.2   Constructing Bytes 0 and 2 of Each Array Element

Since h_1 and h_2 are similar, without any loss of generality we present the case for P_1, and this is valid for Q_1 also. For $0 \le j \le 500$, we can rewrite the keystream generation equation $s_j = h_1(P[j \boxminus 12]) \oplus P[j]$ as follows.

$$Q[u] + Q[v] = s(j + 12) \oplus P_1[j + 12]), \qquad (1)$$

where $u = P[j]^{(0)}$ and $v = P[j]^{(2)}$. The keystream s is known. For a cache block size of 32 bytes, the first 5 most significant bits of each of u and v are known. Thus, $u \gg 3$ and $32 + (v \gg 3)$ denote the cache blocks loaded for computing h_1. Within these blocks (in Q_0), we exhaustively search the elements that would give a sum identical to the right hand side of Equation 1. These additions are across two chunks of 5 bits and so additional carry bits need to be accounted. For each element $P[j]$, there are $(b/4).(b/4) = b^2/16$ calculations. Finding a correct single match gives the unknown bits of bytes 0 and 2 of P_1. Finding more than one match means that we have a set of values out of which one is the correct candidate. Considering the HC-128 keystream is uniformly random, the frequency of such ties would be very low. The procedure is repeated for all elements of P and Q array.

3.3   Finding the Remaining Sixteen Bits for Each Element

Since bytes 1 and 3 of the array elements are never used in h_1 (or h_2), obtaining any information about these bits is not possible by the above cache analysis. If one considers the g_1 (or g_2) function and propagates the known 10 bits across many updates, one can guess some bits considering the carry propagation. However, we could not get much information from such analysis. In the cache attack of HC-256 [18], the advantage was that all the four bytes of the array elements are used inside the h_1 (or h_2) functions, giving leakage of all the 32 bits eventually.

In order to find the remaining 16 bits for each element in case of HC-128, we propose to use the techniques of differential fault analysis [4] in combination with the cache analysis suggested here. According to [4], they need to solve a set of 32 systems of linear equations over $\mathbb{Z}_2$ in 1024 variables. If one performs the cache analysis proposed in this paper first, immediately the problem reduces to 16 systems of linear equations over $\mathbb{Z}_2$ in 1024 variables.

According to [8], the key schedule of HC-128 is reversible and hence once the full state is recovered, the secret key can be easily found.

4   Description of HC-256

The operations used in HC-256 are similar to HC-128 as described in Section 2. Two tables P and Q, each with 1024 many 32-bit elements are used as internal states of HC-256. A 256 bit key array $K[0,\ldots,7]$ and a 256-bit initialization vector $IV[0,\ldots,7]$ are used, where each entry of the array is a 32-bit element. Let s_t denote the keystream word generated at the t-th instance, $t = 0,1,2,\ldots$.

The following six functions are used in HC-256.

$$f_1(x) = (x \ggg 7) \oplus (x \ggg 18) \oplus (x \gg 3),$$
$$f_2(x) = (x \ggg 17) \oplus (x \ggg 19) \oplus (x \gg 10),$$
$$g_1(x,y) = ((x \ggg 10) \oplus (y \ggg 23)) + Q[(x \oplus y) \bmod 1024],$$
$$g_2(x,y) = ((x \ggg 10) \oplus (y \ggg 23)) + P[(x \oplus y) \bmod 1024],$$
$$h_1(x) = Q[x^{(0)}] + Q[256 + x^{(1)}] + Q[512 + x^{(2)}] + Q[768 + x^{(3)}],$$
$$h_2(x) = P[x^{(0)}] + P[256 + x^{(1)}] + P[512 + x^{(2)}] + P[768 + x^{(3)}].$$

The key and IV setup of HC-256 proceeds as follows.

The key and IV are expanded into an array $W[0,\ldots,2559]$ as follows:
$$W[i] = K[i], \qquad\qquad\qquad \text{for } 0 \le i \le 7;$$
$$= IV[i-8], \qquad\qquad\quad \text{for } 8 \le i \le 15;$$
$$= f_2(W[i-2]) + W[i-7]$$
$$\quad + f_1(W[i-15]) + W[i-16] + i, \text{ for } 16 \le i \le 2559.$$

Update the tables P and Q with the array W as follows:
$$P[i] = W[i+512], \text{ for } 0 \le i \le 1023,$$
$$Q[i] = W[i+1536], \text{ for } 0 \le i \le 1023.$$

Run the keystream generation algorithm 1024 steps without generating output.

The keystream generation algorithm is as follows.

```
i = 0;
repeat until enough keystream bits are generated
{
        j = i mod 1024;
        if (i mod)2048 < 1024
        {
            P[j] = P[j] + P[j ⊟ 10] + g₁(P[j ⊟ 3], P[j ⊟ 1023]);
            sᵢ = h₁(P[j ⊟ 12]) ⊕ P[j];
        }
        else
        {
            Q[j] = Q[j] + Q[j ⊟ 10] + g₂(Q[j ⊟ 3], Q[j ⊟ 1023]);
            sᵢ = h₂(Q[j ⊟ 12]) ⊕ Q[j];
        }
        end-if
        i = i + 1;
}
end-repeat
```

5   Fault Attack on HC-256

The model that we use for inserting faults in HC-256 is similar to that used for the attack on HC-128 [4] with a slightly stronger assumption as regards to the fact that one *needs to know the location of the fault*. Such an assumption is not entirely impractical. In [14,15], the authors discuss how to flip precise bits in SRAM and EEPROM, or change the state of any individual CMOS transistor on a chip. We only require a change in at least one of the 32 bits of a word at a specific location. Like [4], we also do not need to know the value of the fault.

In practice, we know that the updates of P and Q occur alternatively. The fault is assumed to be inserted into the array that is not being updated. Any variation in the keystream would imply that a faulty element has been accessed. The block of 1024 keystream generation in which P (or Q) is updated is referred as the P (or Q)-block and the keystream is denoted by s_P (or s_Q). Let the primed variables s'_P and s'_Q denote the 'faulty' keystream, i.e., the keystream generated after fault injection. We denote the location (index) of the fault as f.

In P-block, the keystream is generated as

$$s_{P,j} = h_1(P[j \boxminus 12]) \oplus P[j]$$

$$= \Big(Q\big[(P[j \boxminus 12])^{(0)}\big] + Q\big[256 + (P[j \boxminus 12])^{(1)}\big] + Q\big[512 +$$

$$(P[j \boxminus 12])^{(2)}\big] + Q\big[768 + (P[j \boxminus 12])^{(3)}\big]\Big) \oplus P[j].$$

Suppose we inject a fault at $Q[f]$ before $P[0]$ is updated in P-block. We rerun the key generation algorithm 1024 times to generate 1024 *faulty* keystream words corresponding to the current P-block. We compare $s_{P,j}$ with $s'_{P,j}$ for $j = 0, \ldots,$ 511. Whenever $s_{P,j} \neq s'_{P,j}$, we know that the faulty keystream has been accessed.

The noticeable faults observed in the keystream are either due to a faulty value of Q entering the h_1 function or a faulty value of Q entering the update function of P.

Definition 1. *When a faulty Q (or P) array element enters in h_1 (or h_2), we call this an **opportune** event.*

Definition 2. *When a faulty Q (or P) array element is referred inside g_1 (or g_2), we all this a **traverse** event.*

We consider these cases one by one.

5.1   Faulty Q Entering in Computation of h_1

Suppose an *opportune* event occurs and f is the location of the fault, i.e., $Q[f]$ is the faulty value accessed inside h_1. Here the location of a faulty Q element gives information of a byte of P. The keystream index j where $s_{P,j}$ and $s'_{P,j}$ differs, refers to byte 0 of $P[j \boxminus 12]$ if $0 \leq f \leq 255$, byte 1 of $P[j \boxminus 12]$ if $256 \leq f \leq 511$, byte 2 of $P[j \boxminus 12]$ if $512 \leq f \leq 767$ or byte 3 of $P[j \boxminus 12]$ if $768 \leq f \leq 1023$.

Since all the four bytes of P are used inside h_1 (as indices into Q), one could retrieve all the bytes of P by injecting faults at all the 1024 entries of Q in turn, had the faulty value never entered in the update of P. But in practice, the faulty value enters in the update of P and therefore the keystream indices where $s_{P,j}$ and $s'_{P,j}$ differs do not correspond to distinct bytes of the words of P. Assuming the P and the Q arrays to be uniformly random, we can theoretically estimate how many words of the P array would actually be revealed for the proposed attack model.

Theorem 1. *The expected number of bytes of $P[i]$ leaked through h_1 function is given by $4(\frac{1023}{1024})^{i+1}$, $0 \leq i \leq 1023$.*

Proof. Before $P[i]$ is used in the keystream generation, all the $i + 1$ elements from $P[0]$ to $P[i]$ are updated using the function g. The faulty $Q[f]$ enters in each of these updates with probability $1/1024$, assuming the array elements to be uniformly random. Thus, the probability that it does not enter in any particular one of these updates is $1 - \frac{1}{1024} = \frac{1023}{1024}$. Assuming the events corresponding to $Q[f]$ entering into the updates of different rounds to be independent, the probability that it does not enter in any of the $i + 1$ updates is given by $\alpha_i = (\frac{1023}{1024})^{i+1}$. For $0 \leq b \leq 3$, let $X_{i,b} = 1$, if the byte b of $P[i]$ is revealed successfully; otherwise $X_{i,b} = 0$. The total number of bytes of $P[i]$ revealed is given by $Y_i = \sum_{b=0}^{3} X_{i,b}$. The expectation of $X_{i,b}$ is given by $E[X_{i,b}] = Prob(X_{i,b} = 1) = \alpha_i$, for any b, $0 \leq b \leq 3$. By linearity of expectation, $E[Y_i] = \sum_{b=0}^{3} E[X_{i,b}] = 4\alpha_i$. □

In Fig. 1, we compare the theoretical estimate with the empirical values of the number of bytes of $P[i]$ leaked from the h_1 function, $0 \leq i \leq 1023$, when each element of Q is faulted once. We see that the plots are almost identical. The empirical values were obtained by averaging over 1 million iterations, and each time HC-256 was run with a new randomly generated secret key.

An immediate consequence of Theorem 1 is Corollary 1, that gives the theoretical estimate of the number of words of the array P that are actually leaked.

Corollary 1. *The expected number of words of the array P leaked through h_1 function is 647.*

Proof. Refer to Y_i defined in the proof of Theorem 1. Total number of bytes revealed is given by $\sum_{i=0}^{1023} Y_i$, whose expected value is given by $4\sum_{i=0}^{1023}\left(\frac{1023}{1024}\right)^{i+1}$. Thus, the expected number of words revealed is given by $\sum_{i=0}^{1023}\left(\frac{1023}{1024}\right)^{i+1} = 646.84 \approx 647$. □

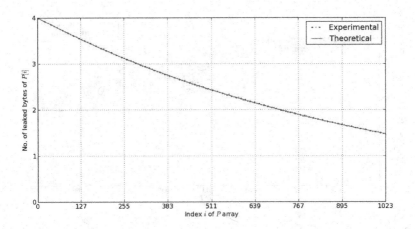

Fig. 1. Number of bytes of P array elements leaked from h_1 function

5.2   Faulty Q Entering in Update of P

Since the update of P involves Q (unlike HC-128), faulty $Q[f]$ is eventually referred inside g_1. When such a *traverse* event happens, it does not yield any more information within the particular update. However, this case assists in finding elements of the previous updates as follows. Recall the update of P.

$$P[j] = P[j] + P[j \boxminus 10] + g_1(P[j \boxminus 3], P[j \boxminus 1023]),$$

where $g_1(x,y) = ((x \ggg 10) \oplus (y \ggg 23)) + Q[(x \oplus y) \bmod 1024]$.

So whenever we observe a mismatch between $s_{P,j}$ and $s'_{P,j}$, that may be due to the fact that $P[j \boxminus 3], \oplus P[j \boxminus 1023] \bmod 1024$ refers to the faulty element of Q. Since the index of the faulty Q element is known, if any one of the elements $P[j \boxminus 3]$ and $P[j \boxminus 1023]$ is known, the other element can be easily computed. Except for $P[0]$, all the elements of the form $P[j \boxminus 1023]$ are from the previously updated P array. Similarly, all the elements of the form $P[j \boxminus 3]$ refer to the updated values of P array, except for $P[0], P[1]$ and $P[2]$. While keeping track of these indices, the elements found in subsequent updates can be used for finding elements of the previous updates. We find that when we propagate the knowledge from the second update into the first update, the probability increases. Similar trend continues as one increases the number of updates. Our experimental results reveal that after faulting four successive updates of P and Q, the first ten bits of approximately 85% elements of P and Q pertaining to first update can be obtained. Fig. 2 shows how the values obtained from the first, the second and the fifth updates help in finding values in the current update. Table 2 gives the numerical data for all the five updates. All the values were obtained by averaging over 10000 simulations with randomly generated secret keys.

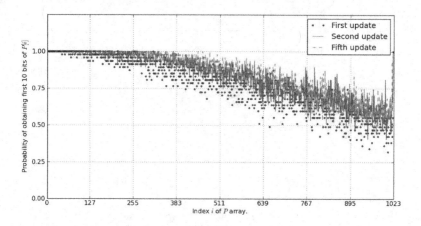

Fig. 2. Probability of finding the first ten bits of P array elements from several updates

Table 2. Number of words with first ten bits leaked vs. number of subsequent updates incorporated

Type	No. of updates	No. of words with first 10 bits leaked
only h fault	1	646.8
both h and g fault	1	805.1
both h and g fault	2	860.0
both h and g fault	3	871.0
both h and g fault	4	875.0
both h and g fault	5	877.6

Thus, we are able to get approx. 877 values of the first ten bits, fourth array update onwards. Thus, a total $647 \times 22 + 8776$ bits ≈ 719 words for each array are known.

5.3   Differentiating the Two Cases and Obtaining Additional Elements

Experiments show that if the opportune event occurs, then the keystream differences ($s_{P,j}$ vs. $s'_{P,j}$) occur at random indices (j), whereas if the traverse event occurs then the keystream differences follow a sequential pattern. This is because a fault in keystream position s_i due to faulty $P[i]$, which in turn is caused via an update involving the faulty $Q[f]$, would result in its being used in the update function of $P[i + 3]$, thereby altering the value of s_{i+3}. This in turn creates a fault in position s_{i+6} by virtue of the faulty value being used in the update of $P[i + 6]$.

Since the first ten bits of both P and Q function are known, by propagating these values across many updates of P array, one can endeavor to find the missing bits by guess and determine strategy. We leave it as an open problem here. It would be interesting to look at the combinatorial aspects of this guess and determine attack.

6   Conclusion

We showed how the cache analysis of HC-256 [18] can be extended to HC-128 and how the differential fault analysis of HC-128 [4] can be extended to HC-256. The first attack leads to half state recovery of HC-128 and when combined with the differential fault analysis can lead to the full state recovery and key recovery of HC-128. With the second attack, we have been able to perform partial state recovery of HC-256. Two interesting future works would be to study the feasibility of using the cache analysis alone to achieve full state recovery of HC-128 and that of mounting the differential fault attack alone to achieve full state recovery of HC-256.

Our findings show that the side channel vulnerability for a particular implementation of a cipher may percolate to its variants also, albeit in a different degree. This vulnerability is still exploitable through refinement of the attack vectors. So, while selecting a cipher variant to thwart side channel vulnerabilities, extra caution must be exercised.

References

1. Bernstein, D.: Cache-timing attacks on AES (2005), http://cr.yp.to/papers.html#cachetiming
2. Boneh, D., Demillo, R.A., Lipton, R.J.: On the Importance of Checking Cryptographic Protocols for Faults. In: Fumy, W. (ed.) EUROCRYPT 1997. LNCS, vol. 1233, pp. 37–51. Springer, Heidelberg (1997)
3. eSTREAM: the ECRYPT Stream Cipher Project, http://www.ecrypt.eu.org/stream
4. Kircanski, A., Youssef, A.M.: Differential Fault Analysis of HC-128. In: Bernstein, D.J., Lange, T. (eds.) AFRICACRYPT 2010. LNCS, vol. 6055, pp. 261–278. Springer, Heidelberg (2010)

5. LAN/MAN Standard Committee. ANSI/IEEE standard 802.11b: Wireless LAN Medium Access Control (MAC) and Physical Layer (phy) Specifications (1999)
6. LAN/MAN Standard Committee. ANSI/IEEE standard 802.11i: Amendment 6: Wireless LAN Medium Access Control (MAC) and Physical Layer (phy) Specifications, Draft 3 (2003)
7. LAN/MAN Standard Committee. ANSI/IEEE standard 802.11i: Amendment 6: Wireless LAN Medium Access Control (MAC) and Physical Layer (phy) Specifications (2004)
8. Liu, Y., Qin, T.: The key and IV setup of the stream ciphers HC-256 and HC-128. In: International Conference on Networks Security, Wireless Communications and Trusted Computing, Wuhan, Hubei China, April 25-26, pp. 430–433 (2009)
9. Maitra, S., Paul, G., Raizada, S., Sen, S., Sengupta, R.: Some observations on HC-128. In: Designs, Codes and Cryptography, vol. 59(1-3), pp. 231–245 (2011)
10. Osvik, D.A., Shamir, A., Tromer, E.: Cache Attacks and Countermeasures: The Case of AES. In: Pointcheval, D. (ed.) CT-RSA 2006. LNCS, vol. 3860, pp. 1–20. Springer, Heidelberg (2006)
11. Paul, G., Maitra, S., Raizada, S.: A Theoretical Analysis of the Structure of HC-128. In: Iwata, T., Nishigaki, M. (eds.) IWSEC 2011. LNCS, vol. 7038, pp. 161–177. Springer, Heidelberg (2011)
12. Sekar, G., Preneel, B.: Improved Distinguishing Attacks on HC-256. In: Takagi, T., Mambo, M. (eds.) IWSEC 2009. LNCS, vol. 5824, pp. 38–52. Springer, Heidelberg (2009)
13. Stankovski, P., Ruj, S., Hell, M., Johansson, T.: Improved distinguishers for HC-128. In: Designs, Codes and Cryptography, vol. 63(2), pp. 225–240 (2012)
14. Skorobogatov, S.P., Anderson, R.J.: Optical Fault Induction Attacks. In: Kaliski Jr., B.S., Koç, Ç.K., Paar, C. (eds.) CHES 2002. LNCS, vol. 2523, pp. 2–12. Springer, Heidelberg (2003)
15. Skorobogatov, S.P.: Semi-invasive attacks - A new approach to hardware security analysis. Technical Report No. UCAM-CL-TR-630, University of Cambridge, Computer Laborator (April 2005), http://www.cl.cam.ac.uk/techreports/UCAM-CL-TR-630.pdf
16. Wu, H.: The Stream Cipher HC-128 (2004), http://www.ecrypt.eu.org/stream/hcp3.html
17. Wu, H.: A New Stream Cipher HC-256. In: Roy, B., Meier, W. (eds.) FSE 2004. LNCS, vol. 3017, pp. 226–244. Springer, Heidelberg (2004), http://eprint.iacr.org/2004/092.pdf
18. Zenner, E.: A Cache Timing Analysis of HC-256. In: Avanzi, R.M., Keliher, L., Sica, F. (eds.) SAC 2008. LNCS, vol. 5381, pp. 199–213. Springer, Heidelberg (2009)
19. Zenner, E.: Cache Timing Analysis of eStream Finalists. Dagstuhl Seminar Proceedings 09031, Symmetric Cryptography (March 9, 2009), http://drops.dagstuhl.de/opus/volltexte/2009/1943

Performance and Security Evaluation of AES S-Box-Based Glitch PUFs on FPGAs

Dai Yamamoto[1,2], Gabriel Hospodar[1], Roel Maes[1], and Ingrid Verbauwhede[1]

[1] KU Leuven ESAT/SCD-COSIC and IBBT
Kasteelpark Arenberg 10, B-3001 Leuven-Heverlee, Belgium
firstname.lastname@esat.kuleuven.be
[2] FUJITSU LABORATORIES LTD,
4-1-1, Kamikodanaka, Nakahara-ku, Kawasaki, 211-8588, Japan
ydai@labs.fujitsu.com

Abstract. Physical(ly) Unclonable Functions (PUFs) are expected to represent a solution for secure ID generation, authentication, and other important security applications. Researchers have developed several kinds of PUFs and self-evaluated them to demonstrate their advantages. However, both performance and security aspects of some proposals have not been thoroughly and independently evaluated. Third-party evaluation is important to discuss whether a proposal performs according to what the developers claim, regardless of any accidental bias. In this paper, we focus on Glitch PUFs (GPUFs) that use an AES S-Box implementation as a glitch generator, as proposed by Suzuki et al. [1]. They claim that this GPUF is one of the most practically feasible and secure delay-based PUFs. However, it has not been evaluated by other researchers yet. We evaluate GPUFs implemented on FPGAs and present three novel results. First, we clarify that the total number of challenge-response pairs of GPUFs is 2^{19}, instead of 2^{11}. Second, we show that a GPUF implementation has low robustness against voltage variation. Third, we point out that the GPUF has "weak" challenges leading to responses that can be more easily predictable than others by an adversary. Our results indicate that GPUFs that use the AES S-Box as the glitch generator present almost no PUF-behavior as both reliability and uniqueness are relatively low. In conclusion, our case study on FPGAs suggests that GPUFs should not use the AES S-Box as a glitch generator due to performance and security reasons.

Keywords: Glitch PUF, FPGA, Security, Performance, Key Generation, Authentication.

1 Introduction

Secure identification/authentication technology using integrated circuits (ICs) is very important for a secure information infrastructure. One is often concerned with finding solutions for anti-counterfeiting devices on medical supplies, prepaid-cards and public ID cards such as passports and driver's licenses. The IC card is a well-known solution for this kind of application. Counterfeiting is

A. Bogdanov and S. Sanadhya (Eds.): SPACE 2012, LNCS 7644, pp. 45–62, 2012.

prevented by storing a secret key on the IC card and using a secure cryptographic protocol to make the key invisible to the outside. In theory, however, the possibility of counterfeiting still remains if the IC design is revealed and reproduced. Recently, interest has been focused on Physical(ly) Unclonable Functions (PUFs) as a solution to the aforementioned issue [2]. In a PUF realized in an IC (silicon PUF), the output value (response) to the input value (challenge) is unique for each individual IC. This uniqueness is provided by random process variations that occur in the manufacturing process of each IC [3] [4]. It is expected that PUFs will represent a breakthrough in technology for anti-counterfeiting devices through its use for ID generation, key generation and authentication protocols, making cloning impossible even when the design is revealed.

The silicon PUFs are basically classified into two categories [5]. One uses the characteristics of memory cells such as SRAM-PUFs [6] [7], Butterfly PUFs [8], Flip-flop PUFs [9], Mecca PUFs [10] and Latch PUFs [11] [12]. The other uses the characteristics of delay variations such as Ring Oscillator PUFs [13], Arbiter PUFs [14] and Glitch PUFs (GPUFs) [1]. This paper focuses on the latter. Ring Oscillator PUFs derive entropy from the difference in oscillator frequencies. Arbiter PUFs have an *arbiter* circuit that generates a response determined by the difference in the signal delay between two paths set by a challenge. However, a machine learning attack can predict responses of Arbiter PUFs by using a number of challenge-response pairs (CRPs), as it has been shown that the relationship between challenges and responses is linear [15]. The GPUF [1] was proposed to solve this problem of ease of prediction. A glitch is a pulse of short duration which may occur before the signal settles to a value. The GPUF generates a one-bit response by using the parity of the number of glitches obtained from an 8-bit AES S-Box implementation used as a glitch generator. Part of the challenges correspond to 8-bit inputs to the S-Box. Since the response to challenges behaves like a non-linear function, the developers claim that machine learning attacks are prevented.

Although PUF developers evaluate their proposals themselves, some of them may either accidentally exaggerate on good results or not mention undesirable ones. Hence it is quite important not only to propose and evaluate new PUFs, but also to get the proposals evaluated and analyzed by third-party researchers.

Our Contributions. In this paper, we evaluate both performance and security aspects of the GPUF developed by Suzuki et al. [1] (i.e. "developers") implemented on FPGAs. The reason why we focus on this PUF is that it is one of the most feasible and secure delay-based PUFs because of the resistance against machine learning attacks. However, it has not been evaluated by other researchers yet. Our main contribution consists of three parts. First, we propose a general method to generate responses because the original paper is somewhat obscure about it. To the best of our knowledge, the developers used only 2^8 challenges as input to the 8-bit AES S-Box glitch generator. Hence they relied on a total of $256 \times 8 = 2,048$ responses since the AES S-Box has 8 1-bit outputs. We point out that glitches normally appear when an 8-bit input value of the S-Box is transitioned from one value to another. The glitches thus depend on the input values both before and after the transition. Consequently, a GPUF based on an 8-bit AES S-Box has $256 \times 256 \times 8 = 2^{19}$ CRPs. It means that the performance results presented by the developers are insufficient as they evaluated only a subset of all CRPs. Second, we evaluate the performance of GPUFs using all CRPs. We clarify that both reliability and uniqueness strongly depend on the Hamming distance between the AES S-Box input values before and after the transition. Therefore, GPUF designers have to carefully select the set of CRPs meeting their security requirements, which increases design costs. Additionally, if the supply voltages are changed within the rated voltage range of FPGAs (1.14V ~ 1.26V), GPUFs present low reliability – meaning that the intra-chip variation is greater than 30%. This value exceeds the error correction range when using a Fuzzy Extractor with a reasonable size of redundant data. This indicates that GPUFs present almost no PUF-behavior. Third, we analyze the security of GPUFs. If the AES S-Box input value after the transition is chosen to be one out of 16 specific values, then the number of glitches is almost zero regardless of the input value before the transition. AES S-Box-based GPUFs have "weak" challenges (like a weak key for a block cipher) leading to responses that are more easily predictable than others by an attacker, which could compromise the whole security of a GPUF-based system.

Organization of the Paper. The rest of the paper is organized as follows. Section 2 gives an outline of the original GPUF proposed by the developers, and our proposed method to generate responses using all CRPs. Section 3 evaluates the performance of the GPUF implemented on an FPGA platform. We evaluate both reliability and uniqueness in various voltages. Section 4 evaluates the security of the GPUF, and discusses weak challenges that should not be used. Finally, in Section 5 we summarize our work and comment on future directions.

2   Glitch PUF

2.1   Original GPUF Proposal by Suzuki et al. [1] [16]

Different GPUFs have been proposed until now. In 2008, Crouch et al. [17] [18] first proposed the concept of extracting a unique digital identification using glitches obtained from a 32-bit combinational multiplier. In 2010, Anderson [19] proposed a glitch-based PUF design specifically targeted for FPGAs. This GPUF generates a one-bit response based on the delay differences between two multiplexer (MUX) chains. Then, a new glitch-based PUF using one AES S-Box as a glitch generator was proposed in 2010 [1], and improved in 2012 [16] by Suzuki et al. In this paper, we focus only on the third GPUF proposal (and refer to it as only GPUF) because of its good performance, good security features – such as resistance against machine learning attacks, and practical advantages as it can be implemented on ASIC and FPGA platforms, as claimed by the authors. Figure 1 presents this GPUF. It uses one 8-bit AES S-Box based on composite

Galois field as a glitch generator. The challenge input to the GPUF has 11 bits and is composed of two parts. The first part of the challenge contains 8 bits inputted from the data registers to the AES S-Box. Each of the 8 output bits of the S-Box generates a different number of glitches due to the complicated non-linearity of the AES S-Box implementation. The second part of the challenge contains 3 bits to select one out of the 8 AES S-Box output bits. A toggle flip-flop (TFF) eventually outputs the GPUF response by evaluating the parity of the number of glitches that appear in the selected AES S-Box output bit. To the best of our knowledge, the developers have evaluated 2^{11} CRPs. The masking scheme is used to select *stable* challenges that output the same responses at normal operating condition (room temperature and standard supply voltage) most of the times. For each challenge, the developers evaluated its response 10 times. A challenge was considered *stable* if all 10 responses were equal. According to their strict methodology, challenges yielding at least one different response were discarded.

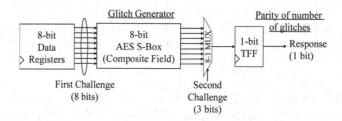

Fig. 1. Glitch PUF

2.2   Our Response Generation Method

In this paper, glitches appear right after the first 8-bit part of the challenge is transitioned from one value (previous 8-bit challenge: C_p) to another (current 8-bit challenge: C_c). Figure 2 depicts a conceptual explanation of two cases. For example, for the same value of C_c (e.g. 31), the number of glitches are respectively 5 or 2 for C_p equal to 246 or 97. Actually, the number of glitches strongly depends on both C_p and C_c according to our experiments (details in Sect. 3). Therefore, we claim that the first part of the GPUF challenge has not 8, but 16 bits (8 bits from C_p and 8 bits from C_c). The combination of all values of C_p and C_c leads to $256 \times 256 = 65,536$ CRPs per S-Box output bit. However, if both C_p and C_c are equal, then no glitch occurs since there is no bit transition, making the responses always equal to zero. Thus, the valid number of CRPs is reduced to $256 \times 255 = 65,280$. As the second part of the challenge has 3 bits, the AES S-Box-based GPUF has in fact a total of $65,280 \times 2^3 = 522,240$ CRPs.

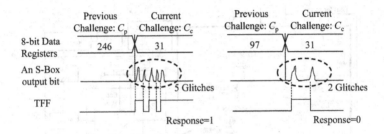

Fig. 2. Number of glitches with respect to C_{P} and C_{C}

3 Performance Evaluation

3.1 Experimental Environment

Figure 3 shows our experimental evaluation system, which uses a Spartan-3E starter kit board [20] with a Xilinx Spartan-3E FPGA (XC3S500E-4FG320C) and a custom-made expansion board with a Xilinx Spartan-6 FPGA (XC6SLX16-2CSG324C). The developers implemented both peripheral circuits such as the block RAM, RS232C module and GPUF circuit on the same FPGA chip. In contrast, we implement the peripheral circuits separately on a Spartan-3E (SP3E) FPGA, and the GPUF circuit on a Spartan-6 (SP6) FPGA. Such configuration enables us to change only the core voltage of the SP6 FPGA chip. The voltage change does not impact the peripheral circuits and does not cause data garbling, which enhances the confidence of our experimental results. An SP6 FPGA chip is put on a socket of the expansion board, being therefore easily replaceable by another chip. A programmable ROM (PROM) is implemented on the expansion board, allowing us to download our circuit design on the PROM through a JTAG port. The core voltage of an SP6 chip can be changed by 0.01V using a stabilized power supply. The two boards are connected with user I/O interfaces through a connector. The clock signal is provided from the SP3E to the SP6 through a SMA cable and port in order to prevent signal degradation. A micro SD adapter and card are also connected to the SP3E board to store the responses from the GPUF. We evaluate 20 GPUFs implemented on 20 SP6 FPGA chips.

Figure 4 shows the details of our circuit designs realized on the SP3E and SP6 FPGA chips. The AES S-Box implementation based on composite Galois field techniques was obtained from the RTL code from [21]. A 50-MHz clock signal generated by an on-board oscillator is applied to a Digital Clock Manager (DCM) primitive yielding a 2.5-MHz clock signal that is applied to the GPUF. The data acquisition process is as follows. When the RS232C module from the SP3E chip receives a start command from a user PC, the module sends a start signal to the CTRL module. The module initializes the values of C_{P} and C_{C} to zero, and stores them into two registers dedicated for C_{P} ($P_1 \sim P_8$) and C_{C} ($C_1 \sim C_8$) on the SP6, respectively. After that, registers storing the inputs to the S-Box ($R_1 \sim R_8$) are transitioned from C_{P} to C_{C} in one cycle. We evaluate not

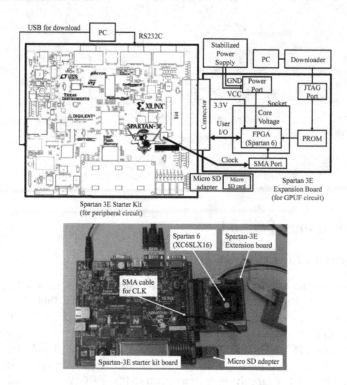

Fig. 3. Experimental evaluation system

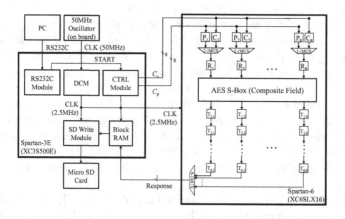

Fig. 4. Circuit design on FPGAs

the parity but the actual number of glitches output from the glitch generator. This does not influence the GPUF performance. The number of glitches is stored into eight 8-bit counters with TFFs ($T_{1,1} \sim T_{8,8}$). Then, the total amount of 64 bits coming from eight 8-bit counters are sent to a block RAM on the SP3 bit-sequentially. The values of the block RAM are sent to a SD write module, and written into a micro SD card. This process is repeated with the same C_p and C_c 100 times as in [1] [16]. Then both C_p and C_c are incremented by 1 from 0 to 255 and the process is repeated 100 times analogously. Note that the responses are meaningful when C_p is not equal to C_c, as mentioned in Sect. 2.2.

In Sect. 3.2, we evaluate the following performance-related figure of merits [22] of GPUFs operating at 1.20V: reliability, uniqueness, uniformity and bit-aliasing. We choose 1.20V as the standard voltage because the rated voltage range of the SP6 FPGA (XC6SLX16-2CSG324C) is 1.20 ± 0.06V (1.14V ~ 1.26V). In the standard voltage of 1.20V our GPUF implementations present performance results in accordance with the developers' ones. Later, in Sect. 3.3 we evaluate our GPUF implementations operating at the maximum allowed FPGA rated voltages of 1.14V and 1.26V.

3.2 Performance at the Standard Voltage of 1.20V

The reliability and uniqueness results of our GPUF implementations are shown in Figs. 5 and 6, respectively. In order to evaluate the reliability, 101 responses are generated per SP6 FPGA chip (see Appendix). One response is used as the reference, and the remaining are used for analysis. The response space size is $65,280 \times 8$ bits. Figure 5 shows a histogram of normalized Hamming distances between the reference response and each repeated one (i.e. $100 \times 20(\mathrm{chips}) = 2,000$ elements). The average error rate when masking is on is approximately 1.38% with a standard deviation (S.D.) of 0.11%, which is much less than the 15% assumed in [23] for stable responses based on a Fuzzy Extractor with a reasonable size of redundant data. Hence our result shows that the GPUF yields highly reliable responses, in accordance with the developers' results. Next, in order to evaluate the uniqueness, a total of 20 responses using all 20 FPGAs (one response per FPGA) is generated. Figure 6 shows a histogram of normalized Hamming distances between every combination of two responses, i.e. $_{20}C_2 = 190$ combinations. This evaluation is a general way of showing the extent to which the responses of the chips are different. The difference in the responses of two arbitrary PUFs is approximately 39.8% with a S.D. of 1.1% when masking is on. GPUF yields responses with a lower level of uniqueness than the ideal difference of 50%. This result also corresponds to the developers' one.

Next, we evaluate both the uniformity and bit-aliasing of GPUFs – a contribution that has not been addressed by the developers in [1] [16]. The uniformity evaluates how uniform the proportion of '0's and '1's is in the response bits of a PUF. For our GPUF implementations, the average uniformity is approximately 50.6% and 50.7% when masking is off and on, respectively. Since the ideal uniformity is 50%, our GPUFs satisfy the requirement for uniformity. The bit-aliasing evaluates how different the proportion of '0's and '1's is in the 20 response bits extracted respectively from the 20 PUFs given the same challenge. The ideal bit-aliasing is also 50% with a S.D. of 0%. Figures 7 (I) and (II) show histograms of the proportion of '1's when masking is off and on, respectively. The bit-aliasing S.D. is approximately 4.7% larger when masking is used than

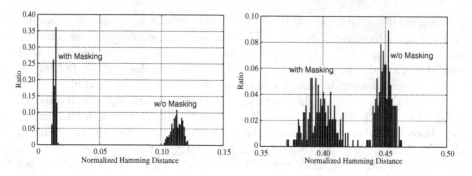

Fig. 5. Reliability   **Fig. 6.** Uniqueness

when it is not used. This is because the masking scheme discards the responses whose proportion of '1's is around 50%. Hence Fig. (II) lacks the peak of the normal distribution. It turns out that there are many responses fixed to 0 or 1 in the GPUF implementations on the 20 chips. This means that GPUFs have many useless CRPs due to the predictability of the responses. Hence GPUF designers should not use all CRPs due to security reasons. This result is implied by the low uniqueness of GPUFs as shown in Fig. 6. The fact that the S.D. becomes larger when masking is being used is related to the lower uniqueness and entropy of responses, as previously mentioned by the developers.

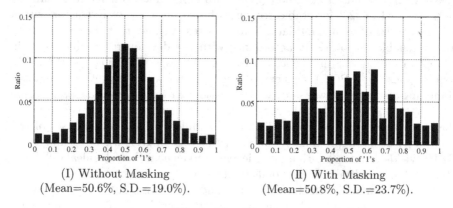

(I) Without Masking
(Mean=50.6%, S.D.=19.0%).

(II) With Masking
(Mean=50.8%, S.D.=23.7%).

Fig. 7. Bit-aliasing

3.3 Performance at Non-standard Voltages (1.14V and 1.26V)

In this section, we evaluate the robustness of the GPUF against voltage variation – the reliability of GPUFs when their supply voltage is changed to 1.14V and 1.26V. Figure 8 (I) shows the response error rates (see Appendix) of our GPUF implementations in comparison to the developers' ones. At 1.14V, our response error rate is approximately 35% when masking is on, differently from the developer's results ($\approx$10%) [16]. A possible reason for the difference in the results could have been caused by our expansion board. However, the proper operation of our expansion board was verified by implementing Latch PUFs on the SP6 FPGAs and confirming that the response error rates are less than 15% even when changes in the supply voltage occur. Consequently, according to our evaluation, the robustness against voltage variation of GPUFs is much lower than the one provided by the developers. This is partly because they evaluated only 256 × 8 CRPs, while we consider all 256 × 255 × 8 CRPs. In fact, if we choose only 256 × 8 CRPs satisfying the following two conditions: the Hamming distance between C_p and C_c being equal to 1 (HD(C_p, C_c)=1), and the different bit position being the least significant bit, then the robustness against voltage variation becomes remarkably better than the developers' results, as shown in Fig. 8 (II). In the following, we discuss the relationship between both reliability and uniqueness to the CRPs. The CRPs are divided into 8 groups based either on each value of HD(C_p, C_c) (excluding HD(C_p, C_c) = 0, as no glitches occur) or on which S-Box bit is used to generate a response.

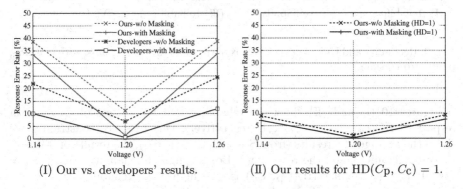

(I) Our vs. developers' results.   (II) Our results for HD(C_p, C_c) = 1.

Fig. 8. Response error rates against various voltages

Figures 9 (I)-(III) and (IV) show the response error rates (reliability) and the uniqueness of CRPs extracted from each S-Box bit (S-Box[0] $\sim$ S-Box[7]), respectively. The reliability is evaluated at three voltages (1.14V, 1.20V and 1.26V), while the uniqueness is evaluated only at the standard voltage of 1.20V. The results when masking is on and off are shown in the left and right histograms, respectively. At 1.14V and 1.26V, the reliability ranges from 30 to 40% depending on the S-Box bit even when masking is on. At 1.20V, the uniqueness ranges from 35 to 45% also depending on the S-Box bit when masking is on. The reliability and uniqueness distributions are thus close to each other, possibly overlapping. Therefore, our GPUF implementations show almost no PUF behavior as an authentication protocol free of errors cannot be implemented. As both reliability and uniqueness of GPUFs strongly depend on the S-Box bits used to generate responses, if GPUFs are used for key generation, suitable challenges should be carefully chosen based on security requirements.

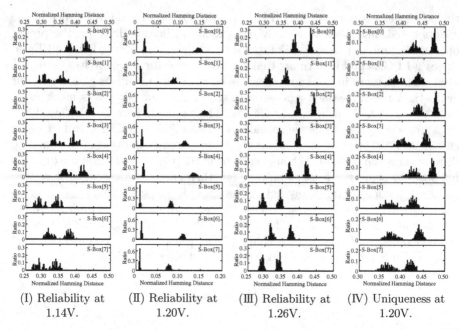

(I) Reliability at 1.14V.   (II) Reliability at 1.20V.   (III) Reliability at 1.26V.   (IV) Uniqueness at 1.20V.

Fig. 9. Reliability and Uniqueness vs. S-Box output bits (left histograms: with masking, right: w/o masking)

Figures 10 (I) and (II) show the reliability and uniqueness of CRPs with respect to $HD(C_p, C_c) = 1, \ldots, 8$, respectively. Due to space constraints, we show: the average of 8 results (from S-Box[0] to S-Box[7]), the results of S-Box[2] (lowest reliability), and the results of S-Box[7] (highest reliability), as shown in Fig. 9 (I). The smaller $HD(C_p, C_c)$ is, the higher the reliability is, and the lower the uniqueness is. This is because if $HD(C_p, C_c)$ is small, the number of changed bits in the S-Box is also small. As a result, the transition from C_p to C_c has little influence on the generation of glitches. As GPUFs perform differently with regard to $HD(C_p, C_c)$, the need for a designer to select appropriate CRPs meeting a system's requirement leads to an additional increase in the design cost. The reliability at 1.20V can be dramatically enhanced by using the masking scheme proposed by the developers. However, the reliability cannot be enhanced effectively at 1.14V and 1.26V using the masking scheme. Consequently, there is no correlation between unstable CRPs at 1.20V and at 1.14V or 1.26V. GPUF designers should thus remove, i.e. mask, CRPs that are unstable not only at 1.20V but also at 1.14V and 1.26V. However, this is not realistic and practical. Such solution not only increases the manufacturing costs as well, but also reduces the number of CRPs, which causes loss of information entropy in the responses.

Finally, we evaluate the side effects of using the masking scheme: how many responses are unstable and therefore discarded. The three types of bar graphs in Fig. 11 show the number of stable responses in three cases: without masking (all responses), with masking at 1.20V (stable responses at 1.20V) and with masking

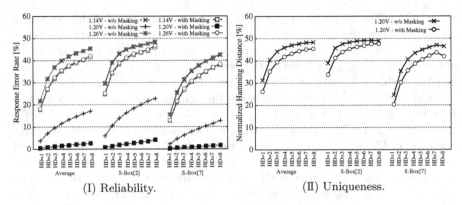

(I) Reliability.   (II) Uniqueness.

Fig. 10. Reliability and Uniqueness vs. HD(C_p, C_c)

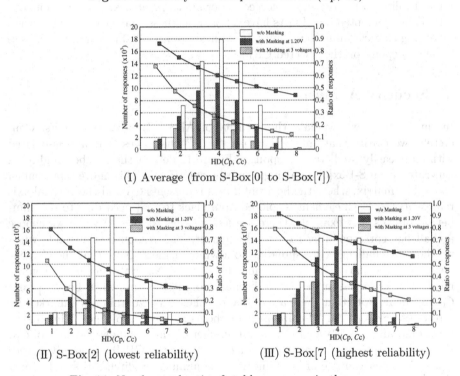

(I) Average (from S-Box[0] to S-Box[7])

(II) S-Box[2] (lowest reliability)   (III) S-Box[7] (highest reliability)

Fig. 11. Number and ratio of stable responses in three cases

at three voltages (stable responses at 1.14V, 1.20V and 1.26V). In fact, the third case is not realistic and practical since the masking processes at all voltages have to be applied. We, however, show this case to evaluate the actual number of valid and stable CRPs in the GPUF. The line graphs in Fig. 11 show the ratio of stable responses in each group of HD(C_p, C_c). We show once more the average results for S-Box[2] and S-Box[7] due to space constraints, over the 20

SP6 FPGAs. The larger HD(C_p, C_c) is, the lower the ratio of stable responses is (i.e. the larger the number of discarded responses is). That is why the larger HD(C_p, C_c) is, the higher the response error rate is, as shown in Fig. 10 (I). Also, there are large gaps between the two lines in Figs. 11 (I)-(III). This means that the stable responses at 1.20V are not always stable at 1.14V and 1.26V. Hence the response error rate is high and the voltage resistance of the GPUF is quite low, as shown in Fig. 10 (I). By comparing Fig. 11 (II) and Fig. 11 (III), the lower the reliability is, the larger the number of discarded responses is. Out of a total of 65,280 × 8 responses, the ratios of stable responses at 1.20V and at the three voltages are 61.7% and 30.1%, respectively. Consequently, GPUFs have in fact a number of useless CRPs that should be removed by the masking scheme. This masking reduces the total number of CRPs or the total pattern of keys generated by multiple GPUFs. The low total number of CRPs or keys might facilitate an attacker to succeed in her modeling attack. In conclusion, our GPUFs implemented on FPGAs have a low robustness against voltage variation according to our evaluation results. In addition, both reliability and uniqueness strongly depend on the selected CRPs.

4   Security Analysis

In this section, we evaluate the security of AES S-Box-based GPUFs. Concretely, we clarify that the GPUF has "weak" challenges that are associated with more easily predictable responses. Figure 12 depicts the number of glitches generated from S-Box[6] on a single specific chip (i=1). This figure represents a 256 × 256 matrix, where the horizontal axis represents C_p and the vertical axis represents C_c. Each element is colored from black to gray according to the number of glitches. For example, there are less glitches ($\approx 0 \sim 1$) when we choose a challenge corresponding to a black element. The response is unstable when we choose a challenge corresponding to a white element. Note that the element means not the parity but the number of glitches. Naturally, a black diagonal line can be observed in this figure because no glitch occurs when both C_p and C_c are equal. Note that there are also a few black "horizontal lines", marked by arrows ($A_1 \sim A_8$). All 20 chips present the same pattern of lines. This means that some values of C_c lead to a small number of glitches independently of C_p. Hence if we use such values of C_c as challenges to the GPUF, then adversaries will have the advantage of knowing that the number of glitches is small, which may help them succeed more easily with an attack aiming at predicting GPUF responses.

The following discusses the reason why such non-secure challenges exist using Fig. 13. An AES S-Box implementation using composite field consists of three sub-parts: isomorph δ, Galois Field (GF) inverter, and a combination module of inverse isomorph δ^{-1} and affine transformation. Let the 8-bit variables x and y be the input and output of the AES S-Box, respectively. Also, let the 8-bit variables a and b be the outputs of the isomorph δ and the GF inverter, respectively. Our goal is to find special values of x making the 6-th output bit of the S-Box ($y[6]$) zero. In step 1 from Fig. 13, according to the properties of

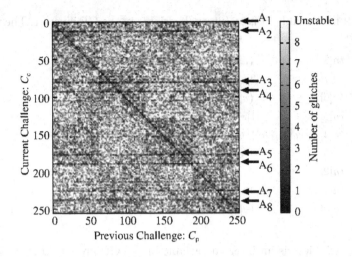

Fig. 12. Number of glitches (S-Box[6], Chip $i=1$)

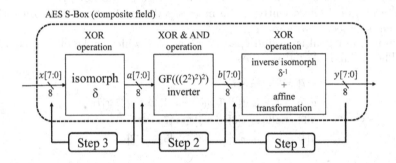

Fig. 13. An AES S-Box implementation using composite field

the combination module, the output value $y[6]$ satisfies:

$$y[6] = {\sim}b[4] \oplus b[5] \oplus b[6] \oplus b[7].$$

Hence $y[6]$ depends on the upper 4 bits of b.

Next, in step 2, we focus on the GF inverter. The value $b[7:4]$, which represents the four most significant bits of b, satisfies:

$$b[7] = tn[0] \oplus tn[1] \oplus tn[3] \oplus tn[4],$$
$$b[6] = tn[0] \oplus tn[2] \oplus tn[3] \oplus tn[5],$$
$$b[5] = tn[0] \oplus tn[1] \oplus tn[7] \oplus tn[8],$$
$$b[4] = tn[0] \oplus tn[2] \oplus tn[6] \oplus tn[7].$$

Here, the 9-bit variable tn is an internal variable in the GF inverter. The variable tn satisfies:

$$
\begin{aligned}
tn[8] &= & (v[3]) & \quad \& \quad (a[7]), \\
tn[7] &= & (v[2] \oplus v[3]) & \quad \& \quad (a[6] \oplus a[7]), \\
tn[6] &= & (v[2]) & \quad \& \quad (a[6]), \\
tn[5] &= & (v[1] \oplus v[3]) & \quad \& \quad (a[5] \oplus a[7]), \\
tn[4] &= (v[0] \oplus v[1] \oplus v[2] \oplus v[3]) & \& \quad (a[4] \oplus a[5] \oplus a[6] \oplus a[7]), \\
tn[3] &= & (v[0] \oplus v[2]) & \quad \& \quad (a[4] \oplus a[6]), \\
tn[2] &= & (v[1]) & \quad \& \quad (a[5]), \\
tn[1] &= & (v[0] \oplus v[1]) & \quad \& \quad (a[4] \oplus a[5]), \\
tn[0] &= & (v[0]) & \quad \& \quad (a[4]).
\end{aligned}
$$

The 4-bit variable v is an internal variable in the GF inverter. Let us focus on the 4-bit variables, $a[4]$, $a[5]$, $a[6]$ and $a[7]$, on the right-hand side of the above-mentioned equations of tn. If the values of the 4-bit variables are all zero, tn also becomes zero. So the glitches caused by the variable v do not propagate to tn, $b[7:4]$ and $y[6]$. Consequently, if the most significant 4 bits of a are zero, then no glitch is expected to appear in $y[6]$.

In step 3, our goal is to find special values of x which make $a[7:4]$ equal to zero. The variable $a[7:4]$ satisfies:

$$
\begin{aligned}
a[7] &= x[5] \oplus x[7], \\
a[6] &= x[1] \oplus x[2] \oplus x[3] \oplus x[4] \oplus x[6] \oplus x[7], \\
a[5] &= x[2] \oplus x[3] \oplus x[5] \oplus x[7], \\
a[4] &= x[1] \oplus x[2] \oplus x[3] \oplus x[5] \oplus x[7].
\end{aligned}
$$

Hence the following holds:

$$
\begin{aligned}
x[1] &= 0, \\
(x[5], x[7]) &= (0,0) \text{ or } (1,1), \\
(x[2], x[3]) &= (0,0) \text{ or } (1,1), \\
(x[4], x[6]) &= \begin{cases} (0,0) \text{ or } (1,1) & (\text{if } x[7] = 0), \\ (0,1) \text{ or } (1,0) & (\text{if } x[7] = 1). \end{cases}
\end{aligned}
$$

Finally, we obtain the 16 patterns of the input x that are expected to generate almost no glitches in the S-Box bit $y[6]$, as shown in Table 1. They correspond to the 16 specific values of C_C marked by the eight arrows in Fig. 12. There are actually 16 black horizontal lines in Fig. 12, but only eight lines corresponding to the eight arrows can be visually observed. This is because the 16 specific values consist of eight pairs of consecutive numbers. In our GPUF implementations, the number of glitches whose challenges C_C and C_P are one of the 16×255 patterns is zero or one, which is smaller than for other challenges. However, the GPUF responses include zero and one with almost the same ratio. This means that such 16 patterns of C_C are secure if the parity of the number of glitches is used as response. Some GPUFs implemented on other kinds of FPGAs or ASICs, however, have a possibility to generate no glitch if using the above values of C_C. Hence we suggest that such values of C_C should not be used.

Table 1. The 16 patterns of the input x generating almost no glitches in $y[6]$

$(x[5], x[7])$	$(x[2], x[3])$	$(x[4], x[6])$	$x[1]$	x (binary) (†)	x (decimal)	Arrows in Fig. 12
(0,0)	(0,0)	(0,0)	0	0000000∗	0, 1	A_1
		(1,1)	0	0101000∗	80, 81	A_3
	(1,1)	(0,0)	0	0000110∗	12, 13	A_2
		(1,1)	0	0101110∗	92, 93	A_4
(1,1)	(0,0)	(0,1)	0	1110000∗	224, 225	A_7
		(1,0)	0	1011000∗	176, 177	A_5
	(1,1)	(0,1)	0	1110110∗	236, 237	A_8
		(1,0)	0	1011110∗	188, 189	A_6

(†) Asterisks mean '0' or '1'.

5 Conclusion

This paper experimentally analyzed GPUFs using a composite field-based AES S-Box implementation as a glitch generator on FPGAs. First, we clarified that the number of glitches depends on both the previous and current states of the registers dedicated to storing the challenge bits that are input to the AES S-Box. As a consequence, GPUFs have a total of 2^{19} CRPs, which is much more than the 2^{11} CRPs evaluated by the GPUF developers [1] [16]. According to our experiments with 20 FPGAs, GPUFs using all 2^{19} CRPs showed a low robustness against voltage variation. Within the rated voltage range of the FPGAs (1.14~1.26V), response error rates approached 35%. The result exceeds the error correction range of a Fuzzy Extractor with a reasonable size of redundant data. Our results also indicated that GPUFs present almost no PUF-behavior as both reliability and uniqueness are relatively low. Finally, we found that our GPUF implementations have 16 × 255 weak challenges leading to almost no glitches regardless of the previous challenge bits stored in the registers. In conclusion, the AES S-Box implementation using composite field may not represent the best option for generating glitches for the GPUF due to issues with robustness against voltage variation and easily predictable responses.

To the best of our knowledge, other well-known AES S-Box implementations, such as sum of product (SOP), product of sum (POS), table lookup (TBL), positive polarity Reed-Miller (PPRM) [24] and 3-stage PPRM [25], are not suitable for GPUFs either. Although SOP, POS or TBL are able to generate glitches, these implementations have larger area size than a composite field-based implementation. Hence these designs are not suitable for PUFs on IC cards with limited resources. PPRM or 3-stage PPRM are designed to reduce the power consumption by preventing the generation of glitches. These are obviously not suitable for GPUFs. Thus we suggest that the AES S-Box should not be used as a glitch generator for GPUFs on FPGAs.

An ASIC implementation of the AES S-Box would probably not behave likewise FPGAs. The performance, such as reliability and uniqueness, has a possibility to improve if GPUFs are implemented on ASICs. Future work should include a discussion of performance and security evaluation of GPUFs on ASICs.

Acknowledgements. This work was supported in part by the Research Council KU Leuven: GOA TENSE (GOA/11/007), by the IAP Programme P6/26 BCRYPT of the Belgian State (Belgian Science Policy), by the European Commission through the ICT programme under contract ICT-2007-216676 ECRYPT II, by the Flemish Government through FWO G.0550.12N and the Hercules Foundation AKUL/11/19 and by the European Commission through the ICT programme under contract FP7-ICT-2011-284833 PUFFIN.

References

1. Suzuki, D., Shimizu, K.: The Glitch PUF: A New Delay-PUF Architecture Exploiting Glitch Shapes. In: Mangard, S., Standaert, F.-X. (eds.) CHES 2010. LNCS, vol. 6225, pp. 366–382. Springer, Heidelberg (2010)
2. Pappu, R.S.: Physical One-Way Functions. PhD thesis, Massachusetts Institute of Technology (2001)
3. Gassend, B., Clarke, D., van Dijk, M., Devadas, S.: Silicon Physical Random Functions. In: Proceedings of CCS 2002, pp. 148–160 (2002)
4. Gassend, B., Clarke, D., Lim, D., van Dijk, M., Devadas, S.: Identification and Authentication of Integrated Circuits. In: Concurrency and Computation: Practice and Experiences, pp. 1077–1098 (2004)
5. Maes, R., Verbauwhede, I.: Physically unclonable Functions: A Study on the State of the Art and Future Research Directions. In: Towards Hardware Intrinsic Security: Foundation and Practice. Information Security and Cryptography, pp. 3–37. Springer, Heidelberg (2010)
6. Guajardo, J., Kumar, S.S., Schrijen, G.-J., Tuyls, P.: FPGA Intrinsic PUFs and Their Use for IP Protection. In: Paillier, P., Verbauwhede, I. (eds.) CHES 2007. LNCS, vol. 4727, pp. 63–80. Springer, Heidelberg (2007)
7. Holcomb, D.E., Burleson, W.P., Fu, K.: Initial SRAM State as a Fingerprint and Source of True Random Numbers for RFID Tags. In: Proceedings of the Conference on RFID Security (2007)
8. Kumar, S.S., Guajardo, J., Maes, R., Schrijen, G.J., Tuyls, P.: Extended Abstract: The Butterfly PUF: Protecting IP on every FPGA. In: Proceedings of HOST 2008, pp. 67–70 (2008)
9. Maes, R., Tuyls, P., Verbauwhede, I.: Intrinsic PUFs from Flip-flops on Reconfigurable Devices. In: 3rd Benelux Workshop on Information and System Security (WISSec 2008), Eindhoven, NL, p. 17 (2008)
10. Krishna, A.R., Narasimhan, S., Wang, X., Bhunia, S.: MECCA: A Robust Low-Overhead PUF Using Embedded Memory Array. In: Preneel, B., Takagi, T. (eds.) CHES 2011. LNCS, vol. 6917, pp. 407–420. Springer, Heidelberg (2011)

11. Su, Y., Holleman, J., Otis, B.: A 1.6pJ/bit 96% Stable Chip-ID Generating Circuit using Process Variations. In: IEEE International on Solid-State Circuits Conference, ISSCC 2007. Digest of Technical Papers, pp. 406–611 (2007)
12. Su, Y., Holleman, J., Otis, B.P.: A Digital 1.6 pJ/bit Chip Identification Circuit Using Process Variations. IEEE Journal of Solid-State Circuits 43(1), 69–77 (2008)
13. Suh, G.E., Devadas, S.: Physical Unclonable Functions for Device Authentication and Secret Key Generation. In: Proceedings of DAC 2007, pp. 9–14 (2007)
14. Lee, J.W., Lim, D., Gassend, B., Suh, G.E., van Dijk, M., Devadas, S.: A Technique to Build a Secret Key in Integrated Circuits for Identification and Authentication Applications. In: Proceedings of the IEEE VLSI Circuits Symposium, pp. 176–179 (2004)
15. Rührmair, U., Sehnke, F., Sölter, J., Dror, G., Devadas, S., Schmidhuber, J.: Modeling Attacks on Physical Unclonable Functions. In: Proceedings of the 17th ACM Conference on Computer and Communications Security, CCS 2010, pp. 237–249. ACM, New York (2010)
16. Shimizu, K., Suzuki, D., Kasuya, T.: Glitch PUF: Extracting Information from Usually Unwanted Glitches. IEICE Transactions 95-A(1), 223–233 (2012)
17. Crouch, J.W., Patel, H.J., Kim, Y.C., Bennington, R.W.: Creating unique identifiers on field programmable gate arrays using natural processing variations. In: Proceedings of FPL 2008, pp. 579–582 (2008)
18. Patel, H.J., Crouch, J.W., Kim, Y.C., Kim, T.C.: Creating a unique digital fingerprint using existing combinational logic. In: Proceeding of ISCAS 2009, pp. 2693–2696 (2009)
19. Anderson, J.H.: A PUF Design for Secure FPGA-Based Embedded Systems. In: Proceedings of the 2010 Asia and South Pacific Design Automation Conference, ASPDAC 2010, pp. 1–6. IEEE Press, Piscataway (2010)
20. Spartan-3E starter kit board, http://www.xilinx.com/products/devkits/HW-SPAR3E-SK-US-G.html
21. AIST (Agency of Industrial Science, Technology), and Tohoku University in Japan. HDL code used for an AES S-Box implementation, http://www.aoki.ecei.tohoku.ac.jp/crypto/items/AES_Comp.v
22. Maiti, A., Gunreddy, V., Schaumont, P.: A Systematic Method to Evaluate and Compare the Performance of Physical Unclonable Functions. Cryptology ePrint Archive, Report 2011/657 (2011)
23. Maes, R., Tuyls, P., Verbauwhede, I.: Low-Overhead Implementation of a Soft Decision Helper Data Algorithm for SRAM PUFs. In: Clavier, C., Gaj, K. (eds.) CHES 2009. LNCS, vol. 5747, pp. 332–347. Springer, Heidelberg (2009)
24. Sasao, T.: AND-EXOR Expressions and Their Optimization. In: Logic Synthesis and Optimization, pp. 287–312. Kluwer Academic Publishers (1993)
25. Morioka, S., Satoh, A.: An Optimized S-Box Circuit Architecture for Low Power AES Design. In: Kaliski Jr., B.S., Koç, Ç.K., Paar, C. (eds.) CHES 2002. LNCS, vol. 2523, pp. 172–186. Springer, Heidelberg (2003)

Appendix

In order to evaluate the reliability, we extract an n-bit ($65,280 \times 8$) reference response (R_i) from i-th FPGA chip ($1 \leq i \leq w$, $w = 20$ in this work) at normal operating condition (room temperature and standard supply voltage of 1.20V). The same n-bit response is extracted at a different operating condition (different temperature and/or supply voltage) with a value R_i'. Then, m samples ($m = 100$ in this work, as in [1] [16]) of R_i' are collected. Here, $R_{i,t}'$ is the t-th ($1 \le t \le m$) sample of R_i'. For the chip i and the sample t, each data element of the reliability histogram is calculated as follows:

$$HD_{i,t} = \frac{1}{n} \sum_{C_p=0}^{255} \sum_{C_c=0}^{255} HD\{R_i'(C_p, C_c), R_{i,t}'(C_p, C_c)\}.$$

Note that we exclude the responses where C_p equals C_c because no glitch occurs. The reliability histograms shown in Fig. 5 and Fig. 9 (I) include 2,000 data elements, resulted from i and t. The response error rate shown in Fig. 8 and Fig. 10 (I) is calculated as follows:

$$ErrorRate = \frac{1}{w \cdot m} \sum_{i=1}^{w} \sum_{t=1}^{m} HD_{i,t}.$$

Relaxing IND-CCA: Indistinguishability against Chosen Ciphertext *Verification* Attack

Sumit Kumar Pandey[1], Santanu Sarkar[1], and Mahabir Prasad Jhanwar[2]

[1] Applied Statistics Unit, Indian Statistical Institute, Kolkata 700 108, India
[2] C R RAO AIMSCS, Hyderabad, India
emailpandey@gmail.com, sarkar.santanu.bir@gmail.com,
mahavir.jhawar@gmail.com

Abstract. The definition of IND-CCA security model for public key encryption allows an adversary to obtain (adaptively) decryption of ciphertexts of its choice. That is, the adversary is given oracle access to the decryption function corresponding to the decryption key in use. The adversary may make queries that do not correspond to a *valid* ciphertext, and the answer will be accordingly (i.e., a special "failure" symbol).

In this article, we investigate the case where we restrict the oracle to only determine if the query made is a valid ciphertext or not. That is, the oracle will output 1 if the query string is a valid ciphertext (do not output the corresponding plaintext) and output 0 otherwise. We call this oracle as *"ciphertext verification oracle"* and the corresponding security model as Indistinguishability against *chosen ciphertext verification attack* (IND-CCVA). We point out that this seemingly weaker security model is meaningful, clear and useful to the extent where we motivate that certain cryptographic functionalities can be achieved by ensuring the IND-CCVA security where as IND-CPA is not sufficient and IND-CCA provides more than necessary. We support our claim by providing nontrivial construction (existing/new) of:

- public key encryption schemes that are IND-CCVA secure but not IND-CCA secure,
- public key encryption schemes that are IND-CPA secure but not IND-CCVA secure.
- public key encryption schemes that are IND-CCA1 secure but not IND-CCVA secure.

Our discoveries are another manifestation of the subtleties that make the study of security notions for public key encryption schemes so attractive and are important towards achieving the definitional clarity of the target security.

Keywords: PKE security notions, IND-CPA, IND-CCA, IND-CCVA.

1 Introduction

The IND-CCA (also known as IND-CCA2) security (security against adaptive chosen ciphertext attacks [16,18,3,8,20]) is now a days considered the *de facto*

A. Bogdanov and S. Sanadhya (Eds.): SPACE 2012, LNCS 7644, pp. 63–76, 2012.
© Springer-Verlag Berlin Heidelberg 2012

level of security required for public key encryption schemes used in practice. Unfortunately, only a handful of approaches are known for constructing encryption schemes that meet this notion of security, thus showing the strongness of this security model. In practice, there are certain cryptographic functionalities for which the security requirement is apparently **less stronger** than IND-CCA. There had been some research [25,24,23] to quantify the gap between the IND-CPA and IND-CCA security.

The most common threat to IND-CCA security is that of a query on a malformed ciphertext causing the decryption oracle to leak damaging information, either about the private key, or about the plaintext. Understanding, the explicit behaviour of the decryption oracle could be the keypoint. In the IND-CCA model, the decryption oracle provides decryption of the ciphertexts of our choice. In this work, we limit the output of the decryption oracle: it will only verify whether or not a query string is a valid ciphertext or not. Consider a setting where a server has the secret key, receives and decrypts ciphertext and sends to the client an accept/reject message depending on whether the ciphertext was valid or not. This setting actually occurs in real life, some schemes can be broken in this setting, and Bleichenbacher's [4] attack is an example of this.

1.1 Background

The security for public key encryption was first formally defined by Goldwasser and Micali [12]. Their notion of *semantic security*, roughly speaking, requires that observation of a ciphertext does not enable an adversary to compute anything about the underlying plaintext message that it could not have computed on its own (i.e., prior to observing the ciphertext). Goldwasser and Micali (see also [10,11]) proved that semantic security is equivalent to the notion of *indistinguishability* that requires (roughly) the following: given a public key pk, a ciphertext C, and two possible plaintexts m_0, m_1, it is infeasible to determine if C is an encryption of m_0 or an encryption of m_1. We will refer to these notions using the commonly accepted term "IND-CPA" security.

IND-CPA security does not guarantee any security against *chosen ciphertext* attacks by which an adversary may obtain decryption of ciphertexts of its choice. Indistinguishability based definitions appropriate for this setting were given by Naor and Yung [16] and Rackoff and Simon [18]. Naor and Yung consider *non-adaptive* chosen ciphertext attack in which the adversary may request decryptions only *before* it obtains the challenge ciphertext. Rackoff and Simon define the stronger notion of security against *adaptive* chosen ciphertext attacks whereby the adversary may request decryptions even after seeing the challenge ciphertext, under the natural limitation that the adversary may not request decryption of the challenge ciphertext it self. We will refer to the later notion as "IND-CCA" security. Lots of research have been done in this direction (see [21] and references there in). Loffus et al. [15] have studied IND-CCA and showed the importance of CCA-like notions in the security of cloud computing. Recently, in [22], CCA has been extended where adversary can not only exploit the decryption oracle queries but also the intermediate calculations stored in hardware (especially RAM). This new notion, where decryption oracle is referred as glass box decryption oracle, is known as Glass-Box-CCA.

1.2 Motivation

In the literature the paradigms that construct IND-CCA secure cryptosystems are few in number. Among them, the paradigms introduced by Naor and Yung in [16] and by Cramer and Shoup in [5,6] are very famous. The proofs of well-formedness of ciphertexts have been shown to underlie the constructions that were instantiated by both of the above paradigms. Informally it speaks of a validity check step for ciphertexts in the decryption algorithm. Infact, Elkind and Sahai have observed [7] that both the above approaches for constructing CCA-secure encryption schemes can be viewed as special cases of a single paradigm. In this paradigm one starts with a CPA-secure cryptosystem in which certain ill-formed ciphertexts are indistinguishable from honestly-generated ciphertexts. A CCA-secure cryptosystem is then obtained by having the sender honestly generate a ciphertext using the underlying CPA-secure scheme, and then append a proof of well-formedness (satisfying certain criteria) to this ciphertext. Thus having a validity check seems a sufficient condition to achieve IND-CCA security and became a common practice until Bleichenbacher's [4] attack showed that this is not the case; the attack broke the IND-CCA security of the underlying scheme using a oracle that confirms just the validity of the ciphertext. Thus for the class of public key encryption schemes with validity check in the decryption could give rise to a meaningful security model (less stronger than IND-CCA) where the adversary has access to a oracle of the above nature. We name this security model as IND-CCVA.

In this article we search for IND-CCVA secure public key encryption schemes. Beside its theoretical importance, there are some practical benefits as well. For example, consider the scenario where one has to pick a encryption scheme between $\mathcal{E}_1$ and $\mathcal{E}_2$, where both are IND-CPA secure but not IND-CCA and both of them are efficient. Suppose $\mathcal{E}_2$ differs with $\mathcal{E}_1$ by having a validity checking step in its decryption algorithm. In this case one may tend to prefer $\mathcal{E}_2$ over $\mathcal{E}_1$, but our findings will show that this may not be a wiser decision always.

1.3 Summary of Our Results

In the definition of IND-CCA security model for public key encryption, the adversary is given oracle access to the decryption function corresponding to the decryption key in use. The adversary may make queries that do not correspond to a *valid* ciphertext, and the answer will be accordingly (i.e., a special "failure" symbol). In this article, we investigate the case where we restrict the oracle to only verify if the query made is a valid ciphertext or not. That is, the oracle will output 1 (not the corresponding plaintext) if the query string is a valid ciphertext and output 0 otherwise. We will denote this oracle by the name "*ciphertext verification oracle*" and the corresponding security model by the name Indistinguishability against *chosen ciphertext verification attack* (IND-CCVA).

We point out that this seemingly weaker security model is meaningful, clear and useful to the extent where we observe that certain cryptographic functionalities can be achieved by ensuring the IND-CCVA security where IND-CPA is not sufficient and IND-CCA provides more than necessary. We further support our claim by providing generic construction of:

- public key encryption schemes that are IND-CCVA secure but not IND-CCA secure,
- public key encryption schemes that are IND-CPA secure but not IND-CCVA secure,
- public key encryption schemes that are IND-CCA1 secure but not IND-CCVA secure.

1.4   Organization

In the following section, we fix notations, recall some notations from number theory, and provide an informal overview of public key encryption and the IND-CCA security model. Formal definition of IND-CCVA security model appear in Section 3. The separation results will appear through sections 4, 5, and 6.

2   Preliminaries

In this section we first fix the notations. We write $x \xleftarrow{\mathcal{R}} X$ to denote the action of assigning a value to the variable x sampled uniformly from the set X. If $\mathcal{A}$ is a probabilistic algorithm which takes an input x, $\mathcal{A}(x)$ denotes the output distribution of $\mathcal{A}$ on input x. Hence, $y \xleftarrow{\mathcal{R}} \mathcal{A}(x)$ denotes the assignment of a value to the variable y from the output distribution of algorithm $\mathcal{A}$ on input x. We can denote any probabilistic algorithm $\mathcal{A}$ by a deterministic algorithm $\mathcal{A}'$ which takes additional input, random coins, uniformly sampled from some set R.

Let n be a positive integer. The number of positive integers less than n and relatively prime to n is denoted $\phi(n)$. We take any string x as a $\{0,1\}$-string. If u and v are two strings, then uv or $u\|v$ denotes the concatenation of strings u and v. $|x|$ denotes the length of the string x.

PKE. A public key encryption scheme $\prod = $ (KeyGen, Enc, Dec) is a triple of algorithms. The key generation algorithm KeyGen takes a security parameter 1^λ and returns a pair (pk, sk) of matching public and secret keys. The encryption algorithm Enc takes a public key pk and a message $m \in \{0,1\}^*$ to produce a ciphertext C. The deterministic decryption algorithm Dec takes sk and ciphertext C to produce either a message $m \in \{0,1\}^*$ or a special symbol $\perp$ to indicate that the ciphertext was invalid. The consistency requirement is that for all $\lambda \in \mathbb{N}$, for all (pk, sk) which can be output by KeyGen(1^λ), for all $m \in \{0,1\}^*$ and for all C that can be output by Enc(pk, m), we have that Dec(sk, C) $= m$.

Remark: In the definition of the decryption algorithm we assume the standard practice that it returns $\perp$ if the input ciphertext is invalid. Our assumption (which is implicit throughout this paper) is a special case of the standard definition where the decryption algorithm may return any arbitrary value (string) for a given invalid ciphertext.

IND-CCA. We recall the definitional template of the IND-CCA security model. In this definition, the underlying experiment picks a public key pk and matching secret key sk, and then provides pk to the adversary $\mathcal{A}$. The latter runs in two phases in both of which $\mathcal{A}$ has access to an oracle for decryption under sk. It ends its first phase by outputting a pair m_0, m_1 of messages. The experiment picks a challenge bit $b \in \{0, 1\}$ at random, encrypts m_b under pk, and returns the resulting challenge ciphertext C^* to $\mathcal{A}$. The latter now enters its second phase, which it ends by outputting a bit $\bar{b}$. We say that $\mathcal{A}$ wins if $b = \bar{b}$. Security requires that the probability of winning minus $\frac{1}{2}$ is negligible.

IND-CCA1. This security notion is slightly milder than IND-CCA; the decryption requests can be made only before the challenge ciphertext (for which the adversary should gain knowledge) is presented.

3   IND-CCVA: Indistinguishability against Chosen Ciphertext Verification Attack

We now present a formal definition of security against chosen ciphertext verification attacks. This is a weaker form of attack when compared to a full CCA attack: the adversary has access to a oracle which is weaker than a decryption oracle. We name this oracle as ciphertext verification oracle and denoted it by $\mathcal{O}_{CV}$. The oracle is described as follows:

$$\mathcal{O}_{CV} : \{0, 1\}^* \to \{0, 1\}$$

The output is 1 if and only if the input string is a *valid ciphertext*. We now describe this new attack model formally as follows. For a public key encryption scheme $\prod$ and an adversary $\mathcal{A}$, consider the following experiment:

The IND-CCVA Experiment

- KeyGen(1^λ) is run to obtain keys (pk, sk).
- Beside the public key pk, the adversary $\mathcal{A}$ is given access to ciphertext verification oracle $\mathcal{O}_{CV}$.
- The adversary outputs a pair of messages m_0, m_1 of the same length from the plaintext space.
- A random bit $b \leftarrow \{0, 1\}$ is chosen, and then a ciphertext $c \leftarrow \text{Enc}_{pk}(m_b)$ is computed and given to $\mathcal{A}$.
- $\mathcal{A}$ continues to interact with $\mathcal{O}_{CV}$.
- Finally, $\mathcal{A}$ outputs a bit $\bar{b}$.
- The output of the experiment is defined to be 1 if $\bar{b} = b$, and 0 otherwise.

We define the advantage of $\mathcal{A}$ in the IND-CCVA experiment as a function of the security parameter as follows:

$$\mathrm{Adv}_{\Pi,\mathcal{A}}^{IND-CCVA}(\lambda) \triangleq |\mathrm{Prob}[\bar{b} = b] - \frac{1}{2}| \tag{1}$$

Definition 1. *A public key encryption scheme Π=(KeyGen, Enc, Dec) has indistinguishable encryption under a decisional chosen ciphertext attack (or is IND-CCVA secure) if for all probabilistic polynomial time adversaries $\mathcal{A}$, we have that $Adv_{\Pi,\mathcal{A}}^{IND-CCVA}(\lambda)$ is negligible.*

Note that our oracle may become constant (always output 1) for certain class of public key encryption schemes. Let Π be a public key encryption scheme with $\mathcal{K}$ as key space, $\mathcal{M}$ as message space, and $\mathcal{C}$ as ciphertext space. In general, we have

$$\cup_{k\in\mathcal{K}}\mathrm{Enc}(\mathcal{M}) \subsetneq \mathcal{C}.$$

The equality between $\cup_{k\in\mathcal{K}}\mathrm{Enc}(\mathcal{M})$ and $\mathcal{C}$ means that any element from $\mathcal{C}$ is a valid ciphertext (encryption of some message under some key). Thus in this case, the verification oracle will always output 1 for any random query from $\mathcal{C}$. This will imply that the IND-CPA and IND-CCVA security are both equivalent for such public key encryption schemes (as oracle is of no use), for example, ElGamal.

In this article we consider public keys encryption schemes with $\cup_{k\in\mathcal{K}}\mathrm{Enc}(\mathcal{M}) \subsetneq \mathcal{C}$. Infact, achieving IND-CCA security requires this kind of setup in general.

Remark: One may note that the security model of IND-CCVA immediately confirms the following:

- IND-CCA implies IND-CCVA and
- IND-CCVA implies IND-CPA

4   The Separating Scheme: IND-CCVA Secure But Not IND-CCA Secure

In this section we describe a public key encryption scheme which was originally proposed by Cramer and Shoup [5] as the light version of their main scheme (the first practical IND-CCA secure scheme). The scheme was shown to be IND-CPA secure by Cramer and Shoup and not IND-CCA secure. We observed that this scheme is infact IND-CCVA secure, thus settling the claim of this section.

4.1   Cramer-Shoup Light Version

- **KG(1^λ):** The key generation algorithm runs as follows.
    - Choose a group G of prime order p, where $2^{\lambda-1} < p < 2^\lambda$
    - Choose $g_1, g_2 \xleftarrow{\mathcal{R}} G$ and $x_1, x_2, z \in \mathbb{Z}_p$.
    - Compute $c = g_1^{x_1} g_2^{x_2}$ and $h = g_1^z$.

- The public key, PK, for this scheme is tuple (g_1, g_2, c, h), with corresponding secret key, SK, is (x_1, x_2, z).
- message space $= G$.

- **ENC**(m, PK): To encrypt a message $m \in G$, the encryption algorithm runs as follows.
  - Choose $r \xleftarrow{\mathcal{R}} \mathbb{Z}_p$.
  - Compute $u_1 = g_1^r$, $u_2 = g_2^r$, $e = h^r m$, $v = c^r$.
  - The ciphertext, $\mathcal{C}$, is (u_1, u_2, e, v).
- **DEC**$(\mathcal{C}, SK, PK)$: Decryption works in the following way: given the ciphertext (u_1, u_2, e, v) and secret key (x_1, x_2, z),
  - It first tests if $u_1^{x_1} u_2^{x_2} \overset{?}{=} v$.
  - If this condition does not hold, the decryption algorithm outputs $\perp$; otherwise, it outputs

$$m = \frac{e}{u_1^z}.$$

Correctness. If (u_1, u_2, e, v) is a valid ciphertext, then we have:

$$u_1^{x_1} u_2^{x_2} = g_1^{r x_1} g_2^{r x_2} = g_1^{x_1} g_2^{x_2 r} = c^r = v \text{ and}$$

$$\frac{e}{u_1^z} = \frac{h^r m^z}{g_1^r} = \frac{g_1^{z r} m}{g_1^{r z}} = \frac{g_1^{r z} m}{g_1^{r z}} = m.$$

4.2 IND-CCVA Security

We show that this scheme is IND-CCVA secure based on the hardness of the Decisional Diffie-Hellman (DDH) problem in G.

DDH problem can be formulated as follows. Let $\mathcal{D}$ be an algorithm that takes triples of group elements as input and outputs a bit. The DDH-advantage of $\mathcal{D}$ is defined as

$$\left| \Pr[x, y \xleftarrow{\mathcal{R}} \mathbb{Z}_p : \mathcal{D}(g^x, g^y, g^{xy}) = 1] - \Pr[x, y, z \xleftarrow{\mathcal{R}} \mathbb{Z}_p : \mathcal{D}(g^x, g^y, g^z) = 1] \right|$$

Then DDH assumption for G assumes that for any efficient algorithm $\mathcal{D}$, it is DDH-advantage is negligible.

Theorem 1. *The scheme described in Section 4.1 is IND-CCVA secure assuming that the DDH assumption holds in G.*

Proof. The proof goes by reduction which shows that if an adversary is able to break the IND-CCVA security, it can be used to solve the DDH problem. Let us assume, there is an adversary $\mathcal{A}$ which can break the IND-CCVA security of the scheme. Using $\mathcal{A}$, we can construct an algorithm $\mathcal{B}$ that solves the DDH problem.

$\mathcal{B}$ is given as input a 4-tuple (g, g^a, g^b, Z), where a, b are chosen randomly from $\mathbb{Z}_p$. The task of $\mathcal{B}$ is to determine whether Z is equal to g^{ab} or a random element of G. $\mathcal{B}$ solves this problem by interacting with $\mathcal{A}$ in the IND-CCVA game as follows.

- **Simulation of Key Generation (KG):** $\mathcal{B}$ proceeds as follows:
  - Sets $g_1 = g$.
  - Chooses $s \xleftarrow{\mathcal{R}} \mathbb{Z}_p$ and sets $g_2 = g_1^s$.
  - Chooses $x_1, x_2 \xleftarrow{\mathcal{R}} \mathbb{Z}_p$ and sets $c = g_1^{x_1} g_2^{x_2}$.
  - Sets $h = g^b$.
  - Finally the 4-tuple (g_1, g_2, c, h) is made available as public key to $\mathcal{A}$ by $\mathcal{B}$.

- **Simulation of Ciphertext Verification Oracle for Ciphertext Validity Check:**
  - Knowledge of (x_1, x_2) ensures that $\mathcal{B}$ can perfectly answer the ciphertext verification queries asked by $\mathcal{A}$.

- **Simulation of Challenge Ciphertext:**
  - In Challenge Phase, $\mathcal{A}$ chooses and outputs two messages m_0 and m_1 to $\mathcal{B}$.
  - $\mathcal{B}$ then chooses a bit $\tau \xleftarrow{\mathcal{R}} \{0, 1\}$ and it proceeds to encrypt m_τ.
  - $\mathcal{B}$ sets

$$u_1 = g^a, \ u_2 = (g^a)^s, \ e = Z \cdot m_\tau \text{ and } v = (g^a)^{x_1}(g^a)^{sx_2}.$$

  - The challenge ciphertext (u_1, u_2, e, v) is given to $\mathcal{A}$ by $\mathcal{B}$.

Finally in the Guess Phase, $\mathcal{A}$ answers a bit τ'. If $\tau = \tau'$ then $\mathcal{B}$ announces the input instance to be a valid DDH tuple, else $(\tau \neq \tau')$ $\mathcal{B}$ announces invalid tuple. This completes the description of $\mathcal{B}$. We show that

$$Adv(\mathcal{B}) = Adv(\mathcal{A}).$$

For this it is enough to show that simulation of challenge ciphertext is perfect given a valid DDH instance. This is true as for valid DDH tuple (i.e., $z = g^{ab}$) we have

- $u_1 = g^a = g_1^a$.
- $u_2 = (g^a)^s = (g^s)^a = g_2^a$.
- $e = Z \cdot m_\tau = g^{ab} \cdot m_\tau = (g^b)^a \cdot m_\tau = h^a \cdot m_\tau$.
- $v = (g^a)^{x_1}(g^a)^{sx_2} = (g^{x_1} g^{sx_2})^a = c^a$.

Thus the simulation of challenge ciphertext is perfect. This proves the theorem. $\qquad \square$

Lemma 1. *The scheme described in Section 4.1 is not IND-CCA secure.*

Proof. In IND-CCA game, if $\mathcal{C} = (u_1, u_2, e, v)$ be the challenge ciphertext, adversary $\mathcal{A}$ chooses any message $m' \neq 1$ (identity in G) and creates another ciphertext $\mathcal{C}' = (u_1, u_2, m'e, v)$ which is indeed different than challenge ciphertext. Decryption oracle returns $m'm$ if $\mathcal{C}'$ is queried to it. $\mathcal{A}$ then easily calculates the original message by calculating $m'mm'^{-1} = m$. Hence, the lemma. $\qquad \square$

5 The Separating Scheme (Known): IND-CPA Secure But Not IND-CCVA Secure

It is well-known that plain-old RSA does not hide partial information about the plaintext, is malleable, and is also insecure against chosen ciphertext attack. Indeed, plain-old RSA is never used in practice, precisely because of these well-known weaknesses. Instead, what people actually use is plain-old RSA with a few modifications attempt to fix these problems.

One idea that is often advocated to improve the security of plain-old RSA is to use a randomized "encoding" or "padding" scheme. That is, we encrypt m as $C = f(m, r)^e$, where $f(m, r)$ encodes the message m using some random bits r. Note that f is not a cryptographic encoding: it is easy for anyone to compute m from $f(m, r)$. The hope is that this enhancement improves the security of RSA. However, if one is not extremely careful, the resulting scheme may become insecure.

One simple way to define $f(m, r)$ is just to concatenate the two bit strings m and r. This is a popular idea. RSA, Inc. has a very popular encryption function, called PKCS #1, which did essentially this until the well-known attack by Bleichenbacher [4] had surfaced. This encryption function is used by the security protocol SSL over internet.

In literature, Bleichenbacher's attack on SSL has been termed as chosen ciphertext attack on RSA's PKCS #1. But we observe that, his attack is actually a chosen ciphertext verification attack. We first describe briefly the RSA encryption standard PKCS #1; refer to [19] for details. It has three block formats: Block types 0 and 1 are reserved for digital signatures, and block type 2 is used for encryption. As we are interested in encryption only, we describe the block 2.

- **KG(1^λ):** Choose primes p, q ($4k$ bit each) and compute $n = pq$ (n is k byte number). Choose e, d, such that $ed \equiv 1 \pmod{\phi(n)}$. The public key, PK, is (n, e) and the secret key, SK, is (p, q, d).
- **ENC(m, PK):** A data block D, consisting of $|D|$ bytes, is encrypted as follows:
  - First, a padding string PS, consisting of $k - 3 - |D|$ nonzero bytes, is generated pseudo-randomly (the byte length of PS is atleast 8).
  - Now, the encryption block $EB = 00||02||PS||00||D$ is formed, is converted into an integer x, and is encrypted with RSA, giving the ciphertext $c = x^e \pmod{n}$.
- **DEC(c, SK, PK)** A Ciphertext c is decrypted as follows:
  - Compute $x' = c^d \pmod{n}$.
  - Converts x' into an encryption block EB'.
  - Check, if the encryption block is PKCS *conforming* (An encryption block EB consisting of k bytes, $EB = EB_1||\ldots||EB_k$, is called PKCS conforming, if it satisfies the following conditions: $EB_1 = 00$, $EB_2 = 02$, EB_3 through EB_{10} are nonzero and at least one of the bytes EB_{11} through EB_k is 00).
  - If the encryption block is PKCS conforming, then output the data block; otherwise an error sign.

5.1   Security

It is well-known that the least significant bit of plain RSA encrypted message is as secure as the whole message [13,1]. In particular, there exists an algorithm that can decrypt a ciphertext if there exists another algorithm that can predict the least significant bit of a message given only the corresponding ciphertext and the public key. Håstad and Näslund extended this result to show that all individual RSA bits are secure [14].

Bleichenbacher's attack assumes that the adversary has access to an oracle that, for every ciphertext, returns whether the corresponding plaintext is PKCS conforming. If the plaintext is not PKCS conforming, the oracle outputs an error sign. Given just these error signs, because of specific properties of PKCS #1, Bleichenbacher showed how a very clever program can decrypt a target ciphertext (the oracle answer will reveal the first two bytes of the corresponding plaintext of the chosen ciphertext). Though, at this point the algorithm of Håstad and Näslund can use this oracle to decrypt the target ciphertext, Bleichenbacher's attack, different from Håstad and Näslund, was aimed at minimizing the number of oracle queries; thus, showing the practicality of the attack.

Hence, all the attacker needs is the verification about the validity of the chosen ciphertext (and not the corresponding whole plaintext). Thus this is clearly a chosen ciphertext verification attack.

6   Separating Schemes: Generic Constructions

In this section we provide generic constructions of public key encryption schemes that are

- IND-CPA secure but not IND-CCVA secure,
- IND-CCVA secure but not IND-CCA secure,
- IND-CCA1 secure but not IND-CCVA secure.

The constructions are based on the existence of (enhanced) trapdoor permutations (see Appendix C in [11]). We refer the reader to [11] (pages 413-422) for the encryption schemes, based on the existence of trapdoor permutations, that are IND-CPA secure but not IND-CCA secure with the property that $\cup_{k \in \mathcal{K}} \text{Enc}(\mathcal{M}) = \mathcal{C}$. Constructions, based on enhanced one-way trapdoor permutation, that are IND-CCA1 secure but not IND-CCA secure are also given in [11] (pages 452-461).

6.1   Generic Construction: IND-CPA Secure But Not IND-CCVA Secure

Let $\mathcal{E}_{CPA}$ be a public key encryption scheme described by the key generation algorithm $KeyGen_{CPA}$, encryption algorithm ENC_{CPA} and decryption algorithm DEC_{CPA}. Now define a new public key encryption $\mathcal{E}$ as follows

- KeyGen: Same as $KeyGen_{CPA}$.
- Enc: Encryption of a message m under a public key PK is give as

$$c = c_1||c_2 = ENC_{CPA}(m, PK)||ENC_{CPA}(m, PK)$$

- Dec: Decryption of a ciphertext $c = c_1||c_2$ with the corresponding secret key SK will proceed as follows:
  - $m'_1 \leftarrow DEC_{CPA}(c_1, SK, PK)$
  - $m'_2 \leftarrow DEC_{CPA}(c_2, SK, PK)$
  - If $m'_1 = m'_2$, return m'_1, else
  - return $\perp$

Theorem 2. *If $\mathcal{E}_{CPA}$ is IND-CPA secure then $\mathcal{E}$ is also IND-CPA secure.*

Proof. Straightforward.

Lemma 2. *Encryption scheme $\mathcal{E}$ is not IND-CCVA secure.*

Proof. We construct an efficient IND-CCVA adversary $\mathcal{A}$ against $\mathcal{E}$. In the challenge phase of the IND-CCVA security game, $\mathcal{A}$ outputs two equal length messages m_0, m_1 and request the challenger to encrypt one of the message. The challenger picks a challange bit $b \in \{0, 1\}$ at random, encrypts m_b under the public key PK, and returns the challenge ciphertext $c_b = c_{b_1}||c_{b_2}$. The adversary $\mathcal{A}$ now picks one of the message, say m_1, and computes $c_1 = ENC_{CPA}(m_1, PK)$. $\mathcal{A}$ now submits the modified ciphertext $\bar{c} = c_1||c_{b_2}$ to the Chosen Ciphertext Verification Oracle. Now $\mathcal{A}$ will return 1 if and only if the oracle returns 1. It is easy to verify that $\mathcal{A}$'s guess is correct with probability 1. Hence the encryption scheme $\mathcal{E}$ is not IND-CCVA secure.

6.2 Generic Construction: IND-CCVA Secure But Not IND-CCA Secure

In [11] (pages 413-422), the one way trapdoor permutation based constructions that are IND-CPA secure but not IND-CCA secure also possesses the following property

$$\cup_{k \in \mathcal{K}} \text{Enc}(\mathcal{M}) = \mathcal{C}.$$

Let us denote this scheme by $\mathcal{E} = (KeyGen, ENC, DEC)$. The IND-CCVA adversary against $\mathcal{E}$ will not gain anything new by using the verification oracle and thus $\mathcal{E}$ is IND-CCVA secure but not IND-CCA secure. But we assumed in this article to work on schemes that satisfy $\cup_{k \in \mathcal{K}} \text{Enc}(\mathcal{M}) \neq \mathcal{C}$. We now give such a construction.

Let us build a new public key encryption $\hat{\mathcal{E}} = (KeyGen_{\hat{\mathcal{E}}}, ENC_{\hat{\mathcal{E}}}, DEC_{\hat{\mathcal{E}}})$ based on $\mathcal{E}$ as follows.

- $KeyGen_{\hat{\mathcal{E}}}$: Same as $KeyGen$.
- $ENC_{\hat{\mathcal{E}}}$: Encryption of a message m under a public key PK is give as

$$\hat{c} = 1||c, \text{ where } c = ENC(m, PK).$$

- $DEC_{\hat{\mathcal{E}}}$: Decryption of a ciphertext $\hat{c}$ with the corresponding secret key SK will proceed as follows:

$$DEC_{\hat{\mathcal{E}}}(\hat{c}, SK, PK) = DEC(c, SK, PK) \text{ if } \hat{c} = 1||c, \text{ otherwise return } \perp.$$

It is easy to check that $\hat{\mathcal{E}}$ is IND-CPA secure but not IND-CCA secure with the added property that every ciphertext need not be valid. Since it is trivial to distinguish valid ciphertexts from invalid ciphertexts (by just looking at the most significant bit), CCVA oracle does not give any extra advantage to the adversary and thus $\hat{\mathcal{E}}$ is IND-CCVA secure.

6.3   Generic Construction: IND-CCA1 Secure But Not IND-CCVA Secure

In this section, we give a generic construction of IND-CCA1 secure encryption scheme which is not IND-CCVA secure. Let $\mathcal{E}_{CCA1}$ be a IND-CCA1 secure encryption scheme. Let (PK, SK) be the public key-secret key pair, ENC_{CCA1} be the encryption algorithm and DEC_{CCA1} be the decryption algorithm of $\mathcal{E}_{CCA1}$. We construct an encryption scheme, say S from S_{CCA1} whose public key-secret key pair is (PK, SK). Encryption algorithm of $\mathcal{E}$, say ENC, takes a message m and outputs ciphertext c.

- $c = c_1||c_2 \leftarrow ENC(m, PK)$

where $c_1 \leftarrow ENC_{CCA1}(m, PK)$, $c_2 \leftarrow ENC_{CCA1}(m, PK)$, and $PK = PK_1$. Decryption algorithm of $\mathcal{E}$, say DEC, for an input $c = c_1||c_2$ is defined as following:

- $m_1' \leftarrow DEC_{CCA1}(c_1, SK, PK)$
- $m_2' \leftarrow DEC_{CCA1}(c_2, SK, PK)$
- If $m_1' = m_2'$, return m_1', else
- return $\perp$

Theorem 3. *If $\mathcal{E}_{CCA1}$ is IND-CCA1 secure then $\mathcal{E}$ is also IND-CCA1 secure.*

Proof. Straightforward.

Lemma 3. *The Encryption scheme $\mathcal{E}$ is not IND-CCVA secure.*

Proof. Similar to the proof of lemma 2.

Remark: The question of an IND-CCVA secure encryption that is not IND-CCA1 may be worth exploring.

Acknowledgements. The authors would like to thank the anonymous reviewers for their comments and suggestions that helped in polishing the technical and editorial content of this paper.

References

1. Alexi, W., Chor, B., Goldreich, O., Schnorr, P.: Bit security of RSA and Rabin functions. SIAM Journal of Computing 17(2), 194–209 (1988)
2. Bellare, M., Rogaway, P.: Optimal Asymmetric Encryption. In: De Santis, A. (ed.) EUROCRYPT 1994. LNCS, vol. 950, pp. 92–111. Springer, Heidelberg (1995)
3. Bellare, M., Desai, A., Pointcheval, D., Rogaway, P.: Relations among Notions of Security for Public-Key Encryption Schemes. In: Krawczyk, H. (ed.) CRYPTO 1998. LNCS, vol. 1462, pp. 26–45. Springer, Heidelberg (1998)
4. Bleichenbacher, D.: Chosen Ciphertext Attacks against Protocols Based on the RSA Encryption Standard PKCS #1. In: Krawczyk, H. (ed.) CRYPTO 1998. LNCS, vol. 1462, pp. 1–12. Springer, Heidelberg (1998)
5. Cramer, R., Shoup, V.: A Practical Public Key Cryptosystem Provably Secure against Adaptive Chosen Ciphertext Attack. In: Krawczyk, H. (ed.) CRYPTO 1998. LNCS, vol. 1462, pp. 13–25. Springer, Heidelberg (1998)
6. Cramer, R., Shoup, V.: Universal Hash Proofs and a Paradigm for Adaptive Chosen Ciphertext Secure Public-Key Encryption. In: Knudsen, L.R. (ed.) EUROCRYPT 2002. LNCS, vol. 2332, pp. 45–64. Springer, Heidelberg (2002)
7. Elkind, E., Sahai, A.: A Unified Methodology For Constructing Public-Key Encryption Schemes Secure Against Adaptive Chosen-Ciphertext Attack, http://eprint.iacr.org/2002/042
8. Dolev, D., Dwork, C., Naor, M.: Non-Malleable Cryptography. SIAM J. Computing 30(2), 391–437 (2000)
9. Freier, A.O., Karlton, P., Kocher, P.C.: The SSL Protocol. Version 3.0
10. Goldreich, O.: A Uniform Complexity Treatment of Encryption and Zero-Knowledge. J. Cryptology 6(1), 21–35 (1993)
11. Goldreich, O.: Foundations of Cryptography. Basic Applications, vol. 2. Cambridge University Press (2004)
12. Goldwasser, S., Micalli, S.: Probabilistic encryption. Journal of Computer and System Sciences 28(2), 270–299 (1984)
13. Goldwasser, S., Micali, S., Tong, P.: Why and how to establish a private code on a public network. In: Proc. 23rd IEEE Symp. on Foundations of Comp. Science, Chicago, pp. 134–144 (1982)
14. Håstad, J., Näslund, M.: The security of individual RSA bits (1998) (manuscript)
15. Loftus, J., May, A., Smart, N.P., Vercauteren, F.: On CCA-Secure Somewhat Homomorphic Encryption. In: Miri, A., Vaudenay, S. (eds.) SAC 2011. LNCS, vol. 7118, pp. 55–72. Springer, Heidelberg (2012)
16. Naor, M., Yung, M.: Public-key cryptosystem provably secure against chosen ciphertext attacks. In: Proc. STOC, pp. 427–437 (1990)
17. Public-Key Cryptography Standards (PKCS) #1 v2.1: RSA Cryptography Standard. RSA Security Inc. (2002)
18. Rackoff, C., Simon, D.: Non-interactive Zero-Knowledge Proof of Knowledge and Chosen Ciphertext Attack. In: Feigenbaum, J. (ed.) CRYPTO 1991. LNCS, vol. 576, pp. 433–444. Springer, Heidelberg (1992)
19. RSA Data Security, Inc. PKCS #1: RSA Encryption Standard. Redwood City, CA. Version 1.5 (November 1993)
20. Shoup, V.: Why chosen ciphertext security matters. Technical Report RZ 3076, IBM Zurich (1998)
21. Vivek, S., Deva Selvi, S., Pandu Rangan, C.: CCA Secure Certificateless Encryption Schemes based on RSA. In: Proc. Secrypt 2011, pp. 208–217 (2011)

22. Vivek, S., Deva Selvi, S., Pandu Rangan, C.: Stronger Public Key Encryption Schemes Withstanding RAM Scraper Like Attacks. ePrint Archive: Report 2012/118 (2012)
23. Hofheinz, D., Kiltz, E.: Secure Hybrid Encryption from Weakened Key Encapsulation. In: Menezes, A. (ed.) CRYPTO 2007. LNCS, vol. 4622, pp. 553–571. Springer, Heidelberg (2007)
24. Hohenberger, S., Lewko, A., Waters, B.: Detecting Dangerous Queries: A New Approach for Chosen Ciphertext Security. In: Pointcheval, D., Johansson, T. (eds.) EUROCRYPT 2012. LNCS, vol. 7237, pp. 663–681. Springer, Heidelberg (2012)
25. Cramer, R., Hanaoka, G., Hofheinz, D., Imai, H., Kiltz, E., Pass, R., Shelat, A., Vaikuntanathan, V.: Bounded CCA2-Secure Encryption. In: Kurosawa, K. (ed.) ASIACRYPT 2007. LNCS, vol. 4833, pp. 502–518. Springer, Heidelberg (2007)

Towards Formal Analysis of Key Control in Group Key Agreement Protocols

Anshu Yadav and Anish Mathuria

Dhirubhai Ambani Institute of Information and Communication Technology,
Gandhinagar, Gujarat, India
{anshu_yadav,anish_mathuria}@daiict.ac.in

Abstract. In group key agreement protocols, it is desired that every honest participant is assured of its contribution to the shared session key. This property ensures that no dishonest insider or a group of dishonest insiders can predetermine the key. In this paper we propose attacks on the Dutta-Barua protocol in which one or more dishonest insiders are able to control the key. We use the algebraic approach given by Delicata and Schneider to formally analyze the attacks on the protocol.

1 Introduction

Group key agreement protocols aim to establish a common shared secret key between members of a group. In such protocols it is desirable to have the contributions of all the honest participants in the session key. In a poorly designed protocol, a dishonest participant or group of dishonest participants may have varying degrees of control over the key. Pieprzyk and Wang in [1] defined different types of control that dishonest participant(s) can have on the session key.

Strong Key Control. A dishonest principal or a group of dishonest principals can select any value of their choice as the group key. They may adjust their public values such that the computed key is the selected value.

Selective Key Control. Contribution of some, but not all, honest members is removed from the session key.

Unfortunately there exist many key agreement protocols that allow dishonest insiders to control the key. For example, strong key control was found in Biswas' protocol [2] by Tseng and Wu [3]. Similarly, attacks were found on Burmester-Desmedt (BD) and Just-Vaudenay (JV) group key agreement protocols by Pieprzyk and Wang in [1].

An unauthenticated static group key agreement protocol, based on basic DH protocol was proposed by Burmester and Desmedt. Later on strong key control by two dishonest insiders was found in the protocol by Pieprzyk and Wang [1]. In [4], Dutta and Barua proposed an authenticated protocol that establishes the same key as the Burmester-Desmedt (BD) protocol [5]. The protocol is claimed to be better than BD in terms of efficiency and security. It involves an extra verification step that aims to detect the presence of a dishonest insider.

A. Bogdanov and S. Sanadhya (Eds.): SPACE 2012, LNCS 7644, pp. 77–93, 2012.
© Springer-Verlag Berlin Heidelberg 2012

We use the Delicata-Schneider (DS) model [6], [7] to analyze key control in DB and BD protocols. The model is based on algebraic approach. It has been used to analyze different classical properties in two party protocols but to the best of our knowledge it has not been used to analyze key control. DB protocol has been analyzed for different security properties in the literature but has not been studied from the point of view of key control. Attacks were found in the dynamic DB protocol in [8,9]. In [10], an unknown key share attack was described on the protocol.

Our Contributions: We show that in the DB protocol a single dishonest insider and two dishonest insiders have selective and strong key control respectively. We also formally show that the protocol is free of key control if all the participants behave honestly in the first phase and a single dishonest insider misbehaves only in the second phase.

In the next section, we describe the BD protocol and an attack against it proposed by Pieprzyk and Wang. We also describe the modification proposed by Dutta and Barua to allow detection of malicious insider. In section 3, we give an overview of the Delicata-Schneider model used for formal analysis. In section 4, we show the formal analysis of the attack on BD in DS model for a group of four members. Analysis of key control in DB in the presence of single and two dishonest insiders is given in section 5. In section 6 we prove, using DS model that the protocol detects a dishonest insider misbehaving in the second phase. We conclude in section 7.

Table 1 shows the notations used throughout the paper.

Table 1. Notations used

p, q : Two large primes such that $q \mid p - 1$	
G : A subgroup of Z_p^*, having prime order q	
g : Generator of group G	
z_I : Ephemeral public key of I	$I \in \{A, B, C\}$
r_I : Ephemeral private key of I	
z_i : message template in DS model	$i \in \mathbb{N}$
r_i : Ephemeral private key of M_i	
t_i : Ephemeral public key of M_i	

2   Review of BD and DB Protocols

2.1   BD Protocol

The protocol proposed by Burmester and Desmedt [5] extends the basic two party Diffie Hellman key agreement protocol to group key agreement. It assumes the presence of authenticated channels. For a group of n members, the protocol assumes that all the members, $M_1, M_2, \ldots, M_n$ are arranged in a circle, such that $M_{n+1} = M_1$ and $M_0 = M_n$.

The protocol consists of two phases:

1. In phase 1, each member, M_i, computes its ephemeral public key $t_i = g^{r_i}$ and sends it to its left and the right neighbors.
2. In phase 2, each member computes $X_i = \left(\frac{t_{i+1}}{t_{i-1}}\right)^{r_i}$ and broadcasts it. We let $K_i^R = t_{i+1}^{r_i}$ and $K_i^L = t_{i-1}^{r_i}$, then $X_i = K_i^R/K_i^L$. The values K_i^R and K_i^L are essentially the pairwise Diffie-Hellman keys shared by M_i with its right and left neighbhours, respectively. Note that $K_{i+1}^L = K_i^R$ and $K_i^L = K_{i-1}^R$.
3. The group key is defined as the product of the pairwise DH keys shared between each pair of adjacent members. After receiving the values X_j, $0 < j \le n$, $j \ne i$, M_i computes the group key as

$$GK = (K_i^L)^n X_i^{n-1} X_{i+1}^{n-2} \cdots X_n^{i-1} X_1^{i-2} \cdots X_{i-2}$$

$$= (K_{i-1}^R)^n \left(\frac{K_i^R}{K_{i-1}^R}\right)^{n-1} \left(\frac{K_{i+1}^R}{K_i^R}\right)^{n-2} \cdots \left(\frac{K_n^R}{K_{n-1}^R}\right)^{i-1} \left(\frac{K_1^R}{K_n^R}\right)^{i-2} \cdots \left(\frac{K_{i-2}^R}{K_{i-3}^R}\right)$$

$$= K_{i-1}^R K_i^R \cdots K_n^R K_1^R \cdots K_{i-2}^R$$

$$= g^{r_1 r_2 + r_2 r_3 + \cdots + r_{n-1} r_n + r_n r_1}$$

As shown by Pieprzyk and Wang [1], the BD protocol fails to ensure contribution of each honest member if there are some dishonest insiders. A single dishonest insider can cheat an honest member to compute the group key which is predetermined by the insider. In case of attack due to single dishonest insider different members compute different key. If there are two dishonest insiders, they can force all the honest members to compute the same predetermined value as the group key. Here we define the attack in the presence of single dishonest insider for a group of four members.

Consider a group of four members, M_1, M_2, M_3, M_4. Suppose M_4 is dishonest and it wants to force M_2 to compute the session key which is predetermined by M_4. It executes the first phase honestly, but in the second phase, it first waits for public ratios, X_1, X_2 and X_3 from all other honest members. Using them it computes X_4' as $t_4/(t_1^{4r_4} X_3^2 X_2^3 X_1^4)$ and broadcasts it. Finally, M_2 computes the session key using this value as $(K_2^L)^4 (X_2)^3 (X_3)^2 X_4'$ $= (g^{r_1 r_2})^4 (X_2)^3 (X_3)^2 (t_4/(t_1^{4r_4} X_3^2 X_2^3 X_1^4)) = t_4 = g^{r_4}$. As r_4 is chosen by M_4, it has strong control of the key.

Note that in the attack described above, M_1 computes the correct key as it does not use X_4 to compute it. It can be seen that different members compute different key. Thus, the attacker does not have control on the keys computed by other members. As the keys are different, it may be argued that it can be detected when the established key is used in further communication. However, as in the case of attack on AGDH protocol [11,12], where the session key does not remain same for all members, we regard the attack described above as a successful one. We say that attacker has key control if the key computed by any honest participant does not have that participant's contribution. Formal derivation of the above attack in DS model is given in section 4.

2.2   DB Protocol

The first phase of Dutta-Barua (DB) protocol [4] is the same as BD. The second phase differs in the computation of the key from X_i values received from other participants. Here we only show the part of the protocol that is different from BD.

– After receiving the X_j values of all the other members in phase 2, M_i computes the right keys of the other members as follows:

$$K_{i+1}^R = K_i^R X_{i+1}$$
$$K_{i+2}^R = K_{i+1}^R X_{i+2}$$
$$\vdots$$
$$K_{i-1}^R = K_{i-2}^R X_{i-1}$$

– M_i compares computed K_{i-1}^R with K_i^L. If the two are same then M_i proceeds further else aborts the protocol. This step is aimed at detecting the presence of a dishonest insider.
– If above step is successful then compute the group key as $GK = \prod_{k=1}^n K_k^R$ $= g^{r_1r_2+r_2r_3+\cdots+r_{n-1}r_n+r_nr_1}$.

In section 5 we will show that the extra verification step above does not suffice to protect against key control attack by dishonest insiders.

3   Delicata-Schneider Model

Delicata and Schneider presented an algebraic approach to provide proofs of security for a class of Diffie-Hellman based protocols [6], [7]. We describe the model in this section. Their model is based on a construct called *message template*, which suitably instantiated, can represent any value that an attacker can derive from the information available to it. A value that cannot be obtained via any possible instantiation of the message template is assumed to be secret.

The messages exchanged in a protocol belong to a group G, in which the Decisional Diffie-Hellman problem is believed to be hard. Let g be the generator of G agreed upon by all principals and e be the identity element. Let C be the adversary. Define two sets: P and E. P consists of all those exponents, x, where C knows g^x, but not the x (excluding the case where x belongs to E). E consists of those random values y, which are known to C.

Power of Adversary
Given initial sets P and E, the adversary can expand the set P as follows: (1) Given $m_1, m_2 \in P$, add $m_1 + m_2$ to P; (2) Given $m \in P$ and $n \in E$, add mn and (mn^{-1}) to P; and (3) Given $m \in P$, add $(-m)$ to P. The attacker's entire knowledge can be represented as the closure of P under deductions of above rules and set E. To represent all possible values derivable by the attacker, a polynomial is defined over the sets E and P, as follows.

1. Let F be a finite family of functions that map elements of E to integer powers: Given $E = \{x_c\}$, for e.g., we may define $F = \{f\}$, where, $f = \{x_c \to -1\}$.
2. Let h be higher order function which, for a member of F, maps elements of P to integers. As an example given $F = \{f\}$, where, $f = \{x_c \to -1\}$, h can be defined as $h(f) = h(\{x_c \to -1\}) = \{r_A \to 1\}$.
3. (*message template*) Fix some E and P then:

$$v(F, h) = \sum_{f \in F}\left(\sum_{p \in P} h_{f,p}.p\right)\left(\prod_{e \in E} e^{f_e}\right)$$

Here v is message template for the system defined by E and P
4. A value m is *realisable* if it can be expressed as $v(F, h)$ for some F and h.

In 2-party DH protocol, a principal U performs some key computation function, k on input z to derive secret Z_{UV}, which is supposed to be shared with V. This is denoted as $Z_{UV} = k_{UV}(z)$. For system given by E and P, a key computation function k is said to provide *secrecy* iff $\forall m.\text{realisable}(m) \Rightarrow \neg\ \text{realisable}(k(m))$.

The analysis using the model proceeds as follows.

- For a given protocol and an adversary, first the sets P and E are initialized according to the knowledge of the adversary. The group identity is always included in P; this ensures that all elements appearing in E are realisable.
- The session secret and the incoming messages for the target victim (in case of an active adversary), are represented in the form of message templates defined over the sets P and E. (These sets can be different for different message templates based on the type of attribute being analyzed.)
- An equation is then formed using above message templates and the key derivation equation. If a solution exists then the adversary is successful else not.

Example: Analysis of IKA in Basic DH

In the protocol, A sends $z_A = g^{r_A}$ to B, B sends $z_B = g^{r_B}$ to A. Key computed by A is $z_B^{r_A} = g^{r_A r_B}$. Suppose, C be an adversary attacking A against implicit key authentication (IKA). The sets representing the knowledge of C can be defined as: $P = \{1, r_A, r_B\}$ and $E = \{r_C\}$, where r_C is chosen by C. (Here 1 denotes the group identity.) To mount the attack, C sends g^{z_1} as input from B to A. Using this, A computes the key as $g^{z_1 r_A}$. Let this value be g^{z_2}. Here, z_1 and z_2 are message templates defined over the sets P and E. For C to be successful, there should exist such values of z_1 and z_2 such that $g^{z_2} = g^{z_1 r_A}$. This gives us following equation

$$z_2 = z_1 r_A \tag{1}$$

Let $z_1 = v(F_1, h_1)$, where $F_1 = \{f_1\}$, $f_1 = \{r_C \to p_1\}$, $h_1(f_1) = \{1 \to n_1, r_A \to n_2, r_B \to n_3\}$. Let $z_2 = v(F_2, h_2)$, where $F_2 = \{f_2\}$, $f_2 = \{r_C \to q_1\}$, $h_2(f_2) = \{1 \to m_1, r_A \to m_2, r_B \to m_3\}$. Thus, $z_1 = (n_1 + n_2 r_A + n_3 r_B)r_C^{p_1}$ and $z_2 = (m_1 + m_2 r_A + m_3 r_B)r_C^{q_1}$. Putting these values in (1), we have

$$(m_1 + m_2 r_A + m_3 r_B)r_C^{q_1} = (n_1 + n_2 r_A + n_3 r_B)r_C^{p_1} r_A \tag{2}$$

One solution to the above equation is: $m_2 = n_1 = q_1 = p_1 = 1$, rest of the values are zero. This results in $z_1 = r_C$ and $z_2 = r_A r_C$. This shows that C can successfully mount the attack by sending $g^{z_1} = g^{r_C}$ as input to A. The key computed is $g^{z_2} = g^{r_A r_C}$. C computes this value as $z_A^{r_C}$.

4   Analysis of Key Control in BD Protocol

Consider a group of four members, M_1, M_2, M_3, M_4. Assume M_4 is dishonest and wants M_2 to compute the session key a value that it has pre-computed. For this it sends some manipulated value of X_4 in the second phase. Let this value be X_4'. To compute this value, it first waits to receive X_1, X_2 and X_3. Let X_4' be equal to g^{z_1}. Here z_1 is the message template defined over following sets: $P_1 = \{1, r_1, r_2, r_3, x_1, x_2, x_3\}$ and $E_1 = \{r_4\}$ (x_1, x_2, x_3 are the exponents of g in X_1, X_2, X_3 respectively). Sets P_1 and E_1 represent M_4's knowledge at the time of computing X_4'. Note that r_2 is the exponent of g in t_2, which is not broadcast. We assume that the attacker eavesdrops on the communication between M_2 and M_1 (M_3) in phase 1 in order to learn t_2. M_2 can exploit knowledge of $t_1, t_2, t_3, X_1, X_2, X_3, r_4$ to compute X_4'. Group key computed by M_2 is $(K_2^L)^4 (X_2)^3 (X_3)^2 X_4' = g^{4r_1 r_2 + 3r_2 r_3 - 3r_1 r_2 + 2r_3 r_4 - 2r_2 r_3 + z_1} = g^{r_1 r_2 + r_2 r_3 + 2r_3 r_4 + z_1}$. Let it be g^{z_2}. Since M_4 wants to compute this value before the protocol starts, z_2 is computed over the sets, P_2 and E_2 that represents the knowledge of M_4 at that time, when it only knows the values chosen by itself. So, $P_2 = \{1\}$ and $E_2 = \{r_4\}$.

For M_4 to be successful there should exist such values for z_1 and z_2 so that the key computed by M_2 using g^{z_1} in the form of X_4' is equal to g^{z_2}. Thus, we have following equation:

$$z_2 = r_1 r_2 + r_2 r_3 + 2r_3 r_4 + z_1 \tag{3}$$

$z_1 = v(F_1, h_1)$ where $F_1 = \{f_{11}, f_{12}\}$; $f_{11} = \{r_4 \to p_{11}\}$, $f_{12} = \{r_4 \to p_{21}\}$;

$$h_1(f_{11}) = \{1 \to n_{10}, r_1 \to n_{11}, r_2 \to n_{12}, r_3 \to n_{13}, x_1 \to n_{14},$$
$$x_2 \to n_{15}, x_3 \to n_{16}\}$$

$$h_1(f_{12}) = \{1 \to n_{20}, r_1 \to n_{21}, r_2 \to n_{22}, r_3 \to n_{23}, x_1 \to n_{24},$$
$$x_2 \to n_{25}, x_3 \to n_{26}\}$$

$z_2 = v(F_2, h_2)$ where $F_2 = \{f_2\}$; $f_2 = \{r_4 \to q_1\}$; $h_2(f_2) = \{1 \to m_1\}$
$z_1 = \sum_{i=1}^{i=2} (n_{i0} + n_{i1} r_1 + n_{i2} r_2 + n_{i3} r_3 + n_{i4} x_1 + n_{i5} x_2 + n_{i6} x_3) r_4^{p_{i1}}$; and $z_2 = m_1 r_4^{q_1}$.

Putting values of z_1 and z_2 in equation (3), we have

$$m_1 r_4^{q_1} = r_1 r_2 + r_2 r_3 + 2r_3 r_4 +$$
$$\sum_{i=1}^{i=2} (n_{i0} + n_{i1} r_1 + n_{i2} r_2 + n_{i3} r_3 + n_{i4} x_1 + n_{i5} x_2 + n_{i6} x_3) r_4^{p_{i1}}$$

Replacing x_i with $r_i r_{i+1} - r_{i-1} r_i$ in the above equation,

$$m_1 r_4^{q_1} = r_1 r_2 + r_2 r_3 + 2 r_3 r_4 + \sum_{i=1}^{i=2} (n_{i0} + n_{i1} r_1 + n_{i2} r_2 + n_{i3} r_3 + n_{i4}(r_1 r_2 - r_4 r_1) +$$
$$n_{i5}(r_2 r_3 - r_1 r_2) + n_{i6}(r_3 r_4 - r_2 r_3)) r_4^{p_{i1}} \quad (4)$$

Following values of the mapping coefficients satisfy the above equation: $n_{20} = m_1 = q_1 = p_{21} = 1$; $n_{21} = -4$; $n_{16} = -2$; $n_{15} = -3$; $n_{14} = -4$; rest of all the coefficients are equal to zero. This solution gives $z_1 = r_4 - 4 r_1 r_4 - 2 x_3 - 3 x_2 - 4 x_1$ and $z_2 = r_4$. Thus, $X_4' = g^{z_1} = g^{r_4 - 4 r_1 r_4 - 2 x_3 - 3 x_2 - 4 x_1}$. It can be seen that $X_4' = g^{r_4}/(t_1^{4 r_4} X_3^2 X_2^3 X_1^4)$. It follows from the analysis thus far that we have derived the attack given by Pieprzyk and Wang described in section 2.1.

5   Analysis of Key Control in DB Protocol

As discussed before, this protocol has a verification step to detect the presence of dishonest insider. In this section we show that the detection fails if there are two or more dishonest insiders or a single dishonest participant misbehaves in the first phase. A single dishonest insider has selective control and two dishonest insiders have strong control over the key. We formally show these results in this section.

Attack with Single Dishonest Participant
As shown above, if any dishonest participant, M_i sends wrong value of X_i, then it would be detected.

But the dishonest member can behave maliciously in the first phase and can send such values to its left and the right neighbors so that the key computed does not contain the contribution of some honest participants. Then, M_i computes X_i value as per the protocol specification and hence the comparison done by the honest participants fails to detect the presence of malicious participant.

The position of the honest members that can be attacked by the dishonest insider are different in case of group of three, four and more than four members. Table 2 lists the maximal group of the honest participants that can be attacked. In all the case without loss of generality we have assumed M_1 to be dishonest. Here we describe the attack in case of five or more members. Attacks for three and four member groups are given in appendix A. In the attacks defined in the presence of a single dishonest insider, the incorrect messages sent by the dishonest insider in the first phase are found heuristically. For other analysis required to analyze the attack, we have used the DS model.

Attack on a Group of Five or More Members. In a group of five or more members, the dishonest participant can remove the contribution of its left and right neighbours from the session key. Consider a group of n members, where M_1 is dishonest. The victims are M_2 and M_n. M_1 first waits for other members to send their ephemeral public key in first phase. Then it computes and sends its ephemeral public keys to its neighbours as:

Table 2. Possible victims against key control for single dishonest insider

Group Size (n)	Malicious participant	Victims
3	M_1	$\{M_2\}$ or $\{M_3\}$
4	M_1	$\{M_2, M_3\}$ or $\{M_3, M_4\}$
> 4	M_1	$\{M_2, M_n\}$

Phase 1:

$M_1 \rightarrow M_2 : t_{12} = t_3^{-1} = g^{-r_3}$ (t_3 is public and hence known to M_1.)

$M_1 \rightarrow M_n : t_{1n} = t_{n-1}^{-1} = g^{-r_{n-1}}$ (t_{n-1} is public and hence known to M_1.)

Here, the ephemeral public values are different for the left and the right neighbours and M_1 does not know the corresponding exponents.

Now, to send X_1 in phase 2, it cannot compute it directly as described in the protocol because it does not know the keys shared with its left and the right neighbours. This is because it does not know the exponents of its own ephemeral public keys sent in phase 1. Note that $\prod_{i=1}^{n} X_i = 1$. Hence, M_1 can compute X_1 as: $X_1 = 1/\prod_{i=2}^{n}(X_i)$

M_1 broadcasts X_1.

Since the value of X_1 is computed correctly, the comparison performed by the honest participants cannot detect the malicious behaviour.

The key computed by every member is the product of the keys shared between each pair of neighbouring participants, i.e. $t_{12}^{r_2} \cdot g^{r_2 r_3 + r_3 r_4 + \cdots + r_{n-2} r_{n-1} + r_{n-1} r_n} \cdot t_{1n}^{r_n}$.

Here $t_{12}^{r_2}$ is the right shared key of M_1 and $t_{1n}^{r_n}$ is the right shared key of M_n. The resulting key will be equal to $g^{-r_3 r_2 + r_2 r_3 + r_3 r_4 + \cdots + r_{n-2} r_{n-1} + r_{n-1} r_n - r_n r_{n-1}} = g^{r_3 r_4 + \cdots + r_{n-2} r_{n-1}}$. Clearly, the victim honest participants, M_2 and M_n have no contribution in this session key.

Note that M_1 does not know its left and right key. So, it cannot compute the session key in the way it is described in the protocol. To compute the key it has to make use of all the available information, (i.e. $X_2, X_3, \ldots, X_n, t_2, t_3, \ldots, t_n$). To check whether this is feasible, we make use of the of formal technique.

Here, M_1 has following information: $X_2, X_3, \ldots, X_n, t_2, t_3, \ldots, t_n$. But it does not know their corresponding exponents.

M_1 does not know any secret exponent of other members.

$P = \{1, x_2, x_3, \ldots, x_n, r_2, r_3, \ldots, r_n\}$. Here, x_i represents the exponent of g in X_i, i.e. $X_i = g^{x_i}$.

$E = \{r_1\}$.

For the adversary to be able to compute the session key, the key must be equal to g^{z_1}, where z_1 is a message template for some F and h defined over the sets P and E.

Thus, we have following equation:

$$z_1 = r_3 r_4 + r_4 r_5 + \cdots + r_{n-2} r_{n-1} \tag{5}$$

Let the mappings for functions F and h be defined as:

$F = \{f_1\}; f_1 = \{r_1 \rightarrow p_1\}$. (Set F can have more than one function. For now we start with one function and if required we can add more functions with appropriate mappings.)

$h(f_1) = \{1 \rightarrow n_1, x_2 \rightarrow n_2, \ldots, x_n \rightarrow n_n, r_2 \rightarrow n_{n+2}, \ldots, r_n \rightarrow n_{n+n}\}$.

Thus, using above mappings, we have:

$$z_1 = v(F, h) = (n_1 + n_2 x_2 + \cdots + n_n x_n + n_{n+2} r_2 + \cdots + n_{n+n} r_n) r_1^{p_1} \tag{6}$$

Putting this value in equation (5), we have

$$(n_1 + n_2 x_2 + \cdots + n_n x_n + n_{n+2} r_2 + \cdots + n_{n+n} r_n) r_1^{p_1} = r_3 r_4 + r_4 r_5 + \cdots + r_{n-2} r_{n-1} \tag{7}$$

Putting the values of $x_1, x_2, \ldots$ in equation (7) and then solving, we get following values for constants:

$n_1 = n_{n-1} = n_n = 0; n_2 = (n-4)/2; n_i = n - (i+1); \forall 3 \le i \le n - 2$

all the remaining values are 0. The above solution implies that M_1 can compute the key as: $X_2^{(n-4)/2} X_3^{n-4} X_4^{n-5} X_5^{n-6} \cdots X_{n-3}^2 X_{n-2}$.

Attack in Presence of Two Dishonest Participants

If there are two or more dishonest participants in the group then they can together broadcast their changed values of X i.e. ratio of right and left shared key so that they remain undetected by the honest participants and also, the group key computed by the honest members is a value that was predetermined by the dishonest participants.

Consider a group of n members. Two members are dishonest. The dishonest members arrange themselves adjacent to each other in the group. Without loss of generality, we assume that M_1 and M_2 are dishonest.

The messages sent by M_1 and M_2 are as described below:

1. M_1 and M_2 select a key $K' = g^r$, which they want to be established as the group session key.
2. In the first phase, both M_1 and M_2 behave honestly and send g^{r_1} and g^{r_2} respectively to their neighbours.
3. In phase 2, M_1 and M_2, first wait to receive X_i values from all the honest participants.
   Then using these values, they generate X_1 and X_2 as follows:
   (a) $X_1 = g^r / (g^{r_2 r_3} g^{r_3 r_4} \cdots g^{r_{n-1} r_n} g^{2 r_n r_1})$
   (b) $X_2 = g^{r_2 r_3} / (g^{r_1 r_n} X_1)$
   (We have shown how to get this particular combination of values and then to compute them from other X_i values in the analysis in appendix B using formal technique.)
4. Broadcast X_1 and X_2.
5. Let K_j^R denote the correct value of right shared key of M_j and $K_j'^R$ the value computed by M_j. Then $K_j'^R = K_j^R$ for $2 \le j \le n$ as the product of X_1 and X_2 is $g^{r_2 r_3} / g^{r_1 r_n}$, which it should actually be in an honest run.
   $K_1^R = K_n^R X_1 = g^{r_1 r_n + r - r_2 r_3 - r_3 r_4 - \cdots - r_{n-1} r_n - 2 r_n r_1}$
   $= g^{r - r_2 r_3 - r_3 r_4 - \cdots - r_{n-1} r_n - r_n r_1}$.

6. All the honest members compute the session key equal to $K' = \prod_{j=1}^{j=n} \left(K_j'^{R} \right)$
$$= g^{(r-r_2r_3-r_3r_4-\cdots-r_{n-1}r_n-r_nr_1)+(r_2r_3+r_3r_4\cdots+r_nr_1)} = g^r.$$

Note that the product of X_1 and X_2 is $g^{r_2r_3}/g^{r_1r_n}$, which it should actually be in an honest run. All the honest participants in their computation for computing the right key of its left neighbour makes use of the same product. Since, the product is correct, the malicious activity remains undetected.

The key computed by all the honest participants is g^r, the preselected value of M_1 and M_2. We have shown this result in the analysis part.

Above attack shows that two or more dishonest participants can strongly control the key as it does not contain the contribution of any honest member. Note that in the attack that we discussed, the dishonest members were assumed to be adjacent to each other. If the two dishonest members are not adjacent then in that case also, none of the honest participant would be able to detect the attack in the verification step. However, key computed by the honest members will be different. Let M_i and M_{i+k}, $i + k > i + 1$ be the dishonest participants. Then we have two subsets of the honest members: first from M_{i+k+1} to M_{i-1}, and the other from M_{i+1} to M_{i+k-1}. The key computed by these two sets will be different in the form of attack we have discussed. One of the group will compute g^r as the group key, while other set of members will have some different key, that depends on the value of z_1. As, it can be noticed that z_1 is not independent of honest members' contribution, the key will also contain the contribution of honest members. But, still the dishonest members can perform the attack against a subset of honest members and none of the honest member can detect this.

6   Detection of a Corrupted Group Member Misbehaving in Second Phase

In this section we show that if the following conditions hold, then the protocol is free of key control.

- There is a single dishonest party;
- The dishonest party misbehaves only in phase 2.

Consider a group of n members, $M_1, M_2, \ldots, M_n$. Here we assume that all the participants execute the first phase honestly and any dishonest participant misbehaves only in the second phase. Assuming this condition to be true we formally prove, using the DS model, that the protocol can detect the presence of a single dishonest insider. Let M_1 be a dishonest participant and M_i, $2 \leq i \leq n$ be a victim honest participant. M_1 wants the session key to be a value that is independent of M_i's contribution. Let this value be g^{z_2}. For this it sends manipulated value of X_1 in the second phase. Let it be g^{z_1}. Here, z_1 and z_2 are message templates. M_1 first waits for X_j from all M_j; $2 \leq j \leq n$. Using these values, it computes $X_1 = g^{z_1}$. Let x_j represents the exponent over g in X_j. Then, for computing X_1, $M_1's$ knowledge can be represented using following sets in the DS model:

$P_1 = \{1, r_2, r_3, \ldots, r_i, \ldots, r_n, x_2, x_3, \ldots, x_i, \ldots, x_n\}; E_1 = \{r_1\}$.
Since M_1 wants the session key g^{z_2} to be independent of M_i's contribution, message template, z_2 is defined over following sets. These sets contain those values that represent the knowledge of M_1 such that the closure of set P_2 does not contain any value that includes M_i's contribution.

$P_2 = \{1, r_2, r_3, \ldots, r_{i-1}, r_{i+1}, \ldots, r_n, (r_{i+1}r_{i+2} - r_{i-1}r_{i-2}), x_2, x_3, \ldots, x_{i-2},$
$x_{i+2}, \ldots, x_n\}; E_2 = \{r_1\}$. In set P_2, we have included the term $(r_{i+1}r_{i+2} - r_{i-1}r_{i-2})$. This term is obtained by simplifying $(x_{i-1} + x_i + x_{i+1})$ which corresponds to the product $X_{i-1}X_iX_{i+1}$. All the individual terms in the product depend on r_i, but the product is independent of it. The attacker knows all these terms, but cannot use any of them alone while computing the key, as it will result in a value with M_i's contribution. But all these values together in the product form can be used.

Let $z_1 = v(F_1, h_1)$, where, $F_1 = \{f_{11}\}; f_{11} = \{r_1 \to p_1\}; h_1(f_{11}) = \{1 \to n_1,$
$r_j \to n_j \ (2 \le j \le n), x_j \to n_{n+j} \ (2 \le j \le n)\}$.
$z_2 = v(F_2, h_2)$, where, $F_2 = \{f_{21}\}; f_{21} = \{r_1 \to q_1\}; h_2(f_{21}) = \{1 \to m_1,$
$r_j \to m_j \ (2 \le j \le n; \ j \ne i), (r_{i+1}r_{i+2} - r_{i-1}r_{i-2}) \to m_{n+1},$
$x_j \to m_{n+j} \ (2 \le j \le n; \ j \ne i-1, i, i+1)\}$.
Thus, $z_1 = (n_1 + \sum_{j=2}^{n} n_j r_j + \sum_{j=2}^{n} n_{n+j} x_j) r_1^{p_1}$; $z_2 = (m_1 + \sum_{j=2;\ j \ne i}^{n} m_j r_j + m_{n+1}(r_{i+1}r_{i+2} - r_{i-1}r_{i-2}) + \sum_{j=2;\ j \ne i-1, i, i+1}^{n} m_{n+j} x_j) r_1^{q_1}$ For M_1 to be successful, there should exist some value of z_1 and z_2 as defined above so that the two equations (8) and (9) are satisfied. The first equation captures the verification step in the protocol, where each participant compares the computed right key of its left neighbour with its own left key and the second equation captures the key computation function. We denote by $K_j'^R$, the right key of M_j as computed by M_i. Then, $K_j'^R = K_{j-1}'^R X_j = K_{j-2}'^R X_{j-1} X_j = \cdots = K_i^R X_{i+1} \cdots X_{j-1} X_j$. Notice that in the computation of $K_j'^R$, for $i + 1 \le j \le n$, M_i does not need X_1. So, $K_j'^R = K_j^R = g^{r_j r_{j+1}}$ for $i \le j \le n$; and $K_j'^R = K_n'^R(X_1 X_2 \cdots X_j) = g^{r_n r_1 + z_1 + r_j r_{j+1} - r_1 r_2}$ for $1 \le j \le i - 1$.

Hence, $K_i^L = g^{r_{i-1} r_i}$ and $K_{i-1}'^R = g^{r_n r_1 + z_1 + r_i r_{i-1} - r_1 r_2}$. Since, K_i^L should be equal to $K_{i-1}'^R$ we have,

$$r_{i-1}r_i = r_n r_1 + z_1 + r_i r_{i-1} - r_1 r_2 \tag{8}$$

Session key computed by M_i is $\prod_{j=1}^{n} K_j'^R = K_i^R \prod_{j=i+1}^{i-1} K_j'^R = K_i^R \prod_{j=i+1}^{n} K_j'^R \prod_{j=1}^{i-1} K_j'^R = g^{r_i r_{i+1} + \sum_{j=i+1}^{n}(r_j r_{j+1}) + \sum_{j=1}^{i-1}(r_n r_1 + z_1 + r_j r_{j+1} - r_1 r_2)}$
$= g^{\sum_{j=1}^{n}(r_j r_{j+1}) + (i-1)z_1 + (i-1)r_1 r_n - (i-1)r_1 r_2}$. This should be equal to g^{z_2}. Hence, we have following equation.

$$z_2 = \sum_{j=1}^{n}(r_j r_{j+1}) + (i-1)z_1 + (i-1)r_1 r_n - (i-1)r_1 r_2 \tag{9}$$

Substituting the value of z_1 in equation (8),

$$r_{i-1}r_i = r_n r_1 + (n_1 + \sum_{j=2}^{n} n_j r_j + \sum_{j=2}^{n} n_{n+j} x_j) r_1^{p_1} + r_i r_{i-1} - r_1 r_2 \tag{10}$$

One possible solution to the above equation is $n_n = -1$, $n_2 = 1$, $p_1 = 1$ rest are
zero. This makes $z_1 = r_1 r_2 - r_n r_1$. Note that all other possible solutions too will
give the same value for z_1. Substituting the value of z_2 and the computed value
of z_1 in equation (9), we have

$$(m_1 + \sum_{j=2;\ j\neq i}^{n} (m_j r_j) + m_{n+1}(r_{i+1}r_{i+2} - r_{i-1}r_{i-2}) + \sum_{\substack{j=2,\\ j\neq i-1,i,i+1}}^{n} (m_{n+j}x_j))r_1^{q_1}$$

$$= \sum_{j=1}^{n}(r_j r_{j+1}) + (i-1)r_1 r_2 - (i-1)r_n r_1 + (i-1)r_1 r_n - (i-1)r_1 r_2 \quad (11)$$

Simplifying equation (11),

$$(m_1 + \sum_{\substack{j=2,\\ j\neq i}}^{n} m_j r_j + m_{n+1}(r_{i+1}r_{i+2} - r_{i-1}r_{i-2}) +$$

$$\sum_{\substack{j=2,\\ j\neq i-1,i,i+1}}^{n} m_{n+j}x_j)r_1^{q_1} = \sum_{j=1}^{n} r_j r_{j+1} \quad (12)$$

Note that the terms $r_i r_{i+1}$ and $r_{i-1}r_i$ on RHS cannot be balanced as there is no
other term containing r_i on either side in the equation except these two. Therefore equation (12) has no solution. This shows that the dishonest participant
cannot find two such messages that simultaneously satisfy both the equations.
This proves that the protocol is free of key control under the given condition.

7   Conclusions

In this paper we considered formal modeling of key control attacks on group key
protocols. As we have shown, the Dutta-Barua protocol suffers from key control
problems. We showed that in the case of a single dishonest participants key
control can be removed if we assume that the parties send the correct ephemeral
public values during the first phase.

Acknowledgements. We thank the three anonymous reviewers for helpful
comments and suggestions. The work of the second author was supported by a
grant from DST (Govt. of India) under the India-Japan co-operative programme.

References

1. Pieprzyk, J., Wang, H.: Malleability attacks on multi-party key agreement protocols in dynamic setting. Progress in Computer Science and Applied Logic 23,
277–288 (2004)
2. Biswas, G.P.: Diffie-hellman technique: extended to multiple two-party keys and
one multi-party key. IET Information Security 2(2), 12–18 (2008)

3. Tseng, Y.M., Wu, T.Y.: Analysis and improvement on a contributory group key exchange protocol based on the diffie-hellman technique. Informatica, Lith. Acad. Sci. 21(2), 247–258 (2010)
4. Dutta, R., Barua, R.: Provably secure constant round contributory group key agreement in dynamic setting. IEEE Transactions on Information Theory 54(5), 2007–2025 (2008)
5. Burmester, M., Desmedt, Y.: A Secure and Efficient Conference Key Distribution System (extended abstract). In: De Santis, A. (ed.) EUROCRYPT 1994. LNCS, vol. 950, pp. 275–286. Springer, Heidelberg (1995)
6. Delicata, R., Schneider, S.A.: A Formal Approach for Reasoning About a Class of Diffie-Hellman Protocols. In: Dimitrakos, T., Martinelli, F., Ryan, P.Y.A., Schneider, S. (eds.) FAST 2005. LNCS, vol. 3866, pp. 34–46. Springer, Heidelberg (2006)
7. Delicata, R., Schneider, S.: An algebraic approach to the verification of a class of diffie-hellman protocols. Int. J. Inf. Sec. 6(2-3), 183–196 (2007)
8. Tan, C.H., Yang, G.: Comments on "provably secure constant round contributory group key agreement in dynamic setting". IEEE Transactions on Information Theory 56(11), 5887–5888 (2010)
9. Teo, J.C.M., Tan, C.H., Ng, J.M.: Security analysis of provably secure constant round dynamic group key agreement. IEICE Transactions 89-A(11), 3348–3350 (2006)
10. Nam, J., Kim, M., Paik, J., Won, D.: Security weaknesses in harn-lin and dutta-barua protocols for group key establishment. TIIS 6(2), 751–765 (2012)
11. Pereira, O.: Modeling and Security Analysis of Authenticated Group Key Agreement Protocols. PhD thesis, Catholic University of Leuven (May 2003)
12. Pereira, O., Quisquater, J.J.: A security analysis of the cliques protocols suites. In: CSFW, pp. 73–81. IEEE Computer Society (2001)

A   Single Dishonest Insider

Group of Three Members:

In this case, M_1 can attack either of its two neighbours. Removing the contribution of both the neighbours results in the group key having value 1, which is generally not accepted. So, we have not considered that condition in other cases too.

Attack:

Following steps shows the messages sent by M_1. Suppose M_2 is the victim.

Phase 1:

$M_1 \rightarrow M_2 : t_{12} = t_3^{-1} = g^{-r_3}$ (t_3 is public and hence known to M_1.)

$M_1 \rightarrow M_3 : t_{13} = g^{r_1}$ (r_1 is chosen by M_1)

Phase 2:

M_1 *cannot compute* K_1^R, *needed to compute* X_1, *therefore, it uses* X_2 *&* X_3 *to compute* X_1.

M_1 computes $X_1 = (X_2 X_3)^{-1}$ $(X_2 = t_3^{r_2}/t_{12}^{r_2} = g^{2r_2 r_3}$

$$\text{and } X_3 = t_{13}^{r_3}/t_2^{r_3} = g^{r_1 r_3 - r_2 r_3})$$

$M_1 \rightarrow *$: X_1.

t_{ij} represents ephemeral public key sent by M_i for M_j.

$X \rightarrow *$ represents broadcast message from X.

Here, it can be seen that K_1^R computed using X_1, X_3 by M_2 is equal to $g^{r_2 r_3} X_3 X_1 = g^{r_2 r_3} g^{r_1 r_3 - r_2 r_3} (g^{2 r_2 r_3} g^{r_1 r_3 - r_2 r_3})^{-1} = g^{-r_2 r_3}$, which is same as $K_2^L = t_{12}^{r_2} = g^{-r_3 r_2}$, hence the malicious act is not caught. Similarly it can be verified that M_3 also gets the two values to be same.

The key computed by M_2 is:
$g^{r_2 r_3}(g^{r_2 r_3} X_3)(g^{r_2 r_3} X_3 X_1) = g^{r_1 r_3}$. It can be verified that the same key is computed by other honest members too. Clearly, this does not have r_2 and thus does not involves the contribution of M_2 as intended by M_1.

M_1 computes the key as: $t_3^{r_1}$

Group of Four Members:
In case of four member group, the dishonest participant can make the session key independent of any two honest participant's contribution who are adjacent to each other. Again suppose M_1 is dishonest. Thus, it can make the session key independent of the contribution of both M_2 and M_3 or M_3 and M_4. Following steps shows the message sent by M_1. Here we have shown the messages sent by M_1 only. All the other messages and notations are as per the protocol standards. Suppose M_2 and M_3 are victims.

Phase 1:
$M_1 \to M_2 : t_{12} = t_3^{-1} = g^{-r_3}$ (t_3 is public and hence known to M_1.)
$M_1 \to M_4 : t_{14} = g^{r_1}/t_3 = g^{r_1 - r_3}$ (r_1 is chosen by M_1)
Phase 2:
M_1 cannot compute K_1^R and K_1^L, needed to compute X_1, therefore it uses X_2, X_3 and X_4 to compute X_1.
M_1 computes $X_1 = (X_2 X_3 X_4)^{-1}$ $(X_2 = t_3^{r_2}/t_{12}^{r_2} = g^{2 r_2 r_3}; X_3 = t_4^{r_3}/t_2^{r_3}$
$\qquad\qquad\qquad\qquad\qquad = g^{r_4 r_3 - r_2 r_3}$ and $X_4 = t_{14}^{r_4}/t_3^{r_4} = g^{r_1 - 2 r_3 r_4})$

$M_1 \to *$: X_1.

Here again, it can be seen that K_1^R computed using X_1, X_3, X_4 by M_2 is equal to
$g^{r_2 r_3} X_3 X_4 X_1 = g^{r_2 r_3} g^{r_4 r_3 - r_2 r_3} g^{r_1 - 2 r_3 r_4} (g^{2 r_2 r_3} g^{r_4 r_3 - r_2 r_3} g^{r_1 - 2 r_3 r_4})^{-1} = g^{-r_2 r_3}$,
which is same as $K_2^L = t_{12}^{r_2} = g^{-r_3 r_2}$, hence the malicious act is not caught. Similarly it can be verified that other honest participants also gets the two values to be same, because X_2 is computed according to the protocol steps.

The key computed is:
$g^{r_2 r_3}(g^{r_2 r_3} X_3)(g^{r_2 r_3} X_3 X_4)(g^{r_2 r_3} X_3 X_4 X_1) = g^{r_1 r_4}$. Clearly, this does not have r_2 and r_3. Thus the key does not involve the contribution of M_2 and M_3 as intended by M_1.

M_1 computes the key as: $t_4^{r_1}$.

B   Two Dishonest Insiders

We have a group of n members, where M_1 and M_2 are dishonest. Suppose they want a fixed value $K' = g^r$ to be established as the session key. In the second phase they behave maliciously.

Suppose $X_1 = g^{z_1}$ and $X_2 = g^{z_2}$. z_1, z_2 are some exponents that can be expressed as message templates in the DS model and the dishonest members should be able to compute g^{z_1} and g^{z_2}.

M_1 and M_2 now have to compute the values for z_1 and z_2 such that both of the following conditions:

1. The test performed by the honest participants does not detect the misbehaviour, i.e. K_i^L is equal to the computed value of K_{i-1}^R by M_i using X_1 and X_2 for all i; where, M_i is an honest member.
2. The session key, GK is $K' = g^r$

are satisfied.

We first find a possible solution w.r.t. to any one honest participant and then verify that the same is true for all other honest participants.

Consider the computations done by M_3:

$K_3^L = g^{r_2 r_3}$ and K_2^{R3} i.e K_2^R as computed by M_3 is $g^{r_3 r_4} X_4 X_5 \cdots X_n X_1 X_2 = g^{r_3 r_4 + (r_4 r_5 - r_3 r_4) + (r_5 r_6 - r_4 r_5) + \cdots + (r_n r_1 - r_{n-1} r_n) + z_1 + z_2} = g^{r_1 r_n + z_1 + z_2}$

The two values, K_3^L and K_2^{R3} must be equal. Hence, we have this equation:

$$r_2 r_3 = r_1 r_n + z_1 + z_2 \tag{13}$$

The right key, K_j^R of M_j, $3 \leq j \leq n$ computed by M_3 does not use either of X_1 or X_2. Hence, M_3 computes these values correctly. For M_1 and M_2, it computes $K_1^R = K_n^R X_1 = g^{r_n r_1 + z_1}$ and $K_2^R = K_1^R X_2 = g^{r_n r_1 + z_1 + z_2}$.

The group key computed by M_3 is $\prod_{j=1}^{j=n} (K_j^R)$, which will be equal to $g^{r_3 r_4 + r_4 r_5 + \cdots + r_{n-1} r_n + r_n r_1 + (r_n r_1 + z_1) + (r_n r_1 + z_1 + z_2)}$. The dishonest participants want it to be equal to g^r. So, we have following equation

$$r = \sum_{i=3}^{n}(r_i r_{i+1}) + (r_n r_1 + z_1) + (r_n r_1 + z_1 + z_2) \tag{14}$$

Solving equation (13) and (14), we get following values of z_1 and z_2:

$z_1 = r - \sum_{i=2}^{n}(r_i r_{i+1}) - r_n r_1$ and

$z_2 = r_2 r_3 + \sum_{i=2}^{n}(r_i r_{i+1}) - r$ from these, values, X_1 and X_2 are computed as g^{z_1} and g^{z_2} respectively.

Now, we verify, using DS model, that if it is possible for M_1 and M_2 to compute these values using the information available to them.

M_1 and M_2 have following values:

1. X_i and t_i, $3 \leq i \leq n$ (Note that M_1 and M_2 do not know the corresponding exponents.)
2. r_1, r_2, r

Suppose x_i represents the exponent over g in X_i, i.e. $X_i = g^{x_i}$. Thus, $x_i = r_i r_{i+1} - r_i r_{i-1}$ for $3 \leq i \leq n$.

Then we have following set definitions for the model:

$$P = \{1, x_3, x_4, \ldots, x_n, r_3, r_4, \ldots, r_n\}$$
$$E = \{r_1, r_2, r\}$$

For M_1 and M_2 to be able to compute g^{z_1} and g^{z_2}, z_1 and z_2 should be equal to some message template defined over sets P and E. Let the above computed value of z_1 is equal to some message template $z_3 = v(F_3, h_3)$ and that of z_2 is $z_4 = v(F_4, h_4)$

Let F_3, h_3, F_4, h_4 be defined as:

$$F_3 = \{f_{31}, f_{32}, f_{33}\}, f_{3k} = \{r_1 \to p_{k1}, r_2 \to p_{k2}, r \to p_{k3}\};$$

$$h(f_{3k}) = \{1 \to n_{k1}, x_3 \to n_{k3}, x_4 \to n_{k4}, \dots, x_i \to n_{ki}, \dots, x_n \to n_{kn},$$
$$r_3 \to n_{kn+3}, \dots, r_i \to n_{kn+i}, r_n \to n_{kn+n}\}$$

for $k = 1, 2, 3$.

$$F_4 = \{f_{41}, f_{42}, f_{43}\}, f_{4k} = \{r_1 \to q_{k1}, r_2 \to q_{k2}, r \to q_{k3}\};$$

$$h(f_{4k}) = \{1 \to m_{k1}, x_3 \to m_{k3}, x_4 \to m_{k4}, \dots, x_i \to m_{ki}, \dots, x_n \to m_{kn},$$
$$r_3 \to m_{kn+3}, \dots, r_i \to m_{kn+i}, r_n \to m_{kn+n}\}$$

for $k = 1, 2, 3$.

Thus, $z_3 = v(F_3, h_3) = \sum_{k=1}^{k=3} (n_{k1} + n_{k3}x_3 + \dots + n_{ki}x_i + \dots + n_{kn}x_n + n_{kn+3}r_3 + n_{kn+4}r_4 + \dots + n_{kn+i}r_i + \dots + n_{kn+n}r_n)r_1^{p_{k1}} r_2^{p_{k2}} r^{p_{k3}}$

and $z_4 = v(F_4, h_4) = \sum_{k=1}^{k=3} (m_{k1} + m_{k3}x_3 + \dots + m_{ki}x_i + \dots + m_{kn}x_n + m_{kn+3}r_3 + m_{kn+4}r_4 + \dots + m_{kn+i}r_i + \dots + m_{kn+n}r_n)r_1^{q_{k1}} r_2^{q_{k2}} r^{q_{k3}}$

So, we have following equations (from $z_1 = z_3$; $z_2 = z_4$):

$$r - \sum_{i=2}^{n} (r_i r_{i+1}) - r_n r_1 = \sum_{k=1}^{k=3} (n_{k1} + n_{k3}x_3 + \dots + n_{ki}x_i + \dots + n_{kn}x_n +$$
$$n_{k(n+3)}r_3 + n_{k(n+4)}r_4 + \dots + n_{k(n+i)}r_i + \dots + n_{k(n+n)}r_n)r_1^{p_{k1}} r_2^{p_{k2}} r^{p_{k3}} \quad (15)$$

$$r_2 r_3 + \sum_{i=2}^{n} (r_i r_{i+1}) - r = \sum_{k=1}^{k=3} (m_{k1} + m_{k3}x_3 + \dots + m_{ki}x_i + \dots + m_{kn}x_n +$$
$$m_{k(n+3)}r_3 + m_{k(n+4)}r_4 + \dots + m_{k(n+i)}r_i + \dots + m_{k(n+n)}r_n)r_1^{q_{k1}} r_2^{q_{k2}} r^{q_{k3}} \quad (16)$$

Equations (15) and (16) can be balanced for following values of the mapping constants.

$n_{11} = p_{13} = 1$;

$n_{23} = 1, n_{24} = 2, \dots, n_{2i} = i - 2, n_{2n} = n - 2$;

$n_{3(n+n)} = -n; p_{31} = 1$. rest of all values are 0 in equation (15).

$m_{11} = -1; q_{13} = 1$;

$m_{23} = -2, m_{24} = -3, \dots, m_{2i} = -(i - 1), m_{2n} = -(n - 1)$;

$m_{3(n+n)} = n; q_{31} = 1$. Rest of all values are 0 in equation (16)

This gives, $z_3 = r + x_3 + 2x_4 + 3x_5 + \cdots + (n-2)x_n - nr_1r_n$
$z_4 = -r - 2x_3 - 3x_4 \cdots - (n-1)x_n + r_nr_1$

Thus, X_1 and X_2 are computed as:
$X_1 = g^r X_3 X_4^2 X_5^3 \cdots X_i^{i-2} \cdots X_n^{n-2}/t_i^{r_1}$
and $X_2 = t_n^{r_1}/(g^r X_3 X_4^2 X_3^3 \cdots X_i^{i-1} \cdots X_n^{n-1})$

Now, we have to verify that K_i^L is equal to the computed value of K_{i-1}^R by M_i using X_1 and X_2. for all i, where, M_i is an honest member.
For this, consider an honest member M_i.
$K_i^L = g^{r_{i-1}r_i}$
$K_{i-1}^R = K_i^R X_{i+1} X_{i+2} \cdots X_n X_1 X_2 X_3 \cdots X_{i-1}$
$= g^{r_i r_{i+1} + (r_{i+1}r_{i+2} - r_i r_{i+1}) + \cdots + (r_n r_1 - r_{n-1}r_n) + z_1 + z_2 + (r_3 r_4 - r_2 r_3) + \cdots + (r_{i-1}r_i - r_{i-1}r_{i-2})}$
$= g^{r_1 r_n + z_1 + z_2 - r_2 r_3 + r_i r_{i-1}}$
$= g^{r_1 r_n + r_2 r_3 - r_n r_1 - r_2 r_3 + r_i r_{i-1}}$ (from equation (13))
$= g^{r_i r_{i-1}}$, which is same as K_i^L.
Thus, we can see that none of the honest member can detect the malicious behaviour, as all of them compute K_{i-1}^R equal to their left key K_i^L

Group Key Computed by M_i
The key computed by M_i is $\prod_{j=i+1}^{i+n-1}(K_j^{Ri})K_i^R$, where K_j^{Ri} is K_j^R as computed by M_i.
$K_j^{Ri} = (\prod_{k=i+1}^{j} X_k)K_i^R$. Note that members are arranged in a circle and therefore, $X_0 = X_n$ and $X_{n+1} = X_1$.
M_i computes correct value of right shared key of all the honest members till n, as their computation does not involve X_1 and X_2.

$$K_j^{Ri} = \qquad K_j^R \qquad\qquad (i \le j \le n) \qquad\qquad (17)$$
$$= \qquad g^{r_1 r_n + z_1} \qquad\qquad (j = 1) \qquad\qquad (18)$$
$$= g^{r_1 r_n + z_1 + z_2 - r_2 r_3 + r_j r_{j+1}} \ (2 \le j < i) \qquad (19)$$

Thus, the group key computed by M_i is:
$g^{\sum_{k=i}^{n}(r_k r_{k+1}) + (r_n r_1 + z_1) + (r_n r_1 + z_1 + z_2) + \sum_{l=3}^{i-1}(r_n r_1 + z_1 + z_2 - r_2 r_3 + r_l r_{l+1})}$
From equation (13), $z_1 + z_2 = r_2 r_3 - r_1 r_n$. Substituting this in the above expression,
$GK_i = g^{\sum_{k=i}^{n}(r_k r_{k+1}) + r_2 r_3 - z_2 + r_2 r_3 + \sum_{l=3}^{i-1}(r_l r_{l+1})}$
$= g^{\sum_{k=3}^{n}(r_k r_{k+1}) + (r_n r_1 + z_1) + (r_n r_1 + z_1 + z_2)} = g^r$. (from equation (14))
Thus, it can be seen that all the honest members accept the predetermined value of dishonest members as the group key. This shows that a pair of dishonest insiders have strong key control in DB protocol.

Some Results on Related Key-IV Pairs of Grain

Subhadeep Banik, Subhamoy Maitra, and Santanu Sarkar

Applied Statistics Unit, Indian Statistical Institute,
203 B T Road, Kolkata 700 108, India
{s.banik_r,subho}@isical.ac.in, sarkar.santanu.bir@gmail.com

Abstract. In this paper we explain how one can obtain Key-IV pairs for Grain family of stream ciphers that can generate output key-streams which are either (i) almost similar in the initial part or (ii) exact shifts of each other throughout the generation of the stream. Let l_P be the size of the pad used during the key loading of Grain. For the first case, we show that in expected 2^{l_P} many invocations of the Key Scheduling Algorithm and its reverse routine, one can obtain two related Key-IV pairs that can produce same output bits in 75 (respectively 112 and 115) selected positions among the initial 96 (respectively 160 and 160) bits for Grain v1 (respectively Grain-128 and Grain-128a). Similar idea works for the second case in showing that given any Key-IV, one can obtain another related Key-IV in expected 2^{l_P} many trials such that the related Key-IV pairs produce shifted key-streams. We also provide an efficient strategy to obtain related Key-IV pairs that produce exactly i-bit shifted key-streams for small i. Our technique pre-computes certain equations that help in obtaining such related Key-IV pairs in 2^i many expected trials.

Keywords: Grain v1, Grain-128, Grain-128a, LFSR, NFSR, Related Key-IV pairs, Sequences, Keystream, Stream Cipher.

1   Introduction

The Grain v1 stream cipher is in the hardware profile of the eStream portfolio [1] that has been designed by Hell, Johansson and Meier in 2005 [12]. It is a synchronous bit oriented cipher, although it is possible to achieve higher throughput at the expense of additional hardware. The physical structure of Grain is simple as well as elegant and it has been designed so as to require low hardware complexity. Following certain attacks on the initial design of the cipher, the modified versions Grain v1 [12], Grain-128 [13] and Grain-128a [2] were proposed after incorporating certain changes. For detailed cryptanalytic results related to this family, the reader may refer to [3–10, 14–17, 19].

Our results in this paper are motivated to study how given a Key-IV, one can efficiently obtain another Key-IV so that the generated output key-streams are

- almost similar in the initial part or
- exact shifts of each other throughout the key-stream generation.

We call these Key-IV pairs "related" following [6, Section 3].

A. Bogdanov and S. Sanadhya (Eds.): SPACE 2012, LNCS 7644, pp. 94–110, 2012.

Since the Grain family of stream ciphers are essentially finite state machines, we can make several interesting observations. Any pair of internal states during the key-stream production stage (say S and S') that differ only in a few bit positions (say not exceeding three), produce very similar key-stream bits at-least in the first few output rounds. The idea therefore is to come up with two distinct Key-IV pairs (K, IV) and (K', IV'), that after the key initialization round, produce the states S, S' respectively. These Key-IV pairs would then produce key-stream which would be initially very similar to one another.

On the other hand, since the state update functions of the cipher are one-to-one and invertible, two distinct Key-IV pairs (K, IV) and (K', IV') will never produce exactly the same state S after the key initialization round. However, it may be possible that the Key-IV pair (K', IV'), after producing a certain number of output bits (say i), lands on the state S which is the same state that (K, IV)) lands on after Key initialization. Since Grain is a finite state machine, the key-stream produced by (K', IV') after these i rounds is exactly the same as that produced by (K, IV). These Key-IV pairs will then produce i bit shifted key-stream.

Though our work does not have any immediate implication towards breaking any cipher of the Grain family, the observations are relevant in cryptographic scenario.

1.1 Structure of Ciphers in Grain Family

The exact structure of the Grain family is explained in Figure 1. It consists of an n-bit LFSR and an n-bit NFSR. Certain bits of both the shift registers are taken as inputs to a combining Boolean function, whence the key-stream is produced. The update function of the LFSR is given by the equation $y_{t+n} = f(Y_t)$, where $Y_t = [y_t, y_{t+1}, \ldots, y_{t+n-1}]$ is an n-bit vector that denotes the LFSR state at the tth clock interval and f is a linear function on the LFSR state bits obtained from a primitive polynomial in $GF(2)$ of degree n. The NFSR state is updated as $x_{t+n} = y_t + g(X_t)$. Here, $X_t = [x_t, x_{t+1}, \ldots, x_{t+n-1}]$ is an n-bit vector that denotes the NFSR state at the tth clock interval and g is a non-linear function of the NFSR state bits.

The output key-stream is produced by combining the LFSR and NFSR bits as $z_t = h'(X_t, Y_t) = \bigoplus_{a \in A} x_{t+a} + h(X_t, Y_t)$, where A is some fixed subset of $\{0, 1, 2, \ldots, n-1\}$.

Key Loading Algorithm (KLA). The Grain family uses an n-bit key K, and an m-bit initialization vector IV, with $m < n$. The key is loaded in the NFSR and the IV is loaded in the 0th to the $(m-1)^{th}$ bits of the LFSR. The remaining m^{th} to $(n-1)^{th}$ bits of the LFSR are loaded with some fixed pad $P \in \{0, 1\}^{n-m}$. Hence at this stage, the $2n$ bit initial state is of the form $K \| IV \| P$.

Key Scheduling Algorithm (KSA). After the KLA, for the first $2n$ clocks, the key-stream produced at the output point of the function h' is XOR-ed to both the LFSR and NFSR update functions, i.e., during the first $2n$ clock intervals, the LFSR and the NFSR bits are updated as $y_{t+n} = z_t + f(Y_t)$, $x_{t+n} = y_t + z_t + g(X_t)$.

Pseudo-Random Key-stream Generation Algorithm (PRGA). After the completion of the KSA, z_t is used as the Pseudo-Random key-stream bit. It is no longer XOR-ed to the LFSR and the NFSR. Therefore during this phase, the LFSR and NFSR are updated as $y_{t+n} = f(Y_t)$, $x_{t+n} = y_t + g(X_t)$.

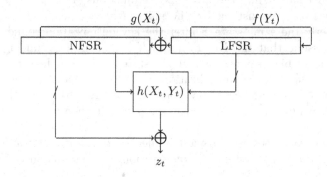

Fig. 1. Structure of Stream Cipher in Grain Family

One may note that given any arbitrary state and the information about its evolution (the number of clocks in KSA or PRGA), one can calculate the corresponding state S_0^K at the beginning of the KSA. This is because the state update functions in both the KSA and PRGA in the Grain family are one-to-one and invertible. Hence one can construct the KSA^{-1} routine that given an input $2n$ bit vector denoting the internal state of the cipher at the end of the KSA, returns the $2n$ bit vector giving internal state of the cipher at the beginning of the KSA. One can similarly describe a PRGA^{-1} routine that inverts one round of the PRGA. Note that this is not any problem in the design, but this is a valid approach for design of stream ciphers with small states.

1.2   Related Key-IV Pairs

Let us now explain our interpretation of related Key-IV pairs. This is in line of what explained in [6, Section 3]. For this we need the construction of the related Key-IV function ϕ as illustrated in Figure 2. Note that we require both routines KSA and KLA to be uniquely reversible for a successful construction of ϕ. The goal of constructing ϕ is to obtain a pair of related Key-IVs (K, IV) and $(K, IV)_\Delta$ such that they produce either almost similar initial key-streams or shifted key-streams throughout the generation. With explicit construction of such functions ϕ, we will show that given any Key-IV (K, IV) in the Grain family, it is possible to find related Key-IV pair $(K, IV)_\Delta$.

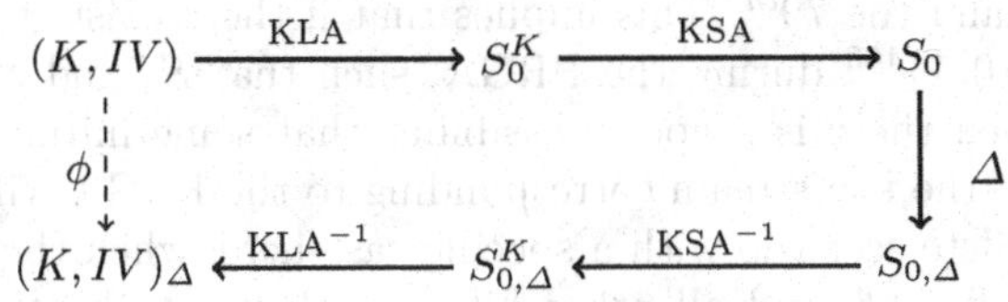

$$(K, IV) \xrightarrow{\text{KLA}} S_0^K \xrightarrow{\text{KSA}} S_0$$

$$\phi \Big\downarrow \qquad\qquad\qquad\qquad\qquad \Big\downarrow \Delta$$

$$(K, IV)_\Delta \xleftarrow{\text{KLA}^{-1}} S_{0,\Delta}^K \xleftarrow{\text{KSA}^{-1}} S_{0,\Delta}$$

Fig. 2. Construction of the Related Key-IV function

2   Related Key-IV Pairs in Grain Family

The general structure of Grain family as explained in Figure 1. In particular, Grain v1 consists of an 80 bit LFSR and an 80 bit NFSR. It uses an 80-bit Key and a 64-bit IV, and a 16-bit pad $P = $ 0x ffff. Certain bits of both the shift registers are taken as inputs to a combining Boolean function, whence the keystream is produced. The update function of the LFSR is given by the equation

$$y_{t+80} = y_{t+62} + y_{t+51} + y_{t+38} + y_{t+23} + y_{t+13} + y_t \overset{\Delta}{=} f(Y_t).$$

The NFSR state is updated as follows

$$x_{t+80} = y_t + g(x_{t+63}, x_{t+62}, x_{t+60}, x_{t+52}, x_{t+45}, x_{t+37}, x_{t+33}, x_{t+28}, x_{t+21}, x_{t+15}$$
$$x_{t+14}, x_{t+9}, x_t),$$

where $g(x_{t+63}, x_{t+62}, \ldots, x_t)$

$$\overset{\Delta}{=} g(X_t) = x_{t+62} + x_{t+60} + x_{t+52} + x_{t+45} + x_{t+37} + x_{t+33} + x_{t+28} + x_{t+21} +$$
$$x_{t+14} + x_{t+9} + x_t + x_{t+63}x_{t+60} + x_{t+37}x_{t+33} + x_{t+15}x_{t+9} +$$
$$x_{t+60}x_{t+52}x_{t+45} + x_{t+33}x_{t+28}x_{t+21} + x_{t+63}x_{t+45}x_{t+28}x_{t+9} +$$
$$x_{t+60}x_{t+52}x_{t+37}x_{t+33} + x_{t+63}x_{t+60}x_{t+21}x_{t+15} +$$
$$x_{t+63}x_{t+60}x_{t+52}x_{t+45}x_{t+37} + x_{t+33}x_{t+28}x_{t+21}x_{t+15}x_{t+9} +$$
$$x_{t+52}x_{t+45}x_{t+37}x_{t+33}x_{t+28}x_{t+21}.$$

The output key-stream is produced by combining the LFSR and NFSR bits as follows

$$z_t = \bigoplus_{a \in A} x_{t+a} + h(y_{t+3}, y_{t+25}, y_{t+46}, y_{t+64}, x_{t+63}) \overset{\Delta}{=} \bigoplus_{a \in A} x_{t+a} + h(X_t, Y_t)$$

where $A = \{1, 2, 4, 10, 31, 43, 56\}$ and $h(s_0, s_1, s_2, s_3, s_4)$
$= s_1 + s_4 + s_0 s_3 + s_2 s_3 + s_3 s_4 + s_0 s_1 s_2 + s_0 s_2 s_3 + s_0 s_2 s_4 + s_1 s_2 s_4 + s_2 s_3 s_4.$

2.1   Search for Related Key-IV Pairs in Grain V1

The non-linear function h that takes inputs from both the linear and non-linear registers to produce the key-stream, taps the 64th bit of the LFSR and no bit in between 65th and the 79th. This implies that if there exist two initial states S_0 and $S_{0,\Delta} \in \{0,1\}^{160}$ during the PRGA, such that S_0 and $S_{0,\Delta}$ differ in a few positions, then there is a good possibility that some initial bits (may not be contiguous) of the key-stream corresponding to the PRGA will be same. We explain the complete scenario with a specific case here, when the last bit of the two states are different, and all other bits are identical. So, this is single-bit differential for the state S_0. However, there are many other such possibilities that may also be explored.

Let us consider that S_0 and $S_{0,\Delta}$ differ only in the 79th LFSR position. In such a case, it is easy to check that they will produce identical key-stream for some initial points. We will also show that it is possible to produce Key-IV pairs (K_0, IV_0) and (K_1, IV_1) with $K_i \in \{0,1\}^{80}$ and $IV_i \in \{0,1\}^{64}$ so that after key-scheduling the pair (K_0, IV_0) produces the initial state S_0 of the key-stream production stage and the pair (K_1, IV_1) produces the initial state $S_{0,\Delta}$ so that S_0 and $S_{0,\Delta}$ differ only in the 79th LFSR position.

First, we will look at a method to compute such related pairs (K_0, IV_0) and (K_1, IV_1). The method works because the KSA is invertible, i.e., given an initial state of the key-stream production stage it is possible to back-track and determine the Key-IV pair that produced it. The following method is, in principle, similar to the technique used by Zhang et al [19]. The basic idea is to generate at random Key-IV pair $K_0, IV_0 \in \{0,1\}^{80} \times \{0,1\}^{64}$ and calculate the initial state S_0 of the PRGA. Then after flipping the y_{79} bit of S_0 we produce the state $S_{0,\Delta}$ and backtrack to find out if there exists a Key-IV pair that produces $S_{0,\Delta}$. We will state the algorithm formally now.

Output: Key-IV pair's that produces almost similar initial key-stream or Failure

1 Randomly choose a Key-IV pair $(K, IV) \in \{0,1\}^{80} \times \{0,1\}^{64}$;
2 Obtain the initial state of the KSA $S_0^K = [K \parallel IV \parallel \text{0x ffff}]$;
3 Run the KSA for 160 clocks to produce an initial state $S_0 \in \{0,1\}^{160}$;
4 Construct $S_{0,\Delta}$ from S_0 by flipping the bit y_{79};
5 Compute $S_{0,\Delta}^K = \text{KSA}^{-1}(S_{0,\Delta})$ as the KSA routine is invertible;
6 If $S_{0,\Delta}^K$ is of the form $[\tilde{K} \parallel \tilde{IV} \parallel \text{0x ffff}]$, return (K, IV) and $(K, IV)_\Delta = (\tilde{K}, \tilde{IV})$ as the related Key-IV pairs;
7 Else return failure;

Algorithm 1: Search for related Key-IV pairs in Grain v1

Given that l_P is the length of the Pad P (which is a specific pattern among all the l_P bit patterns), it is expected that we will be able to obtain related Key-IV pairs in $2^{l_P} = 2^{16}$ many runs of the algorithm (as if obtaining the specific pattern through random search). The next thing that we need to check is the propagation of the single-bit differential into the key-stream of the cipher. This is described in the following technical result.

Theorem 1. *For Grain v1, the two initial states $S_0, S_{0,\Delta} \in \{0,1\}^{160}$ which differ only in the 79th position of the LFSR, produce identical output bits in 75 specific positions among the initial 96 key-stream bits produced during the PRGA.*

Proof. Any input differential introduced in the 79th LFSR position takes 15 clocks before appearing at the 64th position, and hence the first 15 bits z_0 to z_{14} will be exactly the same. In the 16th round, the differential arrives at the 64th position of the LFSR, which contributes an input to the Boolean function h and hence this bit may be different. Hereafter, the differential proceeds to the 63rd LFSR position, which does not provide an input to h and hence in this round the output is the same. In the next round the differential is at the 62nd position, which although does not feed the output function h, provides an input to the LFSR update function, due to which a difference reappears in the 79th position. This new difference will now affect the key-stream after 15 rounds. Thus by keeping track of the propagation of the differential for the first 96 PRGA rounds it is possible to determine which rounds produce the same output bit. At all rounds numbered $k \in [0,95] \setminus \{15, 33, 44, 51, 54, 57, 62, 69, 72, 73, 75, 76, 80, 82, 83, 87, 90, 91, 93, 94, 95\}$, the difference exists only in positions that do not provide input to the Boolean function h and hence at these clocks the key-stream bit produced by the two states are essentially the same. At all other clock rounds the difference appears at positions which provide input to h. Hence the key-stream produced at these clocks may be different. After 96 rounds the input difference is fed to the non-linear update function g of the NFSR, and hereafter the propagation of the difference would depend on the particular NFSR state at that point.   □

2.2   Examples of Related Key-IV Pairs in Grain V1

In case of a practical search for related pairs of Key-IV, we notice that the Algorithm 1 is expected to run 2^{16} times for obtaining one pair of related Key-IV's. Now, this invocation may be accomplished in many ways. First we consider the example for the situation as mentioned in Algorithm 1.

Multiple Key-IV Trials with a Fixed Differential. Consider a fixed differential Δ for all the $(Key - IV)$ pairs. In this case, Algorithm 1 needs to run expected 2^{16} times with different randomly chosen (K, IV)'s to obtain a related Key-IV pair (K, IV) and $(K, IV)_\Delta$. In case of Grain v1, this Δ represents 'flipping the last bit of the LFSR'. With expected 2^{16} queries in each case, we obtained related Key-IV pairs during the experiments. One such example is as follows.

Key	IV	S
bf6689cead5ece39758c	bdfa0025ac44a4fe	52f71a93959ff900ffa9 15c61a47522fffaf8a77
e166bc5aa1952733ab2a	aed6838b948399a0	52f71a93959ff900ffa9 15c61a47522fffaf8a76

One can check that out of the initial 96 key-stream bits, 75 specific bits are same as per Theorem 1 and in particular, 78 many are same in this case.

Single Key-IV Trial with a Multiple Differentials. Now suppose a more practical situation, where a single pair of Key-IV is provided, and one has to produce a related pair of Key-IV corresponding to the one given. In this situation, one may experiment with different values of Δ. If around 2^{16} different Δ's can be used, then given a specific (K, IV) a related Key-IV pair may be expected. In this case, the expected number of invocations of KSA^{-1} is 2^{16}, one for each Δ. However, the number of KSA invocation is only one as we have only a single Key-IV pair for the complete strategy.

In case of Grain v1, we first observed that the single-bit change in the LFSR results towards related initial bits of the key-stream. Similar situation is expected to happen for 1, 2 or 3-bit changes in the LFSR, as the changes are still minor compared to the total size of the state. Thus, we chose a simple family of Δ where at most 3 bits out of the 75 bits of the LFSR are taken; the LFSR has 80 bits and we exclude the 4 bits ($3^{rd}, 25^{th}, 46^{th}, 64^{th}$) that go to the Boolean function h and the 0th bit that goes to the NFSR. One may note that $\binom{75}{1} + \binom{75}{2} + \binom{75}{3} > 2^{16}$ and thus it is expected to obtain a related Key-IV pair.

Below we present an example, where the states differ in three bit positions of the LFSR, namely $47, 52, 54$. Out of the initial 80 key-stream bits produced, 55 are same.

Key	IV	S
bde8d3c319ff4d234706	f363180e262b6cc5	a74e7c7799b00f3c94e1 bf0315b589691f82085a
b223a57ce1578708677a	371d2d93363b014b	a74e7c7799b00f3c94e1 bf0315b589681582085a

2.3   Related Key-IV's in Grain-128

The structure of Grain-128 is similar to its previous versions. The only differences are in the update functions of the LFSR, NFSR and the combining output function. It uses an 128-bit Key and a 96-bit IV, and a 32-bit pad $P = $ 0x ffff ffff. The LFSR of Grain-128 is updated as

$$y_{t+128} = y_{t+96} + y_{t+81} + y_{t+70} + y_{t+38} + y_{t+7} + y_t,$$

where the NFSR is updated as

$$x_{t+128} = y_t + x_t + x_{t+26} + x_{t+56} + x_{t+91} + x_{t+96} + x_{t+3}x_{t+67} + x_{t+11}x_{t+13} +$$
$$x_{t+17}x_{t+18} + x_{t+27}x_{t+59} + x_{t+40}x_{t+48} + x_{t+61}x_{t+65} + x_{t+68}x_{t+84}.$$

The output key-stream bit is produced as

$$z_t = \bigoplus_{j \in B} x_{t+j} + y_{t+93} + h(x_{t+12}, y_{t+8}, y_{t+13}, y_{t+20}, x_{t+95}, y_{t+42}, y_{t+60}, y_{t+79}, y_{t+95})$$

where $B = \{2, 15, 36, 45, 64, 73, 89\}$ and $h(x_0, \ldots, x_8) = x_0 x_1 + x_2 x_3 + x_4 x_5 + x_6 x_7 + x_0 x_4 x_8$.

The key is loaded in the NFSR and the IV is loaded in the 0th to the 95th bits of the LFSR. The remaining 96th to 127th bits of the LFSR are loaded with 1's (the 32-bit pad P, i.e., $l_P = 32$). Here 256 rounds of KSA are executed after which the key-stream is produced. As in Grain v1, here too, the KSA is invertible. After an expected number of $2^{l_P} = 2^{32}$ trials two related Key-IV pairs (K_0, IV_0) and (K_1, IV_1) can be found. For these Key-IV pairs, the KSA gives initial states S_0 and $S_{0,\Delta}$ that differ only in the 127th bit position.

Propagation of the Differential. The following result describes the differential propagation characteristics of the single-bit differential Δ in case of Grain-128.

Theorem 2. *For the Grain-128 stream cipher, two initial states $S_0, S_{0,\Delta} \in \{0,1\}^{256}$ which differ only in the 127th position of the LFSR, produce identical output bits in 112 specific positions among the initial 160 key-stream bits produced during the PRGA.*

Proof. As described in Theorem 1, a similar analysis applies in the case of Grain-128. By tracking the evolution of the single bit differential introduced at the 127th LFSR position, it is possible to determine the clock rounds for which the output key-stream is exactly similar for the related Key-IV pairs which give rise to such a differential after the KSA. In Grain-128, the output key-stream for the following rounds numbered

$$k \in [0, 159] \setminus \{32, 34, 48, 64, 66, 67, 79, 80, 81, 85, 90, 92, 95, 96, 98, 99, 106, 107,$$
$$112, 114, 117, 119, 122, 124, 125, 126, 128, 130, 131, 132, 138, 139,$$
$$142, 143, 144, 145, 146, 148, 149, 150, 151, 153, 154, 155, 156, 157,$$
$$158, 159\}$$

for a related Key-IV pair are identical.   □

Below we present a related Key-IV pair for Grain-128. One can verify that out of the first 160 keystream bits produced by the Key-IV pairs in the given example, 112 specific bits are same as per Theorem 2 and 132 bits are same in total.

Key	IV	S
60287a5ecf99724716a83bf81a9735cf	62b6f21aa5d6511f43cb51f0	7bb026436bc29b585e676e90961830e0
		7e86e48d2370eeda43ddd098a4b3e7d2
dc260a0042112620772443311b933f08	c026cf1526950adee08fbe14	7bb026436bc29b585e676e90961830e0
		7e86e48d2370eeda43ddd098a4b3e7d3

2.4   Related Key-IV's in Grain-128a

The LFSR update functions of Grain-128 and Grain-128a are the same. There is a slight difference in the NFSR update function and the output function. Also Grain-128a uses the pad 0x ffff fffe in the last 32 bits of the LFSR instead of the all 1 pad. The NFSR update function for Grain-128a is given by

$$x_{t+128} = y_t + x_t + x_{t+26} + x_{t+56} + x_{t+91} + x_{t+96} + x_{t+3}x_{t+67} + x_{t+11}x_{t+13} +$$
$$x_{t+17}x_{t+18} + x_{t+27}x_{t+59} + x_{t+40}x_{t+48} + x_{t+61}x_{t+65} + x_{t+68}x_{t+84} +$$
$$x_{t+88}x_{t+92}x_{t+93}x_{t+95} + x_{t+22}x_{t+24}x_{t+25} + x_{t+70}x_{t+78}x_{t+82}.$$

The output key-stream bit is generated as

$$z_t = \bigoplus_{j \in B} x_{t+j} + y_{t+93} + h(x_{t+12}, y_{t+8}, y_{t+13}, y_{t+20}, x_{t+95}, y_{t+42}, y_{t+60}, y_{t+79}, y_{t+94}),$$

where the function h and the set B are same as defined for Grain-128.

It is known that the first 64 output bits of Grain-128a are used for initializing the MAC and thereafter each alternative bit is used as the key-stream and the other bit is used for constructing the MAC. Let us first refer to all these bits as as output bits (these are referred as pre-output stream in [2]) and then analyse the exact scenario. Then we will concentrate on the key-stream bits.

Propagation of the Differential. The following result describes the differential propagation characteristic of the single-bit differential Δ in case of Grain-128a.

Theorem 3. *For the Grain-128a stream cipher, two initial states $S_0, S_{0,\Delta} \in \{0,1\}^{256}$ which differ only in the 127th position of the LFSR, produce identical output bits in 115 specific positions among the initial 160 output bits produced during the PRGA.*

Proof. The proof follows a similar analysis as done for Grain v1 and Grain-128. The output bits for rounds

$$k \in [0, 159] \setminus \{33, 34, 48, 65, 66, 67, 80, 81, 85, 91, 92, 95, 97, 98, 99, 106, 107, 112,$$
$$114, 117, 119, 123, 124, 125, 127, 128, 129, 130, 131, 132, 138, 139,$$
$$142, 143, 144, 145, 146, 149, 150, 151, 154, 155, 156, 157, 159\}$$

for a related Key-IV pair are identical.   □

In case of Grain-128a, the Pad is of length $l_P = 32$ bits, and the number of bits that are same in the key-streams Z and Z_Δ is 115. Thus, the complexity of getting related pairs in these cases is expected 2^{32}. Moreover, 11 bits in the key-stream, the bits $\{34, 66, 81, 92, 98, 124, 128, 130, 145, 150, 156\}$ are always different in Z and Z_Δ. This is because at these rounds the difference appears on one of the NFSR state bits which are linearly added to the output of the $h(\cdot)$ function to produce the keystream.

Out of the initial 160 output bits from Grain-128a, the initial 64 are used for MAC. Thus we are now left with $160 - 64 = 96$ bits. Again out of those, half of them will be used for MAC and half of them will be used as key-stream bits. Thus, we have actually considered 48 key-stream bits. The first 160 output bits are indexed as 0 to 159. Among them the even numbered bits from 64 to 159 are the key-stream bits. One may note that given two related Key-IV pairs, for the initial 48 key-stream bits, 30 will be exactly same, 8 will be exactly complement of each other and rest 10 cannot be determined before-hand.

Below we present a related Key-IV pair for Grain-128a. One can verify that out of the first 48 keystream bits produced by the Key-IV pairs in the given example, 30 specific bits are same as per Theorem 3 and 33 bits are same in total.

Key	IV	S
54fd23a7e54f8fb096a45189b65f0fff	5a7fb7b76c303592b74422c3	36a0589046e177ae325a4b60154084cd fc74e3c99cad9a2f2fcbf394d44f15fd
1c21c39e9404b1c347ee8dc594f3d040	9db86204107b9ac4d401cc2d	36a0589046e177ae325a4b60154084cd fc74e3c99cad9a2f2fcbf394d44f15fc

3 Occurrence of Key-IV Pairs That Produce Shifted Key-Streams

The size of the Key-IV space in Grain being $\{0,1\}^n \times \{0,1\}^m$, one may expect that the cipher produces 2^{n+m} different key-streams. However, many of these key-streams are finite bit-position shifts of one another, that is natural in this kind of design. We have already noted that both the KSA and PRGA routines in the Grain family are invertible. Thus, given any Key-IV in the Grain family, it may be possible to find another Key-IV pair that produces a bit-shifted key-stream.

Let $\psi : \{0,1\}^{2n} \to \{0,1\}^{2n}$ be the state update function during the PRGA of Grain. The goal is to construct a *related key function* $\phi : \{0,1\}^n \times \{0,1\}^m \to \{0,1\}^n \times \{0,1\}^m$ such that (K_0, IV_0) and $\phi(K_0, IV_0)$ produce shifted key-streams. The construction of ϕ in our constrained model of the stream cipher is as in Algorithm 2.

Thus, given any Key-IV in the Grain family, it is possible to find another Key-IV such that both of them produce key-streams which are finite bit shifts of one another, in an expected 2^{l_P} iterations where l_P is the length of the pad P. This holds under the assumption that, after the reverse KSA routine the last l_P bits of the LFSR are uniformly distributed. Hence, it is expected that we will be able to obtain related Key-IV pairs in 2^{l_P} many iterations of the loop.

We present a set of examples here for each of the stream cipher in the Grain family. Given the Key-IV pairs in column 1 of the following table, column 2 gives a related Key-IV pair that produces shifted key-stream. Column 3 gives the length of the shift.

Grain	Key-IV	Key-IV	Shift
v1	4567b66f51b956542319 96b81c6c97ed8853	f0f9d3bc4f2d0001e11d 67e95df014caf50a	72343 $\approx 2^{16.14}$
128	fca5c3705794a26266f58d06f7e87b9f cf74e27475fc36e159069606	990aa66d1d816db4d81cf42ab62937b2 54345cb47fed0997dc1a73d4	236757088 $\approx 2^{27.82}$
128a	2b953abc7427e1c260b2995039766123 81a25f710a9a24aed1644d9f	01f8cda5aa35dece20154a986e24e4d8 4bf4f64d462d379453928a7a	2642097831 $\approx 2^{31.30}$

Output: Key-IV pair that produces shifted key-stream or return failure
1 Randomly choose a Key-IV pair $(K, IV) \in \{0,1\}^n \times \{0,1\}^m$;
2 Obtain the initial state of the KSA $S_0^K = [K \parallel IV \parallel P]$;
3 Run the KSA for $2n$ clocks to produce an initial state $S_0 \in \{0,1\}^{2n}$;
4 Initialize $i = 1$;
5 Construct the state S_i by running one more round of the PRGA;
6 Reverse the KSA routine to generate the initial state $S_i^K = \text{KSA}^{-1}(S_i)$;
7 If S_i^K is of the form $[\tilde{K} \parallel \tilde{IV} \parallel P]$ then return related Key-IV pair (K, IV),
   $(K, IV)_i = (\tilde{K}, \tilde{IV})$, and the shift i;
8 $i \leftarrow i + 1$;
9 If i is greater than some predefined threshold then return failure;
10 Return to step 2 and repeat the process after running another round of the
   PRGA;

Algorithm 2: Related Key-IV function ϕ for shifted key-streams in Grain

3.1 Improved Strategy over [6] for Small Shift

In [6], Key-IV pairs in Grain v1, that produce shifted key-streams, were demonstrated. The idea is as follows. First we demonstrate the idea for for 1-bit shift for simplicity of explanation. If $K_0 \in \{0,1\}^n$ and $IV_0 \in \{0,1\}^m$ denote a Key-IV, then the initial state of the KSA is denoted by $B_0 = K_0$ and $C_0 = IV_0 \parallel P$. After the first round of KSA, the updated initial states are denoted by $B_1 \parallel C_1$.

– If C_1 can be written in the form $IV_1 \parallel P$ for $IV_1 \in \{0,1\}^m$, then $B_1 \parallel C_1 = K_1 \parallel IV_1 \parallel P$ is another valid initial state of the KSA. So if the KSA starts with the state $B_1 \parallel C_1$ instead of $B_0 \parallel C_0$, it may produce one bit-shifted key-streams.
– An added sufficiency condition is required. The 1st output bit produced during the PRGA must be 0 that appears from the KSA initial state B_0, C_0. This is required to ensure that the state after the $2n^{th}$ round of the KSA using $B_1 \parallel C_1$, is the same as the state after the 1st PRGA round using (B_0, C_0).

If both the above conditions are satisfied then (K_0, IV_0) and (K_1, IV_1) will indeed produce 1-bit shifted key-streams. Both the events have a probability of occurrence of $\frac{1}{2}$ and hence a related Key-IV pair may be found with probability $\frac{1}{4}$ by randomly choosing Key-IV pairs. This idea extends to i rounds, so that two Key-IV pairs which produce i-bit shifted key-stream may be obtained with probability $(\frac{1}{4})^i$.

However, in this section we show that the probability may be improved to $(\frac{1}{2})^i$ by explicitly characterizing the structure of the Key-IV which, in every round of KSA out of those i rounds, produce valid internal states.

To analyse this, let us study the KSA in more detail. Given a key IV pair $K_0 = x_0, x_1, \ldots, x_{n-1}$ and $IV_0 = y_0, y_1, \ldots, y_{m-1}$, the state update function during the KSA can be presented in the following way. Consider that $x_i^{[j]}$ ($y_i^{[j]}$) is the value in the ith cell of the NFSR (LFSR) in the jth KSA round. Denote $B_0 \overset{\Delta}{=} x_0^{[0]}, x_1^{[0]}, \ldots, x_{n-1}^{[0]}$, $C_0 \overset{\Delta}{=} y_0^{[0]}, y_1^{[0]}, \ldots, y_{m-1}^{[0]} \parallel P = y_0^{[0]}, y_1^{[0]}, \ldots, y_{n-1}^{[0]}$.

Input: B_0, C_0
Output: B_i, C_i, for $i = 1$ to u

for $i = 1$ *to* u **do**

$\quad y^{[i]} \leftarrow f(Y^{[i-1]})$ where $Y^{[i-1]} = y_0^{[i-1]}, y_1^{[i-1]}, \ldots, y_{n-1}^{[i-1]}$

$\quad x^{[i]} \leftarrow y_0^{[i-1]} + g(X^{[i-1]})$ where $X^{[i-1]} = x_0^{[i-1]}, x_1^{[i-1]}, \ldots, x_{n-1}^{[i-1]}$

$\quad z^{[i]} \leftarrow \bigoplus_{a \in A} x_a^{[i-1]} + h(X^{[i-1]}, Y^{[i-1]})$

$\quad B_i = (x_0^{[i]}, x_1^{[i]}, \ldots, x_{n-2}^{[i]}, x_{n-1}^{[i]}) \leftarrow (x_1^{[i-1]}, x_2^{[i-1]}, \ldots, x_{n-1}^{[i-1]}, x^{[i]} + z^{[i]})$

$\quad C_i = (y_0^{[i]}, y_1^{[i]}, \ldots, y_{n-2}^{[i]}, y_{n-1}^{[i]}) \leftarrow (y_1^{[i-1]}, y_2^{[i-1]}, \ldots, y_{n-1}^{[i-1]}, y^{[i]} + z^{[i]})$

end

Algorithm 3: Obtaining Grain KSA Relations

In Grain v1, for $B_1 \| C_1$ to represent a valid initial state of the KSA it must be of the form $[\tilde{K} \| \tilde{IV} \| P]$, Thus following Algorithm 3, this will occur if $y^{[1]} + z^{[1]} = 1$ in the first iteration of the KSA (where $y^{[i]}, z^{[i]}$ are as defined in Algorithm 3). This implies

$$y_{62} + y_{51} + y_{38} + y_{23} + y_{13} + y_0 + \bigoplus_{a \in A} x_a + h(y_3, y_{25}, y_{46}, y_{64}, x_{63}) = 1, \quad (1)$$

that evaluates to

$$y_{62} = ((y_{25} + x_{63} + 1)y_3 + y_{25}x_{63} + x_{63} + 1)y_{46} + y_{23} + y_{25} + x_{10} + y_{38} + y_{51} +$$
$$x_1 + x_2 + x_{31} + x_{43} + x_4 + x_{56} + y_0 + y_3 + y_{13} + 1.$$

This covers the case of [6] for 1-bit shift. Now, towards the extension, let us consider the case for 2-bit shift.

For both $B_1 \| C_1$ and $B_2 \| C_2$ to be valid initial states, in addition to (1), we need the following condition $(y^{[2]} + z^{[2]} = 1)$ to hold:

$$y_{63} + y_{52} + y_{39} + y_{24} + y_{14} + y_1 + \bigoplus_{a \in A} x_{a+1} + h(y_4, y_{26}, y_{47}, y_{65}, x_{64}) = 1. \quad (2)$$

Solving (1) and (2), we obtain

$$y_{62} = ((y_{25} + x_{63} + 1)y_3 + y_{25}x_{63} + x_{63} + 1)y_{46} + y_{23} + y_{25} + x_{10} + y_{38} + y_{51} +$$
$$x_1 + x_2 + x_{31} + x_{43} + x_4 + x_{56} + y_0 + y_3 + y_{13} + 1,$$

$$y_{63} = ((y_{26} + x_{64} + 1)y_4 + y_{26}x_{64} + x_{64} + 1)y_{47} + y_{24} + y_{26} + x_{11} + y_{39} + y_{52} +$$
$$x_2 + x_3 + x_{32} + x_{44} + x_5 + x_{57} + y_1 + y_4 + y_{14} + 1.$$

Similarly, by solving together equations of the form $y^{[i]} + z^{[i]} = 1$ for each successive round of the KSA, we would be able to determine the necessary conditions that need to be satisfied for each successive internal state $(B_i \| C_i), i = 1, 2, \ldots$ to be valid initial states of the Grain v1 KSA. In Appendix A, we present the equations required for 11-bit shift. Using mathematical tools like SAGE [18], we could arrive at the solution to the simultaneous equations $y^{[i]} + z^{[i]} = 1$ for upto $i = 12$. Beyond that the equations are becoming quite complicated and we need further investigations.

Satisfying these equations are necessary but not sufficient to find a chain of Key-IV pairs that produce shifted key-streams. In order for valid Key-IV pairs derived from $B_0||C_0, B_1||C_1, \ldots, B_i||C_i$ to produce shifted key-streams, the first i output bits produced by the Key-IV derived from $B_0||C_0$ during the PRGA must be zero. By randomly choosing Key-IV pairs satisfying the above conditions, it is expected that after 2^i trials one such pair will be obtained that outputs i zeros in the first i rounds of the PRGA. This is precisely the complexity of the routine needed to find a chain of i such related Key-IV pairs. Thus it improves the complexity of 2^{2i} presented in [6, Section 3].

Example 1. In the Grain family of stream cipher given the Key-IV pairs in column 1 of the following table, column 2 gives a related Key-IV pair that produces shifted key-stream. Column 3 gives the length of the shift. We could successfully obtained related Key-IV pairs for shifts upto 12. Below, we provide examples for 12-bit shifts.

Grain	Key-IV	Key-IV	Shift
v1	8ca87875d334c9de694a 5246f9d65f5eaef9	87875d334c9de694abbc 6f9d65f5eaef9fff	12
128	b8d3dac27cbfeae545a508e9e551c095 bba4d4a0465a4448627e22ed	3dac27cbfeae545a508e9e551c095753 4d4a0465a4448627e22edfff	12

Non-applicability of Such Analysis on Grain-128a. It has already been pointed out in [6, Section 3.4] that such a strategy will not work if the self-similarity of the pad (initialization constant) is eliminated. Subsequently, this has been implemented in Grain 128a [2]. The Grain-128a resists this due to the asymmetric nature of the pad P used during the KLA. In this cipher, the pad length is 32 bits and the value of P =0x ffff fffe, i.e., it consists of 31 ones followed by a zero. Therefore after one round of KSA the last 32 bits of the LFSR may either be 0x ffff fffc or 0x ffff fffd depending on whether the feedback value was 0 or 1. A similar analysis for the first 32 rounds of the KSA will show that it is not possible for the last 32 bits of the LFSR to have the value P =0x ffff fffe in any of these rounds. This is because P is such that it cannot be written in the form $P_s||A$, where P_s is any s bit suffix of P and A is any $(32 - s)$-bit string over $\{0, 1\}$. It is however possible that in the 33rd round of the KSA, the last 32 bits of the LFSR is equal to P. However, finding such Key-IV pairs by solving equations as above may not be possible in real time due to large degree and number of monomials in these equations. If one attempts to find such Key-IV pairs by choosing the initial states randomly, then too the complexity of the task is expected to be $(2^{32})^2 = 2^{64}$.

4   Conclusion

Here we have studied a model of stream cipher where the key and IV are directly loaded in the state variables and the remaining part of the state is filled up with some kind of padding. Considering the length of the padding as l_P, it can be shown that given any Key-IV one can easily construct another pair with expected 2^{l_P} time complexity that produces same bits at a significant amount of initial key-stream. With expected 2^{16} invocations of the KSA and its inverse routine, we could recover related Key-IV pairs of Grain v1 that produce key-streams with 75 identical bits out of the first 96 bits. The effect of our work on Grain-128 and Grain-128a is also similar and we could obtain related Key-IV pairs for both the ciphers within an expected complexity of 2^{32} such that the two output streams match at 112 and 115 bits out of the first 160 bits in Grain-128 (here it is key-stream) and Grain-128a (here it is pre-output stream instead of key-stream) respectively.

Further, we have studied the related Key-IV pairs of Grain that produce shifted key-streams. We demonstrate how one can obtain a related Key-IV in expected 2^{l_P} trials for any given Key-IV such that the pair can generate key-streams that are finite shifts of one another. This idea works for all the versions of Grain. We could also construct Key-IV pairs that produce i-bit shifted key-streams in 2^i many trials and our experiments work for upto $i = 12$. This is applicable for Grain v1 and Grain-128, but not for Grain-128a.

Acknowledgments. The authors like to thank the anonymous reviewers for detailed comments that improved the technical as well as the editorial quality of this paper. The authors also acknowledge detailed comments of Mr. Sourav Sen Gupta in an earlier version of this draft. Further, the authors like to acknowledge the Centre of Excellence in Cryptology at Indian Statistical Institute, supported by Government of India.

References

1. The ECRYPT Stream Cipher Project. eSTREAM Portfolio of Stream Ciphers (revised on September 8, 2008)
2. Ågren, M., Hell, M., Johansson, T., Meier, W.: A New Version of Grain-128 with Authentication. In: Symmetric Key Encryption Workshop 2011. DTU, Denmark (2011)
3. Aumasson, J.P., Dinur, I., Henzen, L., Meier, W., Shamir, A.: Efficient FPGA Implementations of High-Dimensional Cube Testers on the Stream Cipher Grain-128. In: SHARCS - Special-purpose Hardware for Attacking Cryptographic Systems (2009)
4. Berbain, C., Gilbert, H., Maximov, A.: Cryptanalysis of Grain. In: Robshaw, M. (ed.) FSE 2006. LNCS, vol. 4047, pp. 15–29. Springer, Heidelberg (2006)
5. Bjørstad, T.E.: Cryptanalysis of Grain using Time/Memory/Data tradeoffs (v1.0 / 2008-02-25), http://www.ecrypt.eu.org/stream

6. De Cannière, C., Küçük, Ö., Preneel, B.: Analysis of Grain's Initialization Algorithm. In: Vaudenay, S. (ed.) AFRICACRYPT 2008. LNCS, vol. 5023, pp. 276–289. Springer, Heidelberg (2008)
7. Dinur, I., Güneysu, T., Paar, C., Shamir, A., Zimmermann, R.: An Experimentally Verified Attack on Full Grain-128 Using Dedicated Reconfigurable Hardware. In: Lee, D.H. (ed.) ASIACRYPT 2011. LNCS, vol. 7073, pp. 327–343. Springer, Heidelberg (2011)
8. Dinur, I., Shamir, A.: Breaking Grain-128 with Dynamic Cube Attacks. In: Joux, A. (ed.) FSE 2011. LNCS, vol. 6733, pp. 167–187. Springer, Heidelberg (2011)
9. Englund, H., Johansson, T., Turan, M.S.: A Framework for Chosen IV Statistical Analysis of Stream Ciphers. In: Srinathan, K., Rangan, C.P., Yung, M. (eds.) INDOCRYPT 2007. LNCS, vol. 4859, pp. 268–281. Springer, Heidelberg (2007)
10. Fischer, S., Khazaei, S., Meier, W.: Chosen IV Statistical Analysis for Key Recovery Attacks on Stream Ciphers. In: Vaudenay, S. (ed.) AFRICACRYPT 2008. LNCS, vol. 5023, pp. 236–245. Springer, Heidelberg (2008)
11. Fredricksen, H.: A survey of full length nonlinear shift register cycle algorithms. SIAM Rev. 24, 195–221 (1982)
12. Hell, M., Johansson, T., Meier, W.: Grain - A Stream Cipher for Constrained Environments. ECRYPT Stream Cipher Project Report 2005/001 (2005), http://www.ecrypt.eu.org/stream
13. Hell, M., Johansson, T., Maximov, A., Meier, W.: A Stream Cipher Proposal: Grain-128. In: IEEE International Symposium on Information Theory, ISIT 2006 (2006)
14. Khazaei, S., Hassanzadeh, M., Kiaei, M.: Distinguishing Attack on Grain. ECRYPT Stream Cipher Project Report 2005/071 (2005), http://www.ecrypt.eu.org/stream
15. Knellwolf, S., Meier, W., Naya-Plasencia, M.: Conditional Differential Cryptanalysis of NLFSR-Based Cryptosystems. In: Abe, M. (ed.) ASIACRYPT 2010. LNCS, vol. 6477, pp. 130–145. Springer, Heidelberg (2010)
16. Lee, Y., Jeong, K., Sung, J., Hong, S.: Related-Key Chosen IV Attacks on Grain-v1 and Grain-128. In: Mu, Y., Susilo, W., Seberry, J. (eds.) ACISP 2008. LNCS, vol. 5107, pp. 321–335. Springer, Heidelberg (2008)
17. Stankovski, P.: Greedy Distinguishers and Nonrandomness Detectors. In: Gong, G., Gupta, K.C. (eds.) INDOCRYPT 2010. LNCS, vol. 6498, pp. 210–226. Springer, Heidelberg (2010)
18. Stein, W.: Sage Mathematics Software. Free Software Foundation, Inc. (2009), http://www.sagemath.org (Open source project initiated by W. Stein and contributed by many)
19. Zhang, H., Wang, X.: Cryptanalysis of Stream Cipher Grain Family. IACR Cryptology ePrint Archive 2009: 109 (2009), http://eprint.iacr.org/2009/109

Appendix A

The solution for the system $y^{[i]} + z^{[i]} = 1$ for $i = 1, \ldots, 11$ is as follows.

$$x_i = r_{i+1} \quad 0 \le i \le 79$$
$$y_i = r_{i+81} \quad 0 \le i \le 52,$$

where $r_1, r_2, \ldots, r_{133}$ are the degrees of freedom.

$$y_{53} = \Big((r_{108} + r_{66} + 1)r_{129} + 1\Big)r_{86} + \Big(r_{108}r_{66} + r_{66} + 1\Big)r_{129} + r_{106} + r_{108} + r_{121} + r_{13}$$
$$+ r_{34} + r_4 + r_{46} + r_5 + r_{59} + r_7 + r_{83} + r_{96}$$

$$y_{54} = \Big((r_{109} + r_{67} + 1)r_{130} + 1\Big)r_{87} + \Big(r_{109}r_{67} + r_{67} + 1\Big)r_{130} + r_{107} + r_{109} + r_{122} + r_{14}$$
$$+ r_{35} + r_{47} + r_5 + r_6 + r_{60} + r_8 + r_{84} + r_{97}$$

$$y_{55} = \Big((r_{110} + r_{68} + 1)r_{131} + 1\Big)r_{88} + \Big(r_{110}r_{68} + r_{68} + 1\Big)r_{131} + r_{108} + r_{110} + r_{123} + r_{15} +$$
$$r_{36} + r_{48} + r_6 + r_{61} + r_7 + r_{85} + r_9 + r_{98}$$

$$y_{56} = \Big((r_{111} + r_{69} + 1)r_{132} + 1\Big)r_{89} + \Big(r_{111}r_{69} + r_{69} + 1\Big)r_{132} + r_{10} + r_{109} + r_{111} + r_{124}$$
$$+ r_{16} + r_{37} + r_{49} + r_{62} + r_7 + r_8 + r_{86} + r_{99}$$

$$y_{57} = \Big((r_{112} + r_{70} + 1)r_{133} + 1\Big)r_{90} + \Big(r_{112}r_{70} + r_{70} + 1\Big)r_{133} + r_{100} + r_{11} + r_{110} + r_{112}$$
$$+ r_{125} + r_{17} + r_{38} + r_{50} + r_{63} + r_8 + r_{87} + r_9$$

$$y_{58} = \Big[(r_{71} + 1)r_{91} + r_{71} + 1\Big]r_{106} + \Big[(r_{71} + 1)r_{91} + r_{71} + 1\Big]r_{108} + \Big[(r_{71} + 1)r_{91} + r_{71}$$
$$+ 1\Big]r_{83} + \Big[(r_{71} + 1)r_{91} + r_{71} + 1\Big]r_{96} + \Big[(r_{71} + 1)r_{91} + (r_{71} + r_{91})r_{113} + r_{71} + 1\Big]$$
$$r_{121} + \Big[(r_{71} + 1)r_{91} + (r_{71} + r_{91})r_{113} + \Big((r_{66} + 1)r_{71} + ((r_{66} + 1)r_{71} + r_{66} + 1)r_{91} +$$
$$((r_{71} + 1)r_{91} + r_{71} + 1)r_{108} + ((r_{66} + 1)r_{71} + (r_{66} + 1)r_{91} + (r_{71} + r_{91})r_{108})r_{113} + r_{66}$$
$$+ 1\Big)r_{129} + r_{71} + 1\Big]r_{86} + \Big[(r_{66} + 1)r_{71} + \Big((r_{66} + 1)r_{71} + r_{66} + 1\Big)r_{91} + \Big((r_{66}r_{71}$$
$$+ r_{66})r_{91} + r_{66}r_{71} + r_{66}\Big)r_{108} + \Big((r_{66} + 1)r_{71} + (r_{66} + 1)r_{91} + (r_{66}r_{71} + r_{66}r_{91})r_{108}\Big)$$
$$r_{113} + r_{66} + 1\Big]r_{129} + \Big[(r_{71} + r_{91})r_{106} + (r_{71} + r_{91})r_{108} + (r_{71} + r_{91})r_{83} + (r_{71} + r_{91})$$
$$r_{96} + \Big(r_{13} + r_{34} + r_4 + r_{46} + r_5 + r_{59} + r_7\Big)r_{71} + \Big(r_{13} + r_{34} + r_4 + r_{46} + r_5 + r_{59}$$
$$+ r_7\Big)r_{91} + 1\Big]r_{113} + \Big[r_{13} + r_{34} + r_4 + r_{46} + r_5 + r_{59} + r_7\Big]r_{71} + \Big[\Big(r_{13} + r_{34} + r_4 +$$
$$r_{46} + r_5 + r_{59} + r_7\Big)r_{71} + r_{13} + r_{34} + r_4 + r_{46} + r_5 + r_{59} + r_7 + 1\Big]r_{91} + r_{10} + r_{101} + r_{111}$$
$$+ r_{12} + r_{126} + r_{13} + r_{18} + r_{34} + r_{39} + r_4 + r_{46} + r_5 + r_{51} + r_{59} + r_{64} + r_7 + r_{88} + r_9$$

$$y_{59} = \Big[(r_{72} + 1)r_{92} + r_{72} + 1\Big]r_{107} + \Big[(r_{72} + 1)r_{92} + r_{72} + 1\Big]r_{109} + \Big[(r_{72} + 1)r_{92} + r_{72} + 1\Big]$$
$$r_{84} + \Big[(r_{72} + 1)r_{92} + r_{72} + 1\Big]r_{97} + \Big[(r_{72} + 1)r_{92} + (r_{72} + r_{92})r_{114} + r_{72} + 1\Big]r_{122} +$$
$$\Big[(r_{72} + 1)r_{92} + (r_{72} + r_{92})r_{114} + \Big((r_{67} + 1)r_{72} + ((r_{67} + 1)r_{72} + r_{67} + 1)r_{92} + ((r_{72} + 1)$$
$$r_{92} + r_{72} + 1)r_{109} + ((r_{67} + 1)r_{72} + (r_{67} + 1)r_{92} + (r_{72} + r_{92})r_{109})r_{114} + r_{67} + 1\Big)r_{130}$$
$$+ r_{72} + 1\Big]r_{87} + \Big[(r_{67} + 1)r_{72} + ((r_{67} + 1)r_{72} + r_{67} + 1)r_{92} + \Big((r_{67}r_{72} + r_{67})r_{92} + r_{67}$$
$$r_{72} + r_{67}\Big)r_{109} + \Big((r_{67} + 1)r_{72} + (r_{67} + 1)r_{92} + (r_{67}r_{72} + r_{67}r_{92})r_{109}\Big)r_{114} + r_{67} + 1\Big]$$
$$r_{130} + \Big[(r_{72} + r_{92})r_{107} + (r_{72} + r_{92})r_{109} + (r_{72} + r_{92})r_{84} + (r_{72} + r_{92})r_{97} + \Big(r_{14} + r_{35}$$
$$+ r_{47} + r_5 + r_6 + r_{60} + r_8\Big)r_{72} + \Big(r_{14} + r_{35} + r_{47} + r_5 + r_6 + r_{60} + r_8\Big)r_{92} + 1\Big]r_{114}$$
$$+ \Big[r_{14} + r_{35} + r_{47} + r_5 + r_6 + r_{60} + r_8\Big]r_{72} + \Big[(r_{14} + r_{35} + r_{47} + r_5 + r_6 + r_{60} + r_8)r_{72}$$

$+r_{14} + r_{35} + r_{47} + r_5 + r_6 + r_{60} + r_8 + 1\big]r_{92} + r_{10} + r_{102} + r_{11} + r_{112} + r_{127} + r_{13} +$
$r_{14} + r_{19} + r_{35} + r_{40} + r_{47} + r_5 + r_{52} + r_6 + r_{60} + r_{65} + r_8 + r_{89}$

$y_{60} = (r_{73} + 1)r_9 + \big[(r_{73} + 1)r_{93} + r_{73} + 1\big]r_{108} + \big[(r_{73} + 1)r_{93} + r_{73} + 1\big]r_{110} + \big[(r_{73} + 1)$
$r_{93} + r_{73} + 1\big]r_{98} + \big[(r_{73} + 1)r_{93} + (r_{73} + r_{93})r_{115} + r_{73} + 1\big]r_{123} + \big[(r_{73} + 1)r_{93} +$
$(r_{73} + r_{93})r_{115} + r_{73} + 1\big]r_{85} + \big[(r_{73} + 1)r_{93} + (r_{73} + r_{93})r_{115} + \big((r_{68} + 1)r_{73} + ((r_{68} +$
$1)r_{73} + r_{68} + 1)r_{93} + ((r_{73} + 1)r_{93} + r_{73} + 1)r_{110} + ((r_{68} + 1)r_{73} + (r_{68} + 1)r_{93} + (r_{73}$
$+r_{93})r_{110})r_{115} + r_{68} + 1\big)r_{131} + r_{73} + 1\big]r_{88} + \big[(r_{68} + 1)r_{73} + ((r_{68} + 1)r_{73} + r_{68} + 1)r_{93}$
$+\big((r_{68}r_{73} + r_{68})r_{93} + r_{68}r_{73} + r_{68}\big)r_{110} + \big((r_{68} + 1)r_{73} + (r_{68} + 1)r_{93} + (r_{68}r_{73} + r_{68}$
$r_{93})r_{110}\big)r_{115} + r_{68} + 1\big]r_{131} + \big[r_{15} + r_{36} + r_{48} + r_6 + r_{61} + r_7\big]r_{73} + \big[(r_{73} + r_{93})$
$r_{108} + (r_{73} + r_{93})r_{110} + (r_{73} + r_{93})r_{98} + \big(r_{15} + r_{36} + r_{48} + r_6 + r_{61} + r_7\big)r_{73} + \big(r_{15}$
$+r_{36} + r_{48} + r_6 + r_{61} + r_7 + r_9\big)r_{93} + r_{73}r_9 + 1\big]r_{115} + \big[(r_{73} + 1)r_9 + \big(r_{15} + r_{36} +$
$r_{48} + r_6 + r_{61} + r_7\big)r_{73} + r_{15} + r_{36} + r_{48} + r_6 + r_{61} + r_7 + 1\big]r_{93} + r_{103} + r_{11} + r_{113} +$
$r_{12} + r_{128} + r_{14} + r_{15} + r_{20} + r_{36} + r_{41} + r_{48} + r_{53} + r_6 + r_{61} + r_{66} + r_7 + r_{90}$

$y_{61} = (r_{74} + 1)r_{10} + \big[(r_{74} + 1)r_{94} + r_{74} + 1\big]r_{109} + \big[(r_{74} + 1)r_{94} + r_{74} + 1\big]r_{111} + \big[(r_{74} + 1)r_{94}$
$+r_{74} + 1\big]r_{99} + \big[(r_{74} + 1)r_{94} + (r_{74} + r_{94})r_{116} + r_{74} + 1\big]r_{124} + \big[(r_{74} + 1)r_{94} + (r_{74} + r_{94})$
$r_{116} + r_{74} + 1\big]r_{86} + \big[(r_{74} + 1)r_{94} + (r_{74} + r_{94})r_{116} + \big((r_{69} + 1)r_{74} + ((r_{69} + 1)r_{74} + r_{69}$
$+1)r_{94} + ((r_{74} + 1)r_{94} + r_{74} + 1)r_{111} + ((r_{69} + 1)r_{74} + (r_{69} + 1)r_{94} + (r_{74} + r_{94})r_{111})r_{116}$
$+r_{69} + 1\big)r_{132} + r_{74} + 1\big]r_{89} + \big[(r_{69} + 1)r_{74} + ((r_{69} + 1)r_{74} + r_{69} + 1)r_{94} + \big((r_{69}r_{74} + r_{69})$
$r_{94} + r_{69}r_{74} + r_{69}\big)r_{111} + \big(r_{69} + 1)r_{74} + (r_{69} + 1)r_{94} + (r_{69}r_{74} + r_{69}r_{94})r_{111}\big)r_{116} + r_{69}$
$+1\big]r_{132} + \big[r_{16} + r_{37} + r_{49} + r_{62} + r_7 + r_8\big]r_{74} + \big[(r_{74} + r_{94})r_{109} + (r_{74} + r_{94})r_{111} +$
$(r_{74} + r_{94})r_{99} + \big(r_{16} + r_{37} + r_{49} + r_{62} + r_7 + r_8\big)r_{74} + \big(r_{10} + r_{16} + r_{37} + r_{49} + r_{62}$
$+r_7 + r_8\big)r_{94} + r_{10}r_{74} + 1\big]r_{116} + \big[r_{74} + 1)r_{10} + \big(r_{16} + r_{37} + r_{49} + r_{62} + r_7 + r_8\big)r_{74}$
$+r_{16} + r_{37} + r_{49} + r_{62} + r_7 + r_8 + 1\big]r_{94} + r_{104} + r_{114} + r_{12} + r_{129} + r_{13} + r_{15} + r_{16} + r_{21}$
$+r_{37} + r_{42} + r_{49} + r_{54} + r_{62} + r_{67} + r_7 + r_8 + r_{91}$

$y_{62} = \big(r_{106} + r_{64} + 1)r_{84} + r_{106}r_{64} + r_{64} + 1\big)r_{127} + r_{104} + r_{106} + r_{11} + r_{119} + r_{132} + r_2 + r_3 +$
$r_{32} + r_{44} + r_5 + r_{57} + r_{81} + r_{84} + r_{94} + 1$

$y_{63} = \big((r_{107} + r_{65} + 1)r_{85} + r_{107}r_{65} + r_{65} + 1\big)r_{128} + r_{105} + r_{107} + r_{12} + r_{120} + r_{133} + r_3 + r_{33}$
$+r_4 + r_{45} + r_{58} + r_6 + r_{82} + r_{85} + r_{95} + 1$

A Differential Fault Attack on Grain-128a Using MACs

Subhadeep Banik, Subhamoy Maitra, and Santanu Sarkar

Applied Statistics Unit, Indian Statistical Institute,
203 B T Road, Kolkata 700 108, India
{s.banik_r,subho}@isical.ac.in, sarkar.santanu.bir@gmail.com

Abstract. The 32-bit MAC of Grain-128a is a linear combination of the first 64 and then the alternative keystream bits. In this paper we describe a successful differential fault attack on Grain-128a, in which we recover the Secret Key by observing the correct and faulty MACs of certain chosen messages. The attack works due to certain properties of the Boolean functions and corresponding choices of the taps from the LFSR. We present methods to identify the fault locations and then construct a set of linear equations to obtain the contents of the LFSR and the NFSR. Our attack requires less than 2^{11} fault injections and invocations of less than 2^{12} MAC generation routines.

Keywords: Grain v1, Grain-128, Grain-128a, LFSR, MAC, NFSR, Stream Cipher.

1 Introduction

The Grain-128a authentication scheme was proposed in SKEW 2011 [1] by Ågren et al. It was later described in [2]. Any message in $\{0,1\}^*$ can be mapped to a 32-bit tag using this authenticated-encryption scheme. Grain-128a is essentially part of the Grain family which was first proposed by Hell, Johansson and Meier in 2005 [13] as a part of the eStream project. The physical structure of the Grain family is simple as well as elegant and has been designed so as to require low hardware complexity. In response to cryptanalysis against the initial design of the cipher, the modified versions Grain v1 [13], Grain-128 [14] and Grain-128a [1] were proposed in due course. Analysis of this cipher is an area of recent interest as evident from number of cryptanalytic results [3–12, 16–19, 22, 23].

Fault attacks on stream ciphers have received attention in recent cryptographic literature since the work of Hoch and Shamir [15]. For differential fault attack scenario in stream ciphers, the attacker is allowed to inject faults in the internal state, and then by analyzing the difference in the faulty and the fault-free keystreams, he attempts to deduce the complete or partial information about the internal state/Secret Key. The most common method of injecting faults is by using laser shots or clock glitches [20, 21] (see these and the references therein). Though fault attacks usually rely on optimistic assumptions and study the cipher in a model that is weaker than the original version, they are not unrealistic

A. Bogdanov and S. Sanadhya (Eds.): SPACE 2012, LNCS 7644, pp. 111–125, 2012.

as evident from literature. In this paper too, the model we study is a follow up of existing state-of-the-art literature [4, 6, 16]. A detailed justification of the feasibility of such fault model is presented in [6, Section IIIB].

Grain-128 and Grain v1 have been successfully cryptanalyzed by employing fault attacks [4, 6, 16]. In these ciphers, the attacker has the advantage of accessing and analyzing the entire fault-free and faulty keystreams. In Grain-128a, this is not the case as it accommodates authentication too. The scheme does not make the first 64 keystream bits available to the attacker. Thereafter the keystream bits are used for encryption and authentication alternatively. The scheme outputs 32-bit MAC of any message and this can be used by the attacker. In our work, we have described an approach to find the Secret Key used in the authentication scheme by observing the correct and faulty MACs of certain specific messages. In particular, our attack works in the same broad framework described in [4], but due to the added restriction of the first 64 keystream bits and every alternate keystream bit thereafter not being available to the attacker, the ground level details of the attack with respect to fault location identification, construction of linear equations to deduce the LFSR and the NFSR state are entirely different.

We proceed with the description of the Grain family, and in particular Grain-128a, in this section. The implementation of the attack on Grain-128a along with the fault location identification routine is explained in Section 2.

1.1   Brief Description of Grain Family

The exact structure of the Grain family is explained in this section. It consists of an n-bit LFSR and an n-bit NFSR. Certain bits of both the shift registers are taken as inputs to a combining Boolean function, whence the keystream is produced. The update function of the LFSR is given by the equation $y_{t+n} = f(Y_t)$, where $Y_t = [y_t, y_{t+1}, \ldots, y_{t+n-1}]$ is an n-bit vector that denotes the LFSR state at the tth clock interval and f is a linear function on the LFSR state bits obtained from a primitive polynomial in $GF(2)$ of degree n.

We abuse the $+$ notation for Boolean XOR, i.e., GF(2) addition as well as standard arithmetic addition. However, that will be clear from the context.

The NFSR state is updated as $x_{t+n} = y_t + g(X_t)$. Here, the n-bit vector $X_t = [x_t, x_{t+1}, \ldots, x_{t+n-1}]$ denotes the NFSR state at the tth clock interval and g is a non-linear function of the NFSR state bits.

The output keystream is produced by combining the LFSR and NFSR bits as $z_t = h'(X_t, Y_t) = \bigoplus_{a \in A} x_{t+a} + h(X_t, Y_t)$, where A is some fixed subset of $\{0, 1, 2, \ldots, n-1\}$.

The Grain family uses an n-bit Key K, and an m-bit initialization vector IV, with $m < n$. The Key is loaded in the NFSR and the IV is loaded in the 0th to the $(m-1)^{th}$ bits of the LFSR. The remaining m^{th} to $(n-1)^{th}$ bits of the LFSR are loaded with some fixed pad $P \in \{0,1\}^{n-m}$. Hence at this stage, the $2n$ bit initial state is of the form $K||IV||P$. Then, for the first $2n$ clocks, the keystream produced at the output point of the function h' is XOR-ed to both the LFSR and NFSR update functions, i.e., during the first $2n$ clock intervals, the LFSR and the NFSR bits are updated as $y_{t+n} = z_t + f(Y_t)$, $x_{t+n} = y_t + z_t + g(X_t)$. This is the Key Scheduling Algorithm (KSA).

After the completion of the KSA, z_t is no longer XOR-ed to the LFSR and the NFSR but it is used as the Pseudo-Random keystream bit. This is the Pseudo-Random Generation Algorithm (PRGA). Therefore during this phase, the LFSR and NFSR are updated as $y_{t+n} = f(Y_t)$, $x_{t+n} = y_t + g(X_t)$.

For Grain-128a authenticated encryption scheme the exact parameters are as follows. The size of Key $n = 128$ bits and the IV is of size $m = 96$ bits. The value of pad used is $P = \texttt{0xFFFF FFFE}$. The LFSR update rule is given by

$$y_{t+128} \overset{\Delta}{=} f(Y_t) = y_{t+96} + y_{t+81} + y_{t+70} + y_{t+38} + y_{t+7} + y_t.$$

The NFSR state is updated as follows

$$x_{t+128} = y_t + g(x_{t+96}, x_{t+95}, x_{t+93}, x_{t+92}, x_{t+91}, x_{t+88}, x_{t+84}, x_{t+82}, x_{t+78},$$
$$x_{t+70}, x_{t+68}, x_{t+67}, x_{t+65}, x_{t+61}, x_{t+59}, x_{t+48}, x_{t+40}, x_{t+27},$$
$$x_{t+26}, x_{t+25}, x_{t+24}, x_{t+22}, x_{t+13}, x_{t+11}, x_{t+3}, x_t),$$

where $g(x_{t+96}, x_{t+95}, \ldots, x_t)$ is defined as

$$g(X_t) = x_t + x_{t+26} + x_{t+56} + x_{t+91} + x_{t+96} + x_{t+3}x_{t+67} + x_{t+11}x_{t+13}$$
$$+ x_{t+17}x_{t+18} + x_{t+27}x_{t+59} + x_{t+40}x_{t+48} + x_{t+61}x_{t+65} + x_{t+68}x_{t+84}$$
$$+ x_{t+88}x_{t+92}x_{t+93}x_{t+95} + x_{t+22}x_{t+24}x_{t+25} + x_{t+70}x_{t+78}x_{t+82}.$$

The keystream bit z_t is defined as

$$z_t = \bigoplus_{j \in A} x_{t+j} + y_{t+93} + h(x_{t+12}, y_{t+8}, y_{t+13}, y_{t+20}, x_{t+95}, y_{t+42}, y_{t+60}, y_{t+79}, y_{t+94})$$

where $A = \{2, 15, 36, 45, 64, 73, 89\}$ and $h(s_0, \ldots, s_8) = s_0 s_1 + s_2 s_3 + s_4 s_5 + s_6 s_7 + s_0 s_4 s_8$.

Authentication. Assume that we have a message of length L defined by the bits $m_0, \ldots, m_{L-1}$. Set $m_L = 1$ as padding. To provide authentication, two registers, called accumulator and shift register of size 32 bits each, are used. The content of accumulator and shift register at time t is denoted by $a_t^0, \ldots, a_t^{31}$ and $r_t, \ldots, r_{t+31}$ respectively. The accumulator is initialized through $a_0^j = z_j, 0 \le j \le 31$ and the shift register is initialized through $r_j = z_{32+j}, 0 \le j \le 31$. The shift register is updated as $r_{t+32} = z_{64+2t+1}$. The accumulator is updated as $a_{t+1}^j = a_t^j + m_t r_{t+j}$ for $0 \le j \le 31$ and $0 \le t \le L$. The final content of accumulator, $a_{L+1}^0, \ldots, a_{L+1}^{31}$ is used for authentication. Here we follow the description given in [2].

2   Differential Fault Analysis on Grain-128a

We like to point out that to the best of our knowledge there is no existing fault attack on Grain-128a available in literature. Moreover, our attack strategy works using the MAC of certain messages instead of exploiting the keystream bits directly. Before proceeding further, let us now formalize the fault model.

1. The attacker is able to reset the system with the original Key-IV (as in [4, 6]) or the original Key and different IVs (as in [16]) and start the cipher operations again.
2. The attacker can inject a fault at any one random bit location of the LFSR or NFSR. As a result of the fault injection, the binary value in the bit-location (where the fault has been injected) is toggled. The attacker is not allowed to choose the location where he wants to inject the fault. However, as assumed in both [4, 6, 16] the fault in any bit may be reproduced at any later stage of operation, once injected.
3. Similar to [4, 6], the attacker can inject faults in the LFSR only, whereas the NFSR has been used for fault injection in [16].
4. The attacker has full control over the timing of fault injection, i.e., it is possible to inject the fault precisely at any stage of the cipher operation.
5. The attacker can obtain the MAC of any message of his choice including the empty message.

2.1 Obtaining the Location of the Fault

Our attack model assumes that the attacker is allowed to toggle the value at exactly one random location of the LFSR. The attacker, however can not explicitly choose the location where the fault is to be injected. In order for the attack to succeed, it is very important that it will be possible to identify the location of the LFSR where the fault has been induced.

Let $S_0 \in \{0,1\}^{256}$ be the initial state of the Grain-128a PRGA, and S_{0,Δ_ϕ} be the initial state resulting after injecting fault in LFSR location $\phi \in [0, 127]$. Let $Z = [z_0, z_1, \ldots, z_{65}]$ and $Z^\phi = [z_0^\phi, z_1^\phi, \ldots, z_{65}^\phi]$ be the first 66 keystream bits produced by S_0 and S_{0,Δ_ϕ} respectively. Then as per the authentication scheme the MAC $\sigma(\emptyset)$ of the empty message $\emptyset$ is given by the vector

$$\sigma(\emptyset) = [z_0 + z_{32}, z_1 + z_{33}, \ldots, z_{31} + z_{63}],$$

and similarly the MAC for the singular message bit 0 will be given by

$$\sigma(0) = [z_0 + z_{33}, z_1 + z_{34}, \ldots, z_{30} + z_{63}, z_{31} + z_{65}].$$

The corresponding faulty MACs are

$$\sigma^\phi(\emptyset) = [z_0^\phi + z_{32}^\phi, z_1^\phi + z_{33}^\phi, \ldots, z_{31}^\phi + z_{63}^\phi],$$

$$\sigma^\phi(0) = [z_0^\phi + z_{33}^\phi, z_1^\phi + z_{34}^\phi, \ldots, z_{30}^\phi + z_{63}^\phi, z_{31}^\phi + z_{65}^\phi]$$

The task for the fault location identification routine is to determine the fault location ϕ by analyzing the difference between $[\sigma(\emptyset), \sigma(0)]$ and $[\sigma^\phi(\emptyset), \sigma^\phi(0)]$.

Definition 1. *We define a 64-bit vector E_ϕ over GF(2) as follows. Let E_ϕ^1 be the bitwise logical XNOR (complement of XOR) of the MACs of $\sigma(\emptyset)$ and $\sigma^\phi(\emptyset)$, i.e., $E_\phi^1 = 1 + \sigma(\emptyset) + \sigma^\phi(\emptyset)$, (here $+$ should be interpreted as $\oplus$) and similarly $E_\phi^2 = 1 + \sigma(0) + \sigma^\phi(0)$. Then $E_\phi = E_\phi^1 || E_\phi^2$.*

Since S_0 can have 2^{224} values (each arising from a different combination of the 128 bit Key and 96 bit IV, rest 32 padding bits are fixed), each of these choices of S_0 may lead to different patterns of E_ϕ. The bitwise logical AND of all such vectors E_ϕ is denoted as the Signature vector Sgn_ϕ for the fault location ϕ.

Since it is computationally infeasible to generate 2^{224} patterns and compute their logical AND, below we present a technique to achieve this efficiently. Whenever $Sgn_\phi(i)$ is 1 for $0 \le i \le 31$, this implies that the ith MAC bit produced by S_0 and S_{0,Δ_ϕ} for the empty message is equal for all choices of S_0. Similarly if $Sgn_\phi(i)$ is 1 for $32 \le i \le 63$ this implies that the $(i-32)^{th}$ MAC bit produced by S_0 and S_{0,Δ_ϕ} for the zero message is equal for all choices of S_0.

For Grain-128a, two initial states of the PRGA $S_0, S_{0,\Delta_{127}} \in \{0,1\}^{256}$ which differ only in the 127th position of the LFSR, produce identical output bits in 62 specific positions among the initial 66 keystream bits produced during the PRGA. If an input differential is introduced in the 127th LFSR position, then at all rounds numbered $k \in [0,65] \setminus \{33,34,48,65\}$, the difference exists in positions that do not provide input to the Boolean function h and hence at these clocks the keystream bit produced by the two states are essentially the same. At all other clock rounds the difference appears at positions which provide input to h. Hence the keystream produced at these clocks may be different. Since

$$\sigma(\emptyset) = [z_0 + z_{32}, z_1 + z_{33}, \ldots, z_{31} + z_{63}], \ \sigma^\phi(\emptyset) = [z_0^\phi + z_{32}^\phi, z_1^\phi + z_{33}^\phi, \ldots, z_{31}^\phi + z_{63}^\phi],$$

this implies that all bits of $\sigma(\emptyset)$ and $\sigma^{127}(\emptyset)$ are equal except for the bits indexed by $1, 2, 16$. Also since

$$\sigma(0) = [z_0 + z_{33}, z_1 + z_{34}, \ldots, z_{30} + z_{63}, z_{31} + z_{65}] \quad \text{and}$$
$$\sigma^\phi(0) = [z_0^\phi + z_{33}^\phi, z_1^\phi + z_{34}^\phi, \ldots, z_{30}^\phi + z_{63}^\phi, z_{31}^\phi + z_{65}^\phi],$$

we can say that all bits of $\sigma(0)$ and $\sigma^{127}(0)$ are equal except for the bits indexed by $0, 1, 15, 31$. Following the explanation given above, we can write Sgn_{127} in hexadecimal notation, $Sgn_{127} = $ 9FFF 7FFF 3FFE FFFE, which has $64 - 3 - 4 = 57$ many 1's and rest 0's.

Generalizing the above idea, for two PRGA initial states $S_0, S_{0,\Delta_\phi} \in \{0,1\}^{256}$ which differ only in the ϕth LFSR location, an analysis of the differential trails shows that out of the first 66 keystream bits produced by them, the bits at a certain fixed rounds are guaranteed to be equal. Thus by performing the above analysis for all fault locations ϕ ($0 \le \phi \le 127$), it is possible to calculate all the Signature vectors. Table 1 presents the vectors for each fault location ϕ, where the Fault Signature Vectors Sgn_ϕ for $0 \le \phi \le 127$ are written in hexadecimal notation.

Steps for Location Identification. As mentioned above, the task for the fault identification routine is to determine the value of ϕ given the vector E_ϕ, i.e., obtaining a unique Sgn_ϕ. For any l-bit vector V, let $B_V = \{i : 0 \le i < l, V(i) = 1\}$. Now define a relation $\preceq$ in $\{0,1\}^l$ such that for 2 elements $V_1, V_2 \in \{0,1\}^l$, we will have $V_1 \preceq V_2$ if $B_{V_1} \subseteq B_{V_2}$.

Table 1. Signature Vectors for different fault locations

φ	Sgn_ϕ	φ	Sgn_ϕ	φ	Sgn_ϕ	φ	Sgn_ϕ
0	8EFF BEFF 1DFF 7DFE	32	FFF7 EF67 FFF7 EF4E	64	F7F7 ED73 F7EF DCE7	96	D7FF 9DF3 8FFF 3BE7
1	C77F DF7F 8EFF BEFE	33	FFFB F7B3 FFFB F7A7	65	FBFB F6B9 FBF7 EE73	97	EBFF CEF9 C7FF 9DF2
2	E3BF EFBF C77F DF7F	34	FFFD FBD9 FFFD FBD3	66	FDFD FB5C FDFB F739	98	F5FF E77C E3FF CEF9
3	F1DF F7DF E3BF EFBF	35	FFFE FDEC FFFE FDE9	67	FEFE FDAE FEFD FB9D	99	FAFF F3BE F1FF E77D
4	F8EF FBEF F1DF F7DF	36	FFFF 7EF6 FFFF 7EF5	68	FF7F 7ED7 FF7E FDCE	100	FD7F F9DF F8FF F3BE
5	FC77 FD7F F8EF BEFF	37	FFFF B7FB FFFF BF7A	69	FFBF BF6B FFBF 7EE6	101	FEBF FCEF FC7F F9DE
6	FE3B FEFB FC77 FDF7	38	CFFF 9FBD 9FFF 5FBC	70	CFDF 9FB5 9FDF 3F73	102	FF5F FE77 FE3F FCEF
7	CF1D BF7D 9E3B 7EFB	39	E7FF CFDE CFFF AFDE	71	E7EF CFDA CFEF 9FB9	103	FFAF FF3B FF1F FE77
8	678E DFBE 4F1D BF7D	40	73FF E7EF E7FF D7EF	72	F3F7 E7ED E7F7 CFDD	104	FFD7 FF9D FF8F FF3B
9	B3C7 6FDF A78E DFBF	41	B9FF F3F7 73FF EBF7	73	F9FB F3F6 F3FB E7EE	105	FFEB FFCE FFC7 FF9D
10	D9E3 B7EF D3C7 6FDE	42	5CFF F9FB 39FF F5FB	74	7CFD F9FB F9FD F3F7	106	FFF5 FFE7 FFE3 FFCF
11	ECF1 DBF7 E9E3 B7EF	43	AE7F FCFD 9CFF FAFD	75	BE7E FCFD 7CFE F9FB	107	FFFA FFF3 FFF1 FFE6
12	F678 EDFB F4F1 DBF7	44	D73F FE7E CE7F FD7E	76	DF3F 7E7E BE7F 7CFD	108	FFFD 7FF9 FFF8 FFF3
13	7B3C 76FD 7A78 EDFB	45	6B9F FF3F E73F FEBF	77	EF9F BF3F DF3F BE7F	109	FFFE BFFC FFFC 7FF9
14	BD9E 3B7E BD3C 76FD	46	B5CF FF9F 739F FF5F	78	F7CF DF9F EF9F DF3E	110	FFFF 5FFE FFFE 3FFC
15	DECF 1DBF DE9E 3B7F	47	DAE7 FFCF B9CF FFAF	79	7BE7 EFCF 77CF EF9F	111	7FFF AFFF FFFF 1FFE
16	EF67 8EDF EF4F 1DBE	48	ED73 FFE7 DCE7 FFD7	80	BDF3 F7E7 BBE7 F7CF	112	BFFF D7FF 7FFF 8FFE
17	F7B3 C76F F7A7 8EDF	49	F6B9 FFF3 EE73 FFEB	81	CEF9 BBF3 9DF3 7BE7	113	DFFF EBFF BFFF C7FF
18	FBD9 E3B7 FBD3 C76F	50	FB5C FFF9 F739 FFF5	82	E77C DDF9 CEF9 BDF3	114	EFFF F5FF DFFF E3FF
19	FDEC F1DB FDE9 E3B7	51	FDAE 7FFC FB9C FFFA	83	F3BE 6EFC E77C DEF9	115	F7FF FAFF EFFF F1FF
20	7EF6 78ED 7EF4 F1DB	52	7ED7 3FFE FDCE 7FFD	84	F9DF 377E F3BE 6F7D	116	FBFF FDF7 F7FF F8FF
21	BF7B 3C76 BF7A 78ED	53	BF6B 9FFF 7EE7 3FFF	85	FCEF 9BBF F9DF 37BE	117	FDFF FEBF FBFF FC7F
22	DFBD 9E3B DFBD 3C77	54	DFB5 CFFF BF73 9FFE	86	FE77 CDDF FCEF 9BDE	118	FEFF FF5F FDFF FE3F
23	EFDE CF1D EFDE 9E3A	55	EFDA E7FF DFB9 CFFF	87	FF3B E6EF FE77 CDEF	119	FF7F FFAF FEFF FF1F
24	F7EF 678E F7EF 4F1D	56	F7ED 73FF EFDC E7FF	88	FF9D F377 FF3B E6F7	120	FFBF FFD7 FF7F FF8F
25	FBF7 B3C7 FBF7 A78F	57	FBF6 B9FF F7EE 73FF	89	FFCE F9BB FF9D F37B	121	FFDF FFEB FFBF FFC7
26	FDFB D9E3 FDFB D3C6	58	FDFB 5CFF FBF7 39FF	90	FFE7 7CDD FFCE F9BD	122	FFEF FFF5 FFDF FFE3
27	FEFD ECF1 FEFD E9E3	59	FEFD AE7F FDFB 9CFF	91	FFF3 BE6E FFE7 7CDE	123	FFF7 FFFA FFEF FFF1
28	FF7E F678 FF7E F4F1	60	7F7E D73F 7EFD CE7F	92	7FF9 DF37 FFF3 BE6F	124	FFFB FFFD FFF7 FFF8
29	FFBF 7B3C FFBF 7A79	61	BFBF 6B9F BF7E E73F	93	3FFC EF9B 7FF9 DF37	125	7FFD FFFE FFFB FFFC
30	FFDF BD9E FFDF BD3C	62	DFDF B5CF DFBF 739F	94	1FFE 77CD 3FFC EF9B	126	3FFE FFFF 7FFD FFFE
31	FFEF DECF FFEF DE9E	63	EFEF DAE7 EFDF B9CF	95	8FFF 3BE6 9FFE 77CD	127	9FFF 7FFF 3FFE FFFE

So we start with a Key-IV pair K, IV_0 and record the MACs of the empty and zero messages. We then reset the cipher with K, IV_0 and apply a fault at some location ϕ (that is selected randomly and not known at this point) at the beginning of the PRGA, and obtain the corresponding faulty MACs of the empty and zero message. Using these we compute the E_ϕ vector as given in Definition 1. The entire process requires 4 invocations of the MAC routine. Now we check the elements in B_{E_ϕ}. By the definition of Signature vector proposed above, we know that for the correct value of ϕ, $B_{Sgn_\phi} \subseteq B_{E_\phi}$ and hence $Sgn_\phi \preceq E_\phi$. So our strategy would be to search all the Signature vectors and formulate the candidate set $\Psi_0 = \{\psi : 0 \le \psi \le 127, \; Sgn_\psi \preceq E_\phi\}$. If $|\Psi_0|$ is 1, then the single element in Ψ_0 will give us the fault location ϕ. However, this may not necessarily be the case always. If $|\Psi_0| > 1$, we will be unable to decide conclusively at this stage.

In such a scenario we reset the cipher with K, IV_1 (IV_1 different from IV_0) and record the fault-free MAC of the empty and zero messages. We then reset the cipher with K, IV_1 again and apply the fault at the location ϕ (our fault model considers that the fault can be applied at the same location without knowing it) at the beginning of the PRGA round and record the corresponding faulty MACs. Now we recalculate the vector E_ϕ as defined previously. We now search over the Signature vectors in the candidate set Ψ_0 and narrow down the set of possible candidates to $\Psi_1 = \{\psi : \psi \in \Psi_0, \ Sgn_\psi \preceq E_\phi\}$. Clearly, $|\Psi_1| \leq |\Psi_0|$, and so if $|\Psi_1| = 1$ then the fault location ϕ is the single element in Ψ_1. If not, we repeat the above process for another round for a different Key-IV pair K, IV_2. If after k rounds of this process, $|\Psi_{k-1}| = 1$, then the single element in Ψ_{k-1} gives us the desired location ϕ.

With detailed experiments taking on average over 2^{20} uniformly randomly chosen Key-IV pairs, we found that the average value of k is 1.31 to uniquely identify a fault location in the LFSR. Since we are working with the MAC of empty and zero message, thus, for each location we need to inject $\mu = 2 \cdot 1.31 = 2.62$ faults.

Now let us argue that the LFSR fault location can be uniquely identified by the signature scheme proposed here. The signature scheme is based on both the empty and the zero message. Now a simple exhaustive search through the Signature vectors for all fault locations, will show that $Sgn_{\phi_1} \npreceq Sgn_{\phi_2}$ for any two fault locations $0 \leq \phi_1 \neq \phi_2 \leq 127$. This implies that for any value of the fault location $\phi \in [0, 127]$ the fault identification scheme will eventually narrow down the candidate set Ψ_{k-1} to just one element for some value of k.

One may wonder if the Signature vector were to be based on the difference of MAC of just the empty or the 0 message, whether a location identification scheme could have been proposed. The answer is no. Take the signature scheme based on the MAC difference of just the empty message in which $l = 32$. Studying the Signature vectors, one can check that the first 32 bits of $Sgn_{21} = $ BF7B 3C76 and $Sgn_{36} = $ FFFF 7EF6. Note that, for all locations $i \in [0, 31]$ such that $Sgn_{21}(i) = 1$, the value of $Sgn_{36}(i)$ is also 1. This implies that $Sgn_{21} \preceq Sgn_{36}$. Now consider the case with the fault location $\phi = 36$. Then by the definition of the signature vector we have $Sgn_{36} \preceq E_\phi$. Since $\preceq$ is a partial order on $\{0, 1\}^l$, this implies that $Sgn_{21} \preceq E_\phi$ and so whenever $\phi = 36$ the fault location identification routine will never be able to narrow down the set of possible candidates Ψ_k to only $\{36\}$ for any value of k. So the signature scheme can not be based on the MAC difference of the empty message only. If we were to base the signature scheme on the MAC difference of the 0 message bit, then a look at the signature tables will show us that $Sgn_{16} \preceq Sgn_{111}$ and the scheme would fail by the above argument. It will be very interesting to find out a message for which the signature scheme will work just by looking at the fault-free and faulty MACs on it.

3   Determining the LFSR State

Towards this, let us present a few more notations at this point.

1. $S_t = [x_0^t, x_1^t, \ldots, x_{127}^t \ \ y_0^t, y_1^t, \ldots, y_{127}^t]$ is used to denote the internal state of the cipher at the beginning of round t of the PRGA when initialized with the Key-IV pair K, IV_0. Thus x_i^t (y_i^t) denotes the ith NFSR (LFSR) bit at the start of round t of the PRGA. When $t = 0$, we use $S_0 = [x_0, x_1, \ldots, x_{127} \ \ y_0, y_1, \ldots, y_{127}]$ to denote the internal state for convenience.

2. S_t^ϕ is used to denote the internal state of the cipher at the beginning of round t of the PRGA when initialized with the Key-IV pair K, IV_0, if a fault has been injected in LFSR location ϕ at the beginning of the PRGA round.
3. z_i^ϕ denotes the keystream bit produced in the ith PRGA round, after faults have been injected in LFSR location ϕ at the beginning of the PRGA round. z_i is the fault-free i^{th} keystream bit.

We start by making the following observations about the output Boolean function h in Grain-128a:

$$h(s_0, s_1, s_2, s_3, s_4, s_5, s_6, s_7, s_8) + h(s_0, s_1, 1 + s_2, s_3, s_4, s_5, s_6, s_7, s_8) = s_3 \quad (1)$$

$$h(s_0, s_1, s_2, s_3, s_4, s_5, s_6, s_7, s_8) + h(s_0, s_1, s_2, 1 + s_3, s_4, s_5, s_6, s_7, s_8) = s_2 \quad (2)$$

$$h(s_0, s_1, s_2, s_3, s_4, s_5, s_6, s_7, s_8) + h(s_0, s_1, s_2, s_3, s_4, s_5, 1 + s_6, s_7, s_8) = s_7 \quad (3)$$

$$h(s_0, s_1, s_2, s_3, s_4, s_5, s_6, s_7, s_8) + h(s_0, s_1, s_2, s_3, s_4, s_5, s_6, 1 + s_7, s_8) = s_6 \quad (4)$$

Let us now explain in detail how we can obtain the bit-value at a specific location of the LFSR, say for example y_{108}. Note that s_0, s_4 correspond to the NFSR locations $12, 95$ respectively and $s_1, s_2, s_3, s_5, s_6, s_7, s_8$ correspond to the LFSR locations $8, 13, 20, 42, 60, 79, 94$ respectively. Now look at (1) above and note that s_2 corresponds to the LFSR location 13. If two internal states S and S_Δ be such that they differ in the LFSR location 13 (and in no other tap locations that contribute to the keystream bit generation), then the difference of the keystream bit produced by them will be equal to the value in LFSR location 20. Similar analysis can be done corresponding to (2), (3), (4).

Assume that the attacker has injected a fault at location 127 of the LFSR at the beginning of the PRGA. Then at round 48 of the PRGA the input differential travels to location 79 of the LFSR, i.e., at round 48 the original state S_{48} and the faulty state S_{48}^{127} differ in location 79 of the LFSR and in no other location that contributes inputs to the output keystream bit at round 48. Then by equation (4), the sum of the corresponding fault-free and faulty bits produced at round 48 is given by $z_{48} + z_{48}^{127} = y_{60}^{48} = y_{108}$.

Also, at round 16 of the PRGA, the differential does not sit on any LFSR location that contributes input to the output keystream bit at that round. Hence $z_{16} = z_{16}^{127}$.

Now consider the fault-free and faulty MAC (due to the fault at $\phi = 127$ at the beginning of the PRGA) of the empty message $\sigma(\emptyset)$ and $\sigma^{127}(\emptyset)$. From the definition of the MAC of empty message, it can be deduced that the bit number 16 of $\sigma(\emptyset) \oplus \sigma^{127}(\emptyset)$ is given by $z_{16} + z_{48} + z_{16}^{127} + z_{48}^{127} = y_{108}$.

Hence by looking at the difference in the correct and faulty MACs of the empty messages one can deduce the LFSR state bit y_{108} at the beginning of the PRGA.

In Table 2 we give a list of 115 LFSR state bits y_i that can be recovered by observing the difference of the faulty and correct d^{th} ($0 \leq d \leq 31$) MAC bit of the empty message for different values of the fault location ϕ. There are 301 (more than 115) entries in the table and this is due to the fact that there are multiple fault options for identifying some of the LFSR bits.

Table 2. LFSR state bits recovered

ϕ	d	y_i	ϕ	d	y_i	ϕ	d	y_i	ϕ	d	y_i	ϕ	d	y_i	ϕ	d	y_i
0	17	y_{109}	26	13	y_{33}	47	27	y_{40}	66	6	y_{85}	80	1	y_{40}	94	15	y_{75}
1	18	y_{110}	27	7	y_{20}	47	2	y_{54}	66	14	y_{59}	80	20	y_{54}	94	2	y_{113}
2	19	y_{111}	27	14	y_{34}	47	26	y_{118}	66	21	y_{73}	80	27	y_{118}	94	30	y_{122}
3	20	y_{112}	28	8	y_{21}	48	28	y_{41}	67	7	y_{86}	80	28	y_{41}	95	16	y_{76}
4	21	y_{113}	28	15	y_{35}	48	3	y_{55}	67	15	y_{60}	81	2	y_{55}	95	3	y_{114}
5	22	y_{114}	29	9	y_{22}	48	27	y_{119}	67	22	y_{74}	81	21	y_{119}	95	31	y_{123}
6	23	y_{115}	29	16	y_{36}	49	29	y_{42}	68	8	y_{87}	81	17	y_{42}	96	17	y_{77}
7	17	y_{109}	30	10	y_{23}	49	4	y_{56}	68	16	y_{61}	81	28	y_{56}	96	4	y_{115}
7	24	y_{116}	30	17	y_{37}	49	28	y_{120}	68	23	y_{75}	81	29	y_{120}	97	18	y_{78}
8	18	y_{110}	31	11	y_{24}	50	30	y_{43}	69	9	y_{88}	82	3	y_{43}	97	5	y_{116}
8	25	y_{117}	31	18	y_{38}	50	5	y_{57}	69	17	y_{62}	82	22	y_{57}	98	19	y_{79}
9	19	y_{111}	32	12	y_{25}	50	29	y_{121}	69	24	y_{76}	82	18	y_{121}	98	6	y_{117}
9	26	y_{118}	32	19	y_{39}	51	31	y_{44}	70	10	y_{89}	82	29	y_{44}	99	20	y_{80}
10	20	y_{112}	33	13	y_{26}	51	6	y_{58}	70	17	y_{109}	82	30	y_{122}	99	7	y_{118}
10	27	y_{119}	33	20	y_{40}	51	30	y_{122}	70	18	y_{63}	83	4	y_{122}	100	21	y_{81}
11	21	y_{113}	34	14	y_{27}	52	0	y_{45}	70	25	y_{77}	83	23	y_{45}	100	8	y_{119}
11	28	y_{120}	34	21	y_{41}	52	7	y_{59}	71	11	y_{90}	83	19	y_{59}	101	22	y_{82}
12	22	y_{114}	35	15	y_{28}	52	31	y_{123}	71	18	y_{110}	83	30	y_{123}	101	9	y_{120}
12	29	y_{121}	35	22	y_{42}	53	1	y_{46}	71	19	y_{64}	83	31	y_{46}	102	23	y_{83}
13	0	y_{20}	36	16	y_{29}	53	8	y_{60}	71	26	y_{78}	84	5	y_{60}	102	10	y_{121}
13	23	y_{115}	36	23	y_{43}	54	2	y_{47}	72	12	y_{91}	84	24	y_{47}	103	24	y_{84}
13	30	y_{122}	37	17	y_{30}	54	9	y_{61}	72	19	y_{111}	84	20	y_{61}	103	11	y_{122}
14	1	y_{21}	37	24	y_{44}	55	3	y_{48}	72	20	y_{65}	84	31	y_{48}	104	25	y_{85}
14	24	y_{116}	38	18	y_{31}	55	10	y_{62}	72	27	y_{79}	85	6	y_{62}	104	12	y_{123}
14	31	y_{123}	38	25	y_{45}	56	4	y_{49}	73	13	y_{92}	85	25	y_{49}	105	26	y_{86}
15	2	y_{22}	38	17	y_{109}	56	11	y_{63}	73	20	y_{112}	85	21	y_{63}	105	13	y_{124}
15	25	y_{117}	39	19	y_{32}	57	5	y_{50}	73	21	y_{66}	86	7	y_{50}	106	27	y_{87}
16	3	y_{23}	39	26	y_{46}	57	12	y_{64}	73	28	y_{80}	86	26	y_{64}	106	14	y_{125}
16	26	y_{118}	39	18	y_{110}	58	6	y_{51}	74	14	y_{93}	86	22	y_{51}	107	28	y_{88}
17	4	y_{24}	40	20	y_{33}	58	13	y_{65}	74	21	y_{113}	87	8	y_{65}	107	15	y_{126}
17	27	y_{119}	40	27	y_{47}	59	7	y_{52}	74	22	y_{67}	87	27	y_{52}	108	29	y_{89}
18	5	y_{25}	40	19	y_{111}	59	14	y_{66}	74	29	y_{81}	87	23	y_{66}	108	16	y_{127}
18	28	y_{120}	41	21	y_{34}	60	0	y_{79}	75	15	y_{94}	88	9	y_{79}	109	30	y_{90}
19	6	y_{26}	41	18	y_{48}	60	8	y_{53}	75	22	y_{114}	88	28	y_{53}	110	31	y_{91}
19	29	y_{121}	41	20	y_{112}	60	15	y_{67}	75	23	y_{68}	88	24	y_{67}	111	0	y_{92}
20	0	y_{13}	42	22	y_{35}	61	1	y_{80}	75	30	y_{82}	89	10	y_{80}	112	1	y_{93}
20	7	y_{27}	42	29	y_{49}	61	9	y_{54}	76	16	y_{95}	89	29	y_{54}	113	2	y_{94}
20	30	y_{122}	42	21	y_{113}	61	16	y_{68}	76	23	y_{115}	89	25	y_{68}	114	3	y_{95}
21	1	y_{14}	43	23	y_{36}	62	2	y_{81}	76	24	y_{69}	90	11	y_{81}	115	4	y_{96}
21	8	y_{28}	43	30	y_{50}	62	10	y_{55}	76	31	y_{83}	90	30	y_{55}	116	5	y_{97}
21	31	y_{123}	43	22	y_{114}	62	17	y_{69}	77	17	y_{96}	90	26	y_{69}	117	6	y_{98}
22	2	y_{15}	44	24	y_{37}	63	3	y_{82}	77	24	y_{116}	91	12	y_{82}	118	7	y_{99}
22	9	y_{29}	44	31	y_{51}	63	11	y_{56}	77	25	y_{70}	91	31	y_{56}	119	8	y_{100}
23	3	y_{16}	44	23	y_{115}	63	18	y_{70}	78	18	y_{97}	91	27	y_{70}	120	9	y_{101}
23	10	y_{30}	45	25	y_{38}	64	4	y_{83}	78	25	y_{117}	92	13	y_{83}	121	10	y_{102}
24	4	y_{17}	45	0	y_{52}	64	12	y_{57}	78	26	y_{71}	92	0	y_{57}	122	11	y_{103}
24	11	y_{31}	45	24	y_{116}	64	19	y_{71}	79	0	y_{60}	92	28	y_{71}	123	12	y_{104}
25	5	y_{18}	46	26	y_{39}	65	5	y_{84}	79	19	y_{98}	93	14	y_{84}	124	13	y_{105}
25	12	y_{32}	46	1	y_{53}	65	13	y_{58}	79	26	y_{118}	93	1	y_{58}	125	14	y_{106}
26	6	y_{19}	46	25	y_{117}	65	20	y_{72}	79	27	y_{72}	93	29	y_{72}	126	15	y_{107}
															127	16	y_{108}

Finding $y_0, y_1, y_2, \ldots, y_{12}$. The LFSR state bits not present in Table 2 are $y_0, y_1, \ldots, y_{12}$. However it can be verified that $\forall i \in [0, 12]$, by applying a fault at location $\phi = 109 + i$ the $(17 + i)^{th}$ bit in difference of $\sigma(\emptyset)$ and $\sigma^{109+i}(\emptyset)$ is equal to the state bit y_{127}^{1+i}. Since y_{127}^{1+i} is a linear function of $y_0, y_1, \ldots, y_{127}$, we can derive y_0 to y_{12} as follows. By the LFSR update rule of Grain-128a, we have the following 13 equations

$$y_{127}^{1+i} = y_{96+i} + y_{81+i} + y_{70+i} + y_{38+i} + y_{7+i} + y_i, \quad \forall i \in [0, 12].$$

In the last equation y_{12} is the only unknown and its value can be calculated easily. Similarly y_{11} is the only unknown in the previous equation. Solving the equations in this manner one can obtain the entire LFSR state at the beginning of the PRGA.

4   Determining the NFSR State

Once the LFSR internal state of the initial PRGA round is known, one can then proceed to determine the NFSR internal state. In [5] it was shown, that this could have been done efficiently for the initial version of the cipher, i.e., Grain v0. After the attack in [5] was reported, the designers made the necessary changes to Grain v1, Grain-128 and Grain-128a so that for these new ciphers, determining the NFSR state form the knowledge of the LFSR state was no longer straightforward. In order to determine the NFSR bits, we look into the decomposition of the Boolean function h in more detail.

One may note that for Grain-128a, $h(\mathbf{s}) = s_0 \cdot u(\mathbf{s}) + v(\mathbf{s})$, where $u(\mathbf{s}) = s_1 + s_4 s_8$, and $v(\mathbf{s}) = s_2 s_3 + s_4 s_5 + s_6 s_7$. Thus we note that

$$u(s_0, s_1, s_2, s_3, s_4, s_5, s_6, s_7, s_8) + u(s_0, 1 + s_1, s_2, s_3, s_4, s_5, s_6, s_7, s_8) = 1, \quad (5)$$

$$v(s_0, s_1, s_2, s_3, s_4, s_5, s_6, s_7, s_8) + v(s_0, 1 + s_1, s_2, s_3, s_4, s_5, s_6, s_7, s_8) = 0. \quad (6)$$

Also h can be written as $h(\mathbf{s}) = s_4 \cdot U(\mathbf{s}) + V(\mathbf{s})$, where $U(\mathbf{s}) = s_5 + s_0 s_8$, and $V(\mathbf{s}) = s_2 s_3 + s_4 s_5 + s_6 s_7$. We also have

$$U(s_0, s_1, s_2, s_3, s_4, s_5, s_6, s_7, s_8) + U(s_0, s_1, s_2, s_3, s_4, 1 + s_5, s_6, s_7, s_8) = 1, \quad (7)$$

$$V(s_0, s_1, s_2, s_3, s_4, s_5, s_6, s_7, s_8) + V(s_0, s_1, s_2, s_3, s_4, 1 + s_5, s_6, s_7, s_8) = 0. \quad (8)$$

As before, assume the scenario in which the attacker has injected a fault at location 8 of the LFSR at the beginning of the PRGA. Then at this round of the PRGA the input differential travels sits on location 8 of the LFSR, i.e., at round 0 of the PRGA the original state S_0 and the faulty state S_0^8 differ in location 8 of the LFSR and in no other location that contributes inputs to the output keystream bit at round 0. Then by (5,6), the sum of the corresponding fault-free bits produced at round 0 is given by $z_0 + z_0^8 = x_{12}^0 \cdot 1 + 0 = x_{12}$.

Also note that at round 32 of the PRGA the differential does not sit on any LFSR location that contributes input to the output keystream bit at that round. Hence $z_{32} = z_{32}^8$.

Now consider the fault-free and faulty MAC (due to fault at $\phi = 8$ at the beginning of the PRGA) of the empty message $\sigma(\emptyset)$ and $\sigma^8(\emptyset)$. From the definition of MAC of empty message it can be deduced that the bit number 16 of $\sigma(\emptyset) \oplus \sigma^8(\emptyset)$ is given by $z_0 + z_{32} + z_0^8 + z_{32}^8 = x_{12}$.

Hence by looking at the difference in the correct and faulty MACs of the empty messages one is able to deduce the NFSR state bit x_{12} at the beginning of the PRGA. In Table 3 we give an exhaustive list of the NFSR state bits x_i that can be recovered by observing the difference of the faulty and correct d^{th} MAC bit of the empty message for different values of the fault location ϕ.

Table 3. NFSR state bits recovered

ϕ	d	x_i	ϕ	d	x_i	ϕ	d	x_i	ϕ	d	x_i	ϕ	d	x_i	ϕ	d	x_i
8	0	x_{12}	24	16	x_{28}	40	0	x_{44}	49	7	x_{102}	57	15	x_{110}	65	23	x_{118}
9	1	x_{13}	25	17	x_{29}	41	1	x_{45}	49	9	x_{53}	57	17	x_{61}	65	25	x_{69}
10	2	x_{14}	26	18	x_{30}	42	0	x_{95}	50	8	x_{103}	58	16	x_{111}	66	24	x_{119}
11	3	x_{15}	27	19	x_{31}	42	2	x_{46}	50	10	x_{54}	58	18	x_{62}	66	26	x_{70}
12	4	x_{16}	28	20	x_{32}	43	1	x_{96}	51	9	x_{104}	59	17	x_{112}	67	25	x_{120}
13	5	x_{17}	29	21	x_{33}	43	3	x_{47}	51	11	x_{55}	59	19	x_{63}	67	27	x_{71}
14	6	x_{18}	30	22	x_{34}	44	2	x_{97}	52	10	x_{105}	60	18	x_{113}	68	26	x_{121}
15	7	x_{19}	31	23	x_{35}	44	4	x_{48}	52	12	x_{56}	60	20	x_{64}	68	28	x_{72}
16	8	x_{20}	32	24	x_{36}	45	3	x_{98}	53	11	x_{106}	61	19	x_{114}	69	27	x_{122}
17	9	x_{21}	33	25	x_{37}	45	5	x_{49}	53	13	x_{57}	61	21	x_{65}	69	29	x_{73}
18	10	x_{22}	34	26	x_{38}	46	4	x_{99}	54	12	x_{107}	62	20	x_{115}	70	28	x_{123}
19	11	x_{23}	35	27	x_{39}	46	6	x_{50}	54	14	x_{58}	62	22	x_{66}	70	30	x_{74}
20	12	x_{24}	36	28	x_{40}	47	5	x_{100}	55	13	x_{108}	63	21	x_{116}	71	29	x_{124}
21	13	x_{25}	37	29	x_{41}	47	7	x_{51}	55	15	x_{59}	63	23	x_{67}	71	31	x_{75}
22	14	x_{26}	38	30	x_{42}	48	6	x_{101}	56	14	x_{109}	64	22	x_{117}	72	30	x_{125}
23	15	x_{27}	39	31	x_{43}	48	8	x_{52}	56	16	x_{60}	64	24	x_{68}	73	31	x_{126}
															74	0	x_{127}

4.1   Finding the Remaining Bits

From Table 3, all state bits of the NFSR can be found except $x_0, x_1, \ldots, x_{11}$ and $x_{76}, x_{77}, \ldots, x_{94}$. These bits may be found as follows.

Finding $x_{77}, x_{79}, x_{81}, \ldots, x_{93}$. It can be verified that $\forall i \in [0,8]$, by applying a fault at location $\phi = 73 + 2i$ at the beginning of the PRGA, the difference travels to the LFSR location 8 at round $65 + 2i$. It can also be checked that at this PRGA round the differential does not affect any other location that contributes to the output bit, i.e., the states S_{65+2i} and S_{65+2i}^{73+2i} differ in only the LFSR location 8 and no other location that affects the output bit at this round. Then by (5,6)

$$z_{65+2i} + z_{65+2i}^{73+2i} = x_{12}^{65+2i} \cdot 1 + 0 = x_{77+2i}, \quad \forall i \in [0,8].$$

It can also be verified that as a result of applying the fault at $73+2i, \forall i \in [0,8]$ at round 31 of the PRGA, the differential does not affect any location that provides inputs to the output bit. Hence, $z_{31} = z_{31}^{73+2i}$. Now consider the fault-free and faulty MAC of the message 0^{i+1} (string of $i+1$ zeros) obtained by faulting LFSR location $73 + 2i$ at the beginning of the PRGA. From definition

$$\sigma(0^{i+1}) = [z_0 + z_{33+i}, z_1 + z_{34+i}, \ldots, z_{30-i} + z_{63}, z_{31-i} + z_{65}, z_{32-i} + z_{67}, \ldots,$$
$$z_{31} + z_{65+2i}], \quad \forall i \in [0,8]$$

Hence the last bit in difference of $\sigma(0^{i+1})$ and $\sigma^{73+2i}(0^{i+1})$ is equal to

$$z_{31} + z_{65+2i} + z_{31}^{73+2i} + z_{65+2i}^{73+2i} = x_{77+2i}, \quad \forall i \in [0,8].$$

This gives us the values of 9 more state bits. Thus far we have recovered 106 of the 128 NFSR state bits.

Finding x_2. Consider the 0th bit of the fault-free $\sigma(\emptyset)$ given by

$$z_0 + z_{32} = \bigoplus_{t \in B} x_t + y_{93} + y_{125} + h(x_{12}, y_8, y_{13}, y_{20}, x_{95}, y_{42}, y_{60}, y_{79}, y_{94})$$
$$+ h(x_{44}, y_{40}, y_{55}, y_{75}, x_{127}, y_{74}, y_{92}, y_{111}, y_{126}).$$

Here $B = \{2, 15, 36, 45, 64, 73, 89, 34, 47, 68, 77, 96, 105, 121\}$. Note that x_2 is the only unknown linear term in the above equation, and so its value can be calculated immediately.

Finding $x_{78}, x_{80}, x_{82}, \ldots, x_{94}$. Define $x_{127+i} = x_{127}^i, y_{127+i} = y_{127}^i$ for all $i \geq 1$. Again, it can be verified that the ith bit of

$$\sigma(\emptyset) + \sigma^{74+i}(\emptyset) = x_{127+i}, \quad \forall i \in [0,31]. \tag{9}$$

Now consider the 0th bit of $\sigma(0^{2j+1})$ for $0 \leq j \leq 8$, given by $z_0 + z_{33+2j}$

$$z_0 + z_{33+2j} = \bigoplus_{t \in B_j} x_t + y_{93} + y_{126+2j} + h(x_{12}, y_8, y_{13}, y_{20}, x_{95}, y_{42}, y_{60}, y_{79}, y_{94})$$
$$+ h(x_{45+2j}, y_{41+2j}, y_{56+2j}, y_{76+2j}, x_{128+2j}, y_{75+2j}, y_{93+2j}, y_{112+2j},$$
$$y_{127+2j}), \quad \forall j \in [0,8] \text{ and}$$

$$B_j = \{2, 15, 36, 45, 64, 73, 89, 35 + 2j, 48 + 2j, 69 + 2j, 78 + 2j, 97 + 2j,$$
$$106 + 2j, 122 + 2j\}.$$

In the above set of equations any x_k with $k > 127$ may be calculated from (9). Any y_k with $k > 127$ is a linear function of $y_0, \ldots, y_{127}$ which are already known. Hence x_{78+2j} with $0 \leq j \leq 8$ are the only unknown linear terms in each of these equations and their values are also immediately determined.

Finding $x_3, x_4, x_6, x_7, \ldots, x_{11}$. At this point the only unknown state bits are $x_0, x_1, x_3, \ldots, x_{11}, x_{76}$. Consider the pth bit of $\sigma(\emptyset)$ given by $z_p + z_{32+p}$ for $p \in [1,9] \setminus \{3\}$.

$$z_p + z_{32+p} = \bigoplus_{t \in B} x_{t+p} + y_{93+p} + y_{125+p}$$
$$+ h(x_{12+p}, y_{8+p}, y_{13+p}, y_{20+p}, x_{95+p}, y_{42+p}, y_{60+p}, y_{79+p}, y_{94+p})$$
$$+ h(x_{44+p}, y_{40+p}, y_{55+p}, y_{75+p}, x_{127+p}, y_{74+p}, y_{92+p}, y_{111+p}, y_{126+p}),$$
$$\forall p \in [1,9] \setminus \{3\}.$$

In all these equations x_{2+p} is the only unknown term and its value can also be determined immediately (the strategy does not work for $p = 3$ as x_{76} is still unknown).

Finding x_0, x_1, x_5, x_{76}. We are left with x_0, x_1, x_5, x_{76} as the only unknowns. Note that the NFSR update function $g(\cdot)$ in Grain-128a can be written in the form $g(X) = x' + g'(X')$ where x' is the variable that taps the 0th NFSR location. Now consider the following equation for x_{128} which have been derived from the NFSR update rule of GRAIN-128a

$$x_{128} = y_0 + g(x_{96}, x_{95}, x_{93}, x_{92}, x_{91}, x_{88}, x_{84}, x_{82}, x_{78}, x_{70}, x_{68}, x_{67}, x_{65}, x_{61},$$
$$x_{59}, x_{48}, x_{40}, x_{27}, x_{26}, x_{25}, x_{24}, x_{22}, x_{13}, x_{11}, x_3, x_0)$$
$$= y_0 + x_0 + g'(x_{96}, x_{95}, \ldots, x_{11}, x_3).$$

Note that x_0 is the only unknown term in the equation, and hence its value can be determined by solving this equation. Similarly the values of x_1, x_5 may be determined from the update equations for x_{129}, x_{133}. Consider now, the equation for bit number 3 of $\sigma(\emptyset) = z_3 + z_{35}$

$$z_3 + z_{35} = \bigoplus_{t \in C} x_t + y_{96} + y_{128} + h(x_{15}, y_8, y_{16}, y_{23}, x_{98}, y_{45}, y_{63}, y_{82}, y_{97})$$
$$+ h(x_{47}, y_{43}, y_{58}, y_{78}, x_{130}, y_{77}, y_{95}, y_{114}, y_{129}).$$

where $C = \{5, 18, 39, 48, 67, 76, 92, 37, 50, 71, 80, 99, 108, 124\}$. As one can see x_{76} is the only unknown in this equation and thus its value can be determined by solving it. Thus we have determined the whole of S_0.

4.2 Finding the Secret Key and Complexity of the Attack

It is known that the KSA and PRGA routines in the Grain family are invertible. Once we have all the bits of S_0, by running the inverse KSA routine one can recover the Secret Key.

First we need to hit each of the locations of the LFSR. We inject the fault randomly in the LFSR locations and thus, we need $\tau = 128 \cdot \sum_{i=1}^{128} \frac{1}{i} \approx 695.4$

expected number of fault injections. For each of these injected faults, we need to identify the fault locations. Taking the value of μ from Section 2.1 that is the required number of expected faults for each LFSR location, the total number of faults to be injected $= \tau\mu = 695.4 \cdot 2.62 \approx 1822$. Additionally, as described in Section 4, 9 more fault injections are required for the locations $\phi = 73, 75, \ldots, 89$ to recover certain NFSR bits. Therefore, the expected number of faults that our attack needs is $1822 + 9 = 1831 < 2^{11}$.

For each fault during the location identification stage, two MAC invocations are required, that amounts to $1822 \cdot 2 = 3644$. Additionally, 20 more invocations are required during some cases of NFSR bit recovery. Thus the total number of invocations is less than 2^{12}.

5   Conclusion

In this paper we present a differential fault attack on the Grain 128a authenticated encryption scheme using certain properties of the Boolean function h used in the cipher design. The attack requires practical time and space complexity and can be mounted efficiently under the fault model we use. Although there already exist results describing Differential Fault Attack of Grain v1 and Grain-128, the cryptanalysis of Grain-128a is vastly different as the attacker is not able to directly access the first 64 keystream bits and every alternate keystream bit thereafter. Cryptanalysis of the scheme using stricter fault models is an open problem and needs to be explored further.

References

1. Ågren, M., Hell, M., Johansson, T., Meier, W.: A New Version of Grain-128 with Authentication. In: Symmetric Key Encryption Workshop 2011. DTU, Denmark (2011)
2. Ågren, M., Hell, M., Johansson, T., Meier, W.: Grain-128a: a new version of Grain-128 with optional authentication. IJWMC 5(1), 48–59 (2011), This is the Journal Version of [1]
3. Aumasson, J.P., Dinur, I., Henzen, L., Meier, W., Shamir, A.: Efficient FPGA Implementations of High-Dimensional Cube Testers on the Stream Cipher Grain-128. In: SHARCS - Special-purpose Hardware for Attacking Cryptographic Systems (2009)
4. Banik, S., Maitra, S., Sarkar, S.: A Differential Fault Attack on the Grain Family of Stream Ciphers. In: Prouff, E., Schaumont, P. (eds.) CHES 2012. LNCS, vol. 7428, pp. 122–139. Springer, Heidelberg (2012)
5. Berbain, C., Gilbert, H., Maximov, A.: Cryptanalysis of Grain. In: Robshaw, M. (ed.) FSE 2006. LNCS, vol. 4047, pp. 15–29. Springer, Heidelberg (2006)
6. Berzati, A., Canovas, C., Castagnos, G., Debraize, B., Goubin, L., Gouget, A., Paillier, P., Salgado, S.: Fault Analysis of Grain-128. In: IEEE International Workshop on Hardware-Oriented Security and Trust, pp. 7–14 (2009)
7. Bjørstad, T.E.: Cryptanalysis of Grain using Time/Memory/Data tradeoffs (v1.0 / 2008-02-25), http://www.ecrypt.eu.org/stream

8. De Cannière, C., Küçük, Ö., Preneel, B.: Analysis of Grain's Initialization Algorithm. In: Vaudenay, S. (ed.) AFRICACRYPT 2008. LNCS, vol. 5023, pp. 276–289. Springer, Heidelberg (2008)

9. Dinur, I., Güneysu, T., Paar, C., Shamir, A., Zimmermann, R.: An Experimentally Verified Attack on Full Grain-128 Using Dedicated Reconfigurable Hardware. In: Lee, D.H. (ed.) ASIACRYPT 2011. LNCS, vol. 7073, pp. 327–343. Springer, Heidelberg (2011)

10. Dinur, I., Shamir, A.: Breaking Grain-128 with Dynamic Cube Attacks. In: Joux, A. (ed.) FSE 2011. LNCS, vol. 6733, pp. 167–187. Springer, Heidelberg (2011)

11. Englund, H., Johansson, T., Sönmez Turan, M.: A Framework for Chosen IV Statistical Analysis of Stream Ciphers. In: Srinathan, K., Rangan, C.P., Yung, M. (eds.) INDOCRYPT 2007. LNCS, vol. 4859, pp. 268–281. Springer, Heidelberg (2007)

12. Fischer, S., Khazaei, S., Meier, W.: Chosen IV Statistical Analysis for Key Recovery Attacks on Stream Ciphers. In: Vaudenay, S. (ed.) AFRICACRYPT 2008. LNCS, vol. 5023, pp. 236–245. Springer, Heidelberg (2008)

13. Hell, M., Johansson, T., Meier, W.: Grain - A Stream Cipher for Constrained Environments. ECRYPT Stream Cipher Project Report 2005/001 (2005), http://www.ecrypt.eu.org/stream

14. Hell, M., Johansson, T., Maximov, A., Meier, W.: A Stream Cipher Proposal: Grain-128. In: IEEE International Symposium on Information Theory, ISIT 2006 (2006)

15. Hoch, J.J., Shamir, A.: Fault Analysis of Stream Ciphers. In: Joye, M., Quisquater, J.-J. (eds.) CHES 2004. LNCS, vol. 3156, pp. 240–253. Springer, Heidelberg (2004)

16. Karmakar, S., Roy Chowdhury, D.: Fault Analysis of Grain-128 by Targeting NFSR. In: Nitaj, A., Pointcheval, D. (eds.) AFRICACRYPT 2011. LNCS, vol. 6737, pp. 298–315. Springer, Heidelberg (2011)

17. Khazaei, S., Hassanzadeh, M., Kiaei, M.: Distinguishing Attack on Grain. ECRYPT Stream Cipher Project Report 2005/071 (2005), http://www.ecrypt.eu.org/stream

18. Knellwolf, S., Meier, W., Naya-Plasencia, M.: Conditional Differential Cryptanalysis of NLFSR-based Cryptosystems. In: Abe, M. (ed.) ASIACRYPT 2010. LNCS, vol. 6477, pp. 130–145. Springer, Heidelberg (2010)

19. Lee, Y., Jeong, K., Sung, J., Hong, S.: Related-Key Chosen IV Attacks on Grain-v1 and Grain-128. In: Mu, Y., Susilo, W., Seberry, J. (eds.) ACISP 2008. LNCS, vol. 5107, pp. 321–335. Springer, Heidelberg (2008)

20. Skorobogatov, S.P.: Optically Enhanced Position-Locked Power Analysis. In: Goubin, L., Matsui, M. (eds.) CHES 2006. LNCS, vol. 4249, pp. 61–75. Springer, Heidelberg (2006)

21. Skorobogatov, S.P., Anderson, R.J.: Optical Fault Induction Attacks. In: Kaliski Jr., B.S., Koç, Ç.K., Paar, C. (eds.) CHES 2002. LNCS, vol. 2523, pp. 2–12. Springer, Heidelberg (2003)

22. Stankovski, P.: Greedy Distinguishers and Nonrandomness Detectors. In: Gong, G., Gupta, K.C. (eds.) INDOCRYPT 2010. LNCS, vol. 6498, pp. 210–226. Springer, Heidelberg (2010)

23. Zhang, H., Wang, X.: Cryptanalysis of Stream Cipher Grain Family. IACR Cryptology ePrint Archive 2009:109, http://eprint.iacr.org/2009/109

Breaking HITAG 2 Revisited

Vincent Immler

Ruhr University Bochum, Germany
vincent.immler+space2012@rub.de

Abstract. Many Radio Frequency IDentification (RFID) applications such as car immobilizers and access control systems make use of the proprietary stream cipher HITAG 2 from the company NXP. Previous analysis has shown that the cipher is vulnerable to different attacks due to the low complexity of the cipher and its short 48-bit secret key. However, all these attacks either rely on expensive reconfigurable hardware, namely the Field Programmable Gate Array (FPGA) cluster COPACOBANA, or are impractical. In this paper we develop the first bit-sliced OpenCL implementation for the exhaustive key search of HITAG 2 that runs on off-the-shelf hardware. Our implementation is able to reveal the secret key of a HITAG 2 transponder in less than 11 hours on a single Tesla C2050 card in the worst case. The speed of our approach can be further improved due to its scalability, i.e., we estimate a speed of less than one hour on a heterogeneous platform cluster consisting of CPUs and GPUs that can be realized with a budget of less than 5,000 €. This result enables anyone to obtain the secret key with only two sniffed communications in shorter time and with significantly less cost compared to systems such as the COPACOBANA.

Keywords: Brute-force Attacks, HITAG2, GPU, Cryptanalysis, OpenCL.

1 Introduction

Since a strong increase of car theft in the early nineties all major car manufacturers incorporated electronic immobilizers. These systems usually consist of an RFID transponder in the car key and a reader around the ignition lock. Each time the car is started, the transponder is being read by the reader and verified if it is a genuine key. Early systems just used plain messages for authentication, while later systems started to have encryption schemes implemented.

One particular immobilizer system makes use of the proprietary stream cipher HITAG 2 from NXP. According to the NXP website, it is still in production and deployed in many areas which emphasizes the importance of this system. Previous analysis has shown the vulnerability of the cipher, nevertheless it is still being advertised to offer "main stream security" [8].

All existing attacks focus on obtaining recorded communications to determine the key via an analytical attack or exhaustive key search. Obtaining these

A. Bogdanov and S. Sanadhya (Eds.): SPACE 2012, LNCS 7644, pp. 126–143, 2012.

recorded communications is fairly simple, as anyone being in possession of the car and the key can record the communication. This is even of interest for legitimate car owners in case they want to have a cheap extra key for their car.

Due to that, some companies offer key copy machines and sniffing devices such as SILCA's P-Box and SNOOP[10], which may eventually copy keys using the HITAG 2 cipher, though the inner working mechanism is not known publicly.

1.1   Previous Work

HITAG 2 was kept secret by the manufacturer but it was reverse engineered and presented in 2008 [5]. Together with the description of the cipher, a reference program was made available and allowed further research. On that score, several attacks evolved. A type of successful attack is based on algebraic attacks.

One such attack was carried out by Nicolas Courtois, Sean O'Neil, and Jean-Jacques Quisquater in their paper "Practical Algebraic Attacks on the HITAG2 Stream Cipher" which was presented at the Information Security Conference (ISC) in 2009 [6]. The first part of their work details the weaknesses of HITAG 2 with regard to algebraic attacks and explains the principle on how to transform the problem into a Satisfiability (SAT) problem, which may then be solved using the SAT solver MiniSat 2.0. The second part of their paper presents different attacks of which the following was the most practical: 14 bits of the key are fixed/guessed; for four known IVs the problem is then represented in equations solvable by a SAT solver. According to their paper, the attack takes 2 days which was recently confirmed by Mate Soos, developer of CryptoMiniSat2 [11].

Another algebraic attack by Karsten Nohl and Henryk Plötz presented during the HAR2009 lacks detailed information about the restrictions of their attack, which is successful in 6 hours on a standard PC [7]. Hence, we did not take their result into further consideration.

An attack by using the brute-force technique was implemented by Petr Stembera on the FPGA cluster COPACOBANA [12]. The runtime of the attack is less than 2 hours (103.5 minutes) in the worst case and requires two recorded authenticator values. All successful attacks are summarized in Table 1 and compared to the estimation of a brute-force attack implemented in software, running on a single CPU requiring approximately 800 operations per key [12].

Other attacks by time-memory-trade-off (TMTO) [2] are not feasible in real world attacks (because of the amount of required keystream) and protocol weaknesses as shown in [4] cannot be applied to recover the key (plus, the memory page containing the key can be locked against reading).

Table 1. Summary of known attacks on the HITAG 2 cipher

Publication	Method	Runtime	Prerequisites	Platform
[6]	Algebraic attack	2 days	4 authenticators	PC (2 GHz)
[12]	Brute-force	2 hours	2 authenticators	FPGA cluster
[12]	Brute-force	4 years (est.)	2 authenticators	PC (1.8 GHz)

1.2   Contribution of This Paper

Our paper explains the steps necessary to realize an OpenCL implementation to break HITAG 2 by exhaustive key search. We show how to efficiently compute and verify all possible key candidates by using a bit-sliced approach, hence breaking the stream cipher in less than 11 hours on a single Tesla C2050 graphics card.

We also demonstrate the benefit of using a heterogenous computing environment consisting of CPUs and GPUs by estimating the runtime of our approach on heterogenous cluster systems. Our analysis shows that our implementation outperforms any previous attack. It runs on off-the-shelf hardware and can be realized with a budget of less than 5,000 €, thus setting a new lower bound in cost, speed, and practicability for cloning car keys.

1.3   Outline

At first, we introduce the fundamentals of bit-slicing and the cipher itself in Section 2. Afterwards, in Section 3, we sketch the important properties of OpenCL and the available hardware architectures. We then pinpoint the implementation details in Section 4 and explain how to efficiently map the attack to the hardware.

Finally, in Section 5 we conduct practical experiments and measure the execution time of our implementation on different hardware platforms. In addition to that, we evaluate the practical feasibility of realizing a heterogenous cluster in comparison to the costs and speed of the COPACOBANA.

2   Fundamentals

In the following section we introduce the bit-slicing technique that enables us to efficiently implement the cipher, which is explained thereafter. In addition to that, we describe the authentication protocol and the messages that need to be recorded for a successful attack.

2.1   Bit-Slicing

Many algorithms, especially stream ciphers, operate on bits instead of bytes or words, which would be optimal for n bit wide registers of general purpose processors. To allow an efficient implementation of these hardware-oriented algorithms, Eli Biham introduced a concept named bit-slicing [3]. The idea is to perform a chunk-wise serial to parallel bit transposition of the input blocks, thus obtaining a matrix where the n-th column represents the n-th input block and each n-th row containing all bits of the n-th bit position of each input block. By doing this bit-slicing, one achieves a Single Instruction Multiple Data (SIMD) processing of the input data, hence processing more than one data block at a time per computation. The rearrangement can be fitted to the native register width of the underlying processing unit. For many algorithms the bit-slice implementation

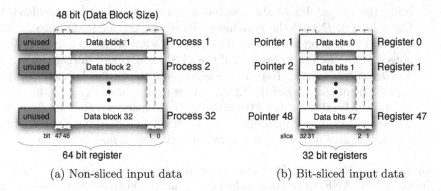

48 bit (Data Block Size)

bit 47 46 ... 1 0

64 bit register

slice 32 31 ... 2 1

32 bit registers

(a) Non-sliced input data   (b) Bit-sliced input data

Fig. 1. Comparison of the different data representations. To the left is the non-sliced form, to the right the bit-sliced form. Each slice represents one block of data and each bit position is put into a single register.

is the fastest, even with the extra cost of the rearrangement. For illustration purposes, we assume a data block size of 48 bit as can be seen in Figure 1a.

Since the register width of current processors is either 32 or 64 bit[1], it is necessary to partition all input data blocks accordingly to the targeted platform. For n bit registers this means packing all bits of the same input position within the n input blocks together in one register. This process is then repeated for all bit positions and results in a representation as depicted in Figure 1b.

For algorithms using functions other than bitwise operations, it is necessary to modify these functions accordingly to only use bitwise operations (if possible). Moreover, the rearrangement must be done for the plaintext, as well as the key (for cryptographic schemes). Furthermore, it is necessary to transpose the ciphertext to ensure compatibility with non-sliced implementations (if required).

2.2 HITAG 2 Stream Cipher and Protocol

Stream Cipher: The HITAG 2 cipher is a bit-oriented stream cipher and used to encrypt transmissions within the HITAG 2 protocol. The cipher, as shown in Figure 2, consists of a 48 bit secret key, a 48 bit Linear Feedback Shift Register (LFSR), and a non-linear output function with 20 input bits and 1 output bit per clock.

This output function can be considered as two different levels of multiplexors. The four input bits to the functions f_a and f_b serve as address bits and select one of the contained data bits. The function f_c works respectively. To generate key stream, one has to run through an initial processing which is now explained:

1. *LFSR initialization*: At first, the LFSR is being initialized by loading the 32 bit serial number (SN) and bits 0..15 of the key into the LFSR.

---

[1] In this paper, we always assume a native register width of 32 bit.

2. *State randomization*: Subsequently, the LFSR is clocked 32 times, each time using the output bit of the non-linear output function as a feedback bit Exclusive OR (XOR) the remaining bits of the key XOR the Initialization Vector (IV) (one bit each cycle). This process is illustrated in Figure 2. Please note that the feedback function of the LFSR is not used during this stage.

3. *Keystream generation:* To generate keystream, the feedback function (which is an XOR of all taps) of the LFSR is now in use, in addition to the output function. All other parts of the cipher remain inactive. The first 32 output bits are inverted and represent an authenticator used during a protocol run. The consecutively generated keystream is then used for encryption.

Alternatively, the output function can be described as an S-box, in Algebraic Normal Form (ANF) or in boolean logic. This ultimately leads to the description for the bit-sliced filter functions[2], as given in [13]:

- Filter function f_a: $(\sim(((a|b)\&c)\hat{\ }(a|d)\hat{\ }b))$
- Filter function f_b: $(\sim(((d|c)\&(a\hat{\ }b))\hat{\ }(d|a|b)))$
- Filter function f_c: $(\sim((((((c\hat{\ }e)|d)\&a)\hat{\ }b)\&(c\hat{\ }b))\hat{\ }(((d\hat{\ }e)|a)\&((d\hat{\ }b)|c))))$

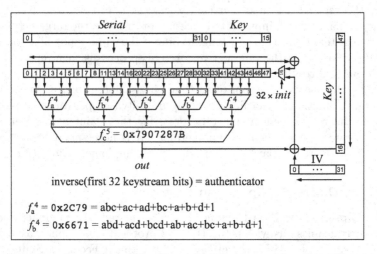

Fig. 2. Graphical description of the HITAG 2 cipher comprising the different components, namely the LFSR and the filter functions f_a, f_b, f_c[13]

Protocol: Within the HITAG 2 protocol, there are two modes for authentication: password and crypto [9]. During the password based authentication, a password in plaintext is being transmitted. Obviously, this mode offers no protection

---

[2] Here, the operands $\sim$, $\&$, $|$ and $\hat{\ }$ represent the equivalent bitwise operands of the C programming language. The variables a, b, c, and d denote the input values that are determined by the tap position of the LFSR.

against eavesdropping. We therefore concentrate our effort on the crypto mode authentication, as it is sketched in Figure 3.

This authentication mode works as follows: If a HITAG 2 transponder is placed within the interrogation zone of a reader, the transponder needs a certain time to power up and is in a wait state. The reader now issues a `Start_Auth` command which consists of the 5 bits: '11000'. The transponder responds with its 32 bit serial number (SN) and a preceding 5 bit header, where all bits are set to '1'. The base station then chooses an IV (32 bit) and generates the authenticator which consists of the first 32 bitwise inverted keystream bits.

During the reception of the IV and authenticator $Auth_B$, the transponder computes the same authenticator (denoted as $Auth_T$) and checks if $Auth_B$ matches the one that was computed. If they match, the transponder responds with a header and the encryption of Page 3 (a configuration memory page).

A successful authentication implies an entity authentication of the reader towards the transponder and causes the transponder to go in an authorized state. This state permits to read/write the tag using encrypted communication.

To break the authentication protocol, we only need to record two pairs of IV and authenticator and may even use an emulation device to trigger the output of a valid IV and authenticator pair (for a given serial number). If the key is successfully recovered, it is easy to decrypt previously recorded communication. In case no memory read/write locks are set, one may read/write the transponder memory or emulate the complete device using the recovered key.

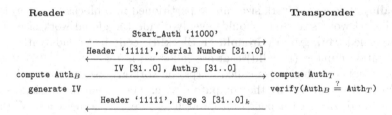

Fig. 3. Authentication messages of the HITAG 2 protocol in crypto mode [9]

3   Overview of OpenCL

In the past decade, multicore processors emerged and both CPUs as well as GPUs have undertaken a swift development, especially GPUs in adding massively parallel computational power. In contrast to the programming language CUDA which is only geared towards GPU platforms, is OpenCL a framework that executes across heterogeneous platforms consisting of CPUs and GPUs.

Therefore, it is beyond scope to cover all details of all platforms that are able to run OpenCL. However, they share a common abstraction layer as it is depicted in Figure 4. In this architecture, a host device is the control instance for several compute devices, for example, a CPU or GPU.

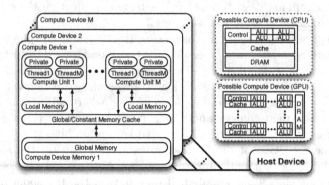

Fig. 4. This figure illustrates the generic OpenCL architecture and the different memory address spaces

These compute devices can be organized in different sets, namely a platform or a context, to ease the management and identify the correct device. The memory of the compute devices is partitioned into four different address spaces: `private`, `local`, `constant`, `global` which is primarily based on recent GPU architectures. To run a program on these devices, a pre-compiled function called kernel is loaded onto the device and executed by a user-specified number (which is the global work size). Each thread is assigned a global identification number (GlobalId). The global work size can be partitioned into blocks by a parameter named local work size that (should) evenly divide the global work size. These blocks, called work-group (GroupId or BlockId), contain threads with a local identification number (LocalId) that are called work-item.

Work-items or sub-sets (so called warps) of work-groups are executed on the compute units provided by the compute device. The actual parallelism is realized by the device and depends on its architecture and kernel code. Within a work-group, inter-thread communication may take place using `local` memory. Each work-item uses its own `private` memory space for computations. Globally available memory is the read-only `constant` memory and the read-write `global` memory.

Limitations of OpenCL may vary due to the different hardware architectures. For GPU devices, memory size and bandwidth, inefficient memory access patterns and cache size are common limitations. Path divergencies of work-items under branching also result in performance penalties. Due to that, it is important to tailor the kernel to a specific device family to address these problems.

4   Implementation

At first, we reason about the techniques used to implement the cipher in Section 4.1. Afterwards, an overview of the system used for our implementation is given in Section 4.2. A difficulty to overcome is the cost of the bit transposition because of the bit-slicing, especially for the key candidates, which is shown in Section 4.3. In a next step, we describe the computation that is carried out by our kernel in Section 4.4.

4.1 Implementation Considerations

To efficiently implement a brute-force attack, we make the following important observation about the cipher: Keys that have a common part (from their 'beginning' on) may share steps of the cipher setup. As an example, keys that have their 16 least significant bit in common may operate on a memory copy of the LFSR that is initialized only once. By taking this idea to the maximum extent, we could possibly use many nested for-loops, each time using a memory copy of the upper loop and using each loop index as next portion of the key.

Alternatively, instead of having (too) many loops, we can also make use of the general idea to initialize the LFSR of the cipher up to a certain point, where we can load this partially initialized LFSR onto a compute device and finish the computation (thus, using parallelization). On our compute device, we can then simply use the identification numbers of each work-item or work-group as potential key guess.

Also relevant for the efficient implementation is to have fast building blocks in software. This can be achieved by using bit-slicing. The LFSR of the cipher is denoted as the array `lfsr[48]`, representing 32 LFSR states of the cipher in parallel. Furthermore, we need to implement the bit-sliced non-linear output function and the feedback function of the LFSR. The latter is simply implemented by 15 XOR operations (cf. function `hitag2bs_round`, Appendix D), whereas the former is realized by the bit-sliced filter functions f_a, f_b, f_c, and results in 46 boolean operations (cf. function `f20bs`, Appendix D).

Also necessary to implement is the 'clocking' of the LFSR. In hardware, this causes a shift of each bit to the next position. In software, an array shift fulfills the same purpose if operating on bit-sliced data. However, by unrolling all subsequent function calls one can omit the array shift by manually adjusting the indices to imitate the shift, thus saving a significant amount of operations[3].

4.2 System Overview

Our system consists of one host device and an arbitrary count of compute devices. On the host device, we perform the necessary steps to access the compute devices and partially initialize/randomize the LFSR to finish the computation on the compute device. This process is described as pseudo-code in Algorithm B.1.

Together with the partially randomized LFSR data, we load the kernel onto the compute device that finishes the cipher computation up to the point, where the output is compared to the sliced authenticator. The result of the computation is then retrieved by the host device and evaluated, i.e., the result contains the

---

[3] Due to that, by referring to 'clocking' we mean the processing of the LFSR (and inputs) accordingly to the cipher description.

number of possible key candidates found (a counter) and information to recover the key on the host to verify it. The computation carried out by the kernel is described in detail in Section 4.4.

We highlight the fact that with one authenticator and IV pair, one may find up to $2^{48}/2^{32} = 2^{16}$ key candidates. These candidates are therefore verified against a second authenticator and IV pair. This verification takes place in parallel to the continuous execution of the kernel(s) and causes only negligible overhead.

4.3   Key Space Partitioning

To circumvent the transformation overhead of the key challenges, we carefully partitioned the key space of 2^{48} based on the ideas given in [1]. Moreover, we are able to distribute the load between host and compute device to benefit from the shared computational cost during the initialization phase.

The details of this process are given in Appendix A and result in a partitioned key space as it is illustrated in Figure 5. We emphasize that the computational cost on the host is minimal by using memory copies.

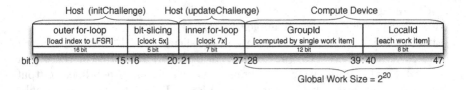

Fig. 5. This figure illustrates the partitioned key space and how the different parts of the systems are used to create the key challenges

4.4   Kernel Implementation

The purpose of the kernel is to finalize the state randomization and then to interleave the authenticator generation with a verification to stop execution if all key candidates have been shown invalid.

The input arguments of the kernel are in sequential order: precomputed LFSR, remaining bits of IV, precomputed key guess XOR IV for each work group, sliced authenticator, result data. For a detailed analysis, the actual (annotated) code is given in Appendix D with only obvious gaps to keep it short.

Finalize State Randomization: As a first step, only the first work item of each work group further randomizes the LFSR by processing the key and IV bits in addition to performing the bit-sliced non-linear output function. The resulting 12 output slices are stored in `local` memory. Consistency is guaranteed by using a synchronization barrier to allow other work items in the same group to access the previously computed output slices.

Afterwards, the last portion of the key is loaded from **constant** memory (precomputed on the host) and processed by each work item of a group. This puts the LFSR in a state ready for keystream generation.

Keystream Generation and Output Verification: The keystream generation consists of the round function and is also fully unrolled. Each time the round
function is carried out we get one output slice which is a 32 bit value. This value
represents 32 times 1 output bit per key candidate per cipher clock cycle.

To verify this output and track the valid key candidates, we make use of the
Not Exclusive Or (NXOR) logical function by applying this operation to the
output of the round function and one register of the authenticator. Afterwards,
we AND the result with a bit mask which is initialized with 0xFFFFFFFF. By doing
so, we keep ones in all the bit positions where a valid key candidate remains.

After 8 times 'clocking' the LFSR, we check if any key candidates are left
(bit mask must be non-zero). If not, we terminate. If key candidates are left, we
repeat the process until we generated 32 slices of output, each time checking after
8 outputs if any key candidates are left by checking the bit mask. By checking
only every 8th mask, we reduce path divergencies (by minimizing if-else clauses)
that are costly on GPU hardware.

The concept of the bit mask was also introduced to directly verify the sliced
output by only causing 3 extra operations per slice. Finally, if the mask is still
non-zero after all steps, we increment a counter and return the mask(s) and the
globalId(s) of the thread, to be able to recover the possible key candidate.

4.5 Analysis of Our Kernel Implementation

To rate our kernel and verify the efficiency, it is our goal to have very few operations per key. To estimate this, we carry out the following simplified calculation.

The state randomization within the kernel is split in two stages. The first
contributes only $12 \cdot 46/256 = R_1 \approx 2$ to the overall operations (first thread of a
group only). The second is executed by each thread resulting in $8 \cdot 46 = R_2 = 368$.
The subsequent key stream generation results in $32 \cdot (46 + 3 + 15) = C = 2048$,
completely disregarding the fact that with each if clause the amount of threads
actually running significantly reduces (but possibly inducing serialization). Taking the bit-slicing into consideration, we can divide the sum of $R_1 + R_2 + C =
2418$ by 32 which yields approximately 75.56 operations per key.

While running on SIMT architectures (e.g., Tesla C2050), we could possibly
further divide this number by the number of processors (e.g., 448), resulting
in hypothetical 0.169 operations per key. Besides the fact that we ignored the
operations contributed by the host, we did not consider amongst other factors:
architectural properties (possible serialization on GPU, dual dispatch units on
Fermi), memory operations, and cache size.

However, this estimation indicates that our implementation is highly efficient
in terms of operations per key. All this can be implemented using 63 registers (C2050) with negligible register spilling, resulting in an occupancy of each
streaming processor (SM) of 33 % (with 2 active thread blocks per SM).

5   Experimental Results and Costs

In this section we conduct practical experiments on different hardware platforms and present the obtained results. We evaluate the practical feasibility of realizing a heterogeneous cluster running on off-the-shelf hardware to break the cipher.

5.1   Throughput Evaluation on a Single Device

Our evaluation aimed at comparing the speed of our OpenCL implementation on the different architectures offered by Nvidia, AMD and Intel. For each GPU platform, minor modifications to the kernel were applied to optimize the result. For CPUs, more significant changes were necessary, e.g., we changed the data type from 32 bit to 64 bit and as a consequence, the overall distribution between host and compute device. The platform details are given in Appendix C.

It was not our goal to write native assembly code (e.g., PTX, IL, x86 assembly), even though we expect a certain performance benefit from that. Instead, we analyzed the speed by using our generic OpenCL kernel as starting point, to find out how well the attack performs on the different architectures.

Further changes were manual loop unrolling on AMD hardware, as we noticed a significant speedup by doing so. Due to the manually unrolled code, it is neither possible to change the global nor local work size on the fly.

Our obtained results are shown in Table 2. The first three columns specify the brand, device, and name (type) of the architecture followed by the number of compute units and cores provided by each platform. The last column shows the kernel runtime and already includes the overhead to set, write, and read the kernel arguments as well as the time to execute the function `updateChallenge`. Any other computational overhead is negligible.

As one can see, a single Tesla C2050 is the fasted compute device, however the keys per € ratio of the GTX295 is much better. In terms of keys per watt, the mobile graphics chipset 6750M offers a competitive ratio of $2^{25.7}$, even compared to the COPACOBANA ($2^{26.17}$). Of course, the overall runtime is different.

Table 2. Comparison of the evaluated compute devices, their technical specifications and the obtained runtimes per kernel execution (including overhead)

Chipset Brand Device	Architecture Name (Type)	#CUs[a]	#Cores[b]	Clock [MHz]	TDP [W]	Release [Date]	Kernel [ms]
NVIDIA GTX295	GT200 (SIMT)	30	$30 \cdot 16 = 480$	1242	289	Jan 2009	7.5
NVIDIA C2050	GF100 (SIMT)	14	$14 \cdot 32 = 448$	1150	238	Nov 2009	4.5
AMD 6750M	TeraScale2 (VLIW)	6	$6 \cdot 16 \cdot 5 = 480$	600	25	Jan 2011	24.5
INTEL 2820QM	Sandy Bridge (SIMD)	8	4	2300	45	Jan 2011	50[c]
INTEL 2xE5540	Nehalem (SIMD)	$2 \cdot 8$	$2 \cdot 4 = 8$	2530	80	Q1' 2009	30[c]

[a] Compute Unit (CU): NVIDIA: Streaming Multiprocessor (SM), AMD: SIMD Engine, Intel: Siblings.

[b] Cores: NVIDIA: Streaming Processor (SP), AMD: Stream Core (SC), Intel: Core.

[c] Runtime of 100 ms resp. 60 ms scaled with 1/2 for comparison reasons (due to 64 bit registers).

5.2 Cost Evaluation of a Heterogeneous Platform Cluster

A great advantage of using OpenCL is the possibility to realize a heterogeneous platform cluster consisting of CPUs and GPUs. Hence, one is able to better utilize the given hardware in comparison to GPU only clusters. We now consider the financial effort to break the cipher by realizing such a cluster with a budget of less than 5,000 €.

By considering the throughput results for a single device, we estimate the runtime of a particular cluster to show that we can easily outperform the COPA-COBANA with less budget using off-the-shelf hardware. For our cost estimation, we assume that one workstation contains two video cards and one CPU.

Table 3 shows the results of our cost analysis. The first two columns report the models of both GPU and CPU, followed by two columns reporting the price of each device. The next column is a cost analysis and presents the number of workstations affordable within the given price range.

Table 3. Overview of two different heterogeneous cluster systems with cost and runtime estimation to break HITAG 2

Device GPU CPU	Cost/Device GPU CPU	# of Workstations Affordable with budget of 5000 €	Estimated Runtime [hours]
GTX295 i7-860	299 229	5	0.5
GTX295 i3-540	299 76	6	0.3

For our analysis, we suppose an overhead of 150 € per workstation, plus the costs for two graphics cards and the CPU. Because we lacked suitable hardware, we assumed a moderate performance gain by 10% when using the i7-860 and a gain by 5% when using the i3-540. We emphasize that no communication between the workstations is required, thus no performance penalty affects the scalability.

6 Conclusion

In this paper, we propose the first bit-sliced OpenCL implementation of HITAG 2 to perform an exhaustive key search on heterogeneous platforms. We present results of our experimental evaluation and show that breaking the cipher is a matter of hours on a single GPU. We emphasize that our hardware setup was rather outdated and more recent hardware would perform even more promising.

Due to the nature of our approach, we can easily make use of more hardware resources and provide data on building a heterogeneous cluster to break the cipher within an hour using off-the-shelf hardware. Given the fact that we did not use platform dependable code, we can assume that future versions may run even faster by using hand-written IL or PTX assembly code. In order to improve the results on CPUs, vector data types could be used to exploit the width of SSE or AVX registers.

References

1. Agosta, G., Barenghi, A., De Santis, F., Pelosi, G.: Record Setting Software Implementation of DES using CUDA. In: Proceedings of the 2010 Seventh International Conference on Information Technology: New Generations, ITNG 2010, pp. 748–755. IEEE Computer Society, Washington, DC (2010)
2. Bachani, R.: Time-memory-data cryptanalysis of the HiTag2 stream cipher. Master's thesis, Technical University of Denmark (2008), http://code.google.com/p/cryptanalysis-of-hitag2/
3. Biham, E.: A Fast New DES Implementation in Software, pp. 260–272. Springer (1997)
4. Bogdanov, A., Paar, C.: On the Security and Efficiency of Real-World Lightweight Authentication Protocols (2008)
5. Courtois, N.T., O'Neil, S.: FSE Rump Session – Hitag 2 Cipher (2008), http://fse2008rump.cr.yp.to/00564f75b2f39604dc204d838da01e7a.pdf (August 30, 2012)
6. Courtois, N.T., O'Neil, S., Quisquater, J.-J.: Practical Algebraic Attacks on the Hitag2 Stream Cipher. In: Samarati, P., Yung, M., Martinelli, F., Ardagna, C.A. (eds.) ISC 2009. LNCS, vol. 5735, pp. 167–176. Springer, Heidelberg (2009)
7. Henryk Plötz, K.N.: Breaking Hitag 2 (August 2009), https://har2009.org/program/attachments/113_breaking_hitag2_part1_hardware.pdf
8. NXP. HITAG 2 transponder IC, http://www.nxp.com/products/identification_and_security/smart_label_and_tag_ics/hitag/series/HITAG_2_TRANSPONDER_IC.html#overview (August 30, 2012)
9. NXP. HT2 Transponder Family Communication Protocol – Revision 2.1, http://www.proxmark.org/files/index.php?dir=Documents%2F125+kHz+-+Hitag%2F&download=HT2protocol.pdf (August 30, 2012)
10. SILCA. Die neueste Silca Transponder Technologie, http://www.silca.de/media/112090/v4/File/silca-id46-solution-rw4.pdf (August 30, 2012)
11. Soos, M.: Cracking Industrial Ciphers at a Whim (April 2011), http://50-56-189-184.static.cloud-ips.com/wordpress/wp-content/uploads/2011/04/hes2011.pdf (August 30, 2012)
12. Stembera, P.: Cryptanalysis of Hitag-2 Cipher. Master's thesis, Czech Technical University in Prague (2011), https://dip.felk.cvut.cz/browse/pdfcache/stembpe1_2011dipl.pdf (August 30, 2012)
13. Unknown. Hitag2 Stream Cipher C Implementation and Graphical Description (2006-2007), http://cryptolib.com/ciphers/hitag2/ (June 14, 2012)

A Details of Key Space Partitioning

We continue with the description of the key space partitioning and make use of the C syntax. The array keyChallenge[48] shall (fictively) contain the key candidates in bit-sliced representation. In detail, we start with:

– The *outer-for-loop* (from 0 to $2^{16} - 1$): This loop contains the function
`initChallenge` that takes the index of the loop as key candidate. Each
candidate is sliced and used as the quantity of the key that is directly loaded
into the LFSR together with the serial number. Of course, loading the serial
number can be done once and a memory copy used for all loop iterations.

```
for(i=0; i<32; i++) { // slice serial number and load into LFSR
    if(serial&1) { lfsr[i] = ~lfsr[i]; }
    serial >>= 1;
}
// ... keyGuess is the index of the outer-for-loop ...
for(i=0; i<16; i++) { // slice index and load into LFSR
    if(keyGuess&1) { lfsr[32+i] = ~lfsr[32+i]; }
    keyGuess >>= 1;
}
// ... keyGuess represents keyChallenge[0..15]
```

– The next 5 bits are all possible values in this range (read column-wise), due
to bit-slicing and the native register width of 32 bit ($2^5 = 32$, for GPUs):

```
fixedBits[0]=0x55555555; // 01010101010101010101010101010101 //=keyChallenge[16]
fixedBits[1]=0x33333333; // 00110011001100110011001100110011 //=keyChallenge[17]
fixedBits[2]=0x0F0F0F0F; // 00001111000011110000111100001111 //=keyChallenge[18]
fixedBits[3]=0x00FF00FF; // 00000000111111110000000011111111 //=keyChallenge[19]
fixedBits[4]=0x0000FFFF; // 00000000000000001111111111111111 //=keyChallenge[20]
```

These bits are fixed and can be directly clocked into the LFSR on the host as
part of the function `initChallenge`. This step represents the first 5 out of
32 clock cycles to randomize the state of the LFSR. We later take advantage
of the fact that we can check for the valid keys by verifying a bit mask.

– The *inner-for-loop* (from 0 to $2^7 - 1$): These 7 bit represent the number of
kernel calls within each outer loop and are clocked into the LFSR by applying
the function `updateChallenge`.

– For the remaining 20 bit, the kernel is sent to the compute device. Hence,
our global work size is 2^{20}, whereas:

   • 12 bit are represented by the blockId and

   • 8 bit by the localId (the maximum size of a work group on some devices).
Together, they specify the unique key challenges of each work item. We
stress that the global work size was limited to 2^{20} due to the fact that some
compute devices refused to work with larger values (e.g., AMD 6750M).

We notice that the 8 bit determining the localId are a fixed index for each
thread and thus can be precomputed by XORing all (sliced) indices with the
corresponding (sliced) IV bits. This precomputed data is then loaded onto
the device as array `workGroupSlices` (size of $256 \cdot 8 \cdot 32$ bit).

B   Pseudocode of the Host Attack Algorithm

To implement this algorithm, we wrote two functions, namely `initChallenge`
and `updateChallenge`. These functions are incorporated in the basic structure
of our program which consists of the set-up stage and two for-loops.

The first for-loop named *outer-for-loop* represents the LFSR initialization and calls the function `initChallenge`. The *inner-for-loop* creates a memory copy of the data provided by the outer-for-loop and continues the state randomization (clocking the LFSR) by calling the function `updateChallenge`.

The pseudo-code implementation can be further improved by using the idea of nested for-loops, each time operating on a memory copy of the upper loop.

Algorithm B.1: Host Attack Algorithm

Input : SN, $(IV_1, Auth_1)$, $(IV_2, Auth_2)$, `fixedBits[5]`
Output: Key
1 Discover and set up compute device;
2 Create sliced representation of IV_1 and $Auth_1$;
3 Precomputation of `workGroupSlices`;
4 **for** $i \leftarrow 0$ **to** $2^{16} - 1$ **do**
5 | $\text{lfsr}_i \leftarrow$ initChallenge(i, `fixedBits`, SN);
6 | **for** $j \leftarrow 0$ **to** $2^7 - 1$ **do**
7 | | $\text{lfsr}_j \leftarrow$ memcpy(lfsr_i);
8 | | $\text{lfsr}_j \leftarrow$ updateChallenge(j, lfsr_j);
9 | | Send data to compute device;
10 | | *counter* $\leftarrow$ Retrieve result data if kernel finishes;
11 | | **if** *counter* > *0* **then**
12 | | | verify data with $(IV_2, Auth_2)$ in parallel and continue execution;
13 | | **end**
14 | **end**
15 **end**
16 return key;

C   Platform Specifications

The specifications of the platforms used for testing are as follows:

- MacBook Pro: Intel i7 2820QM, AMD 6750M, OS X 10.7.4, Apple LLVM compiler 3.1
- Server #1: 2x Intel Xeon X5680 3.33 GHz, Nvidia Tesla C2050, Ubuntu 11.10, Driver 290.10
- Server #2: 2x Intel Xeon E5540 2.53 GHz, Nvidia GTX295, Ubuntu 10.04, Driver 295.40

D   Kernel Implementation

The following source code is a working kernel to be executed on GPUs:

```
/* C preprocessor defines for the filter functions */
#define ht2bs_4a(a,b,c,d)  (~(((a|b)&c)^(a|d)^b))
#define ht2bs_4b(a,b,c,d)  (~(((d|c)&(a^b))^(d|a|b)))
#define ht2bs_5c(a,b,c,d,e) (~((((((c^e)|d)&a)^b)&(c^b))^(((d^e)|a)&((d^b)|c))))

__kernel void
hitag_worker(__constant const unsigned int *preSlicedLFSR,   // 48*32 bit
             __constant const unsigned int *ivInput,         // 12*32 bit
             __constant const unsigned int *workGroupSlices, // 256*8*32 bit, __global on GF100
             __constant const unsigned int *cmpSlicedArray,  // 32*32 bit
             __global unsigned int *numCollisions)           // [0]=cnt, [>0]=data
{
    const unsigned int lid = get_local_id(0);    // 0 ... 255
    unsigned int keyChallenge[20];               // store key challenges (note: index is shifted)
    unsigned int lfsr[48];                        // store LFSR state
    unsigned int bitMask = 0xFFFFFFFF;            // check for valid key candidates

    __local unsigned int groupPreComp[12];

    if (lid==0) { // Execute the following code only for the first work item of each work group
        unsigned int blockId = get_group_id(0);   // 0 ... ((2^20)/(2^8))

        /* Assign key challenges based on blockId (0 ... 2^12) */
        keyChallenge[ 0] = (blockId&1) ? 0xFFFFFFFF : 0x00000000;
        blockId >>= 1;
        // [...] unrolled code [...]
        keyChallenge[10] = (blockId&1) ? 0xFFFFFFFF : 0x00000000;
        blockId >>= 1;
        keyChallenge[11] = (blockId&1) ? 0xFFFFFFFF : 0x00000000;

        /*
        Continue state randomization and store result in local memory.
        The following code is basically the unrolled version of:

        // for (j = 0; j < 47; j++) lfsr[j] = lfsr[j+1]; // extra shift done on host
        for(i=0; i<12; i++) {
            for (j = 0; j < 47; j++) lfsr[j] = lfsr[j+1];
            lfsr[47] = ivInput[i] ^ keyChallenge[i] ^ f20bs(lfsr);
        }
        */

        groupPreComp[11] = ivInput[ 0] ^ keyChallenge[ 0] ^ ht2bs_5c(
            ht2bs_4a(preSlicedLFSR[ 1],preSlicedLFSR[ 2],preSlicedLFSR[ 4],preSlicedLFSR[ 5]),
            ht2bs_4b(preSlicedLFSR[ 7],preSlicedLFSR[11],preSlicedLFSR[13],preSlicedLFSR[14]),
            ht2bs_4b(preSlicedLFSR[16],preSlicedLFSR[20],preSlicedLFSR[22],preSlicedLFSR[25]),
            ht2bs_4b(preSlicedLFSR[27],preSlicedLFSR[28],preSlicedLFSR[30],preSlicedLFSR[32]),
            ht2bs_4a(preSlicedLFSR[33],preSlicedLFSR[42],preSlicedLFSR[43],preSlicedLFSR[45]));
        groupPreComp[ 0] = ivInput[ 1] ^ keyChallenge[ 1] ^ ht2bs_5c(
            ht2bs_4a(preSlicedLFSR[ 2],preSlicedLFSR[ 3],preSlicedLFSR[ 5],preSlicedLFSR[ 6]),
            ht2bs_4b(preSlicedLFSR[ 8],preSlicedLFSR[12],preSlicedLFSR[14],preSlicedLFSR[15]),
            ht2bs_4b(preSlicedLFSR[17],preSlicedLFSR[21],preSlicedLFSR[23],preSlicedLFSR[26]),
            ht2bs_4b(preSlicedLFSR[28],preSlicedLFSR[29],preSlicedLFSR[31],preSlicedLFSR[33]),
            ht2bs_4a(preSlicedLFSR[34],preSlicedLFSR[43],preSlicedLFSR[44],preSlicedLFSR[46]));
        // [...] unrolled code [...]
        groupPreComp[10] = ivInput[11] ^ keyChallenge[11] ^ ht2bs_5c(
            ht2bs_4a(preSlicedLFSR[12],preSlicedLFSR[13],preSlicedLFSR[15],preSlicedLFSR[16]),
            ht2bs_4b(preSlicedLFSR[18],preSlicedLFSR[22],preSlicedLFSR[24],preSlicedLFSR[25]),
            ht2bs_4b(preSlicedLFSR[27],preSlicedLFSR[31],preSlicedLFSR[33],preSlicedLFSR[36]),
            ht2bs_4b(preSlicedLFSR[38],preSlicedLFSR[39],preSlicedLFSR[41],preSlicedLFSR[43]),
            ht2bs_4a(preSlicedLFSR[44],groupPreComp[ 5],groupPreComp[ 6],groupPreComp[ 8]));
    }
    barrier(CLK_LOCAL_MEM_FENCE); // Synchronize all work items of work group
```

```
/* Hint: Use for-loops for NVIDIA, manually unrolled loops for AMD-GPU. */
for(unsigned int i=0; i<11; i++) { lfsr[i] = groupPreComp[i]; }
lfsr[47] = groupPreComp[11];
for(unsigned int i=11; i<47; i++) { lfsr[i] = preSlicedLFSR[i]; }

keyChallenge[12] = workGroupSlices[lid+(256*0)];   // coalesced if global mem
keyChallenge[13] = workGroupSlices[lid+(256*1)];   // coalesced if global mem
// [...] unrolled code [...]
keyChallenge[19] = workGroupSlices[lid+(256*7)];   // coalesced if global mem

lfsr[11] = keyChallenge[12] ^ ht2bs_5c(ht2bs_4a(lfsr[13],lfsr[14],lfsr[16],lfsr[17]),
                                       ht2bs_4b(lfsr[19],lfsr[23],lfsr[25],lfsr[26]),
                                       ht2bs_4b(lfsr[28],lfsr[32],lfsr[34],lfsr[37]),
                                       ht2bs_4b(lfsr[39],lfsr[40],lfsr[42],lfsr[44]),
                                       ht2bs_4a(lfsr[45],lfsr[ 6],lfsr[ 7],lfsr[ 9]));
lfsr[12] = keyChallenge[13] ^ ht2bs_5c(ht2bs_4a(lfsr[14],lfsr[15],lfsr[17],lfsr[18]),
                                       ht2bs_4b(lfsr[20],lfsr[24],lfsr[26],lfsr[27]),
                                       ht2bs_4b(lfsr[29],lfsr[33],lfsr[35],lfsr[38]),
                                       ht2bs_4b(lfsr[40],lfsr[41],lfsr[43],lfsr[45]),
                                       ht2bs_4a(lfsr[46],lfsr[ 7],lfsr[ 8],lfsr[10]));
// [...] unrolled code [...]
lfsr[18] = keyChallenge[19] ^ ht2bs_5c(ht2bs_4a(lfsr[20],lfsr[21],lfsr[23],lfsr[24]),
                                       ht2bs_4b(lfsr[26],lfsr[30],lfsr[32],lfsr[33]),
                                       ht2bs_4b(lfsr[35],lfsr[39],lfsr[41],lfsr[44]),
                                       ht2bs_4b(lfsr[46],lfsr[47],lfsr[ 1],lfsr[ 3]),
                                       ht2bs_4a(lfsr[ 4],lfsr[13],lfsr[14],lfsr[16]));

read_mem_fence(CLK_LOCAL_MEM_FENCE);

/*
We now compute 32 bits of output (the authenticator) and immediately
check the output bits against the expected value. We make special use
of the NXOR to track the valid key candidates (result in bitMask).

The following code is basically the unrolled version of:
for(i=0; i<8; i++) { bitMask &= (~(cmpSlicedArray[i+ 0] ^ hitag2bs_round(lfsr))); }
if(bitMask!=0)
    for(i=0; i<8; i++) { bitMask &= (~(cmpSlicedArray[i+ 8] ^ hitag2bs_round(lfsr))); }
if(bitMask!=0)
    for(i=0; i<8; i++) { bitMask &= (~(cmpSlicedArray[i+ 16] ^ hitag2bs_round(lfsr))); }
if(bitMask!=0)
    for(i=0; i<8; i++) { bitMask &= (~(cmpSlicedArray[i+ 24] ^ hitag2bs_round(lfsr))); }
*/

lfsr[19] ^= lfsr[21] ^ lfsr[22] ^ lfsr[25] ^ lfsr[26] ^ lfsr[27] ^ lfsr[35] ^ lfsr[41] ^
       lfsr[42] ^ lfsr[45] ^ lfsr[1] ^ lfsr[12] ^ lfsr[13] ^ lfsr[14] ^ lfsr[17] ^ lfsr[18];
bitMask &= (~(cmpSlicedArray[0] ^ ht2bs_5c(ht2bs_4a(lfsr[21],lfsr[22],lfsr[24],lfsr[25]),
                                           ht2bs_4b(lfsr[27],lfsr[31],lfsr[33],lfsr[34]),
                                           ht2bs_4b(lfsr[36],lfsr[40],lfsr[42],lfsr[45]),
                                           ht2bs_4b(lfsr[47],lfsr[ 0],lfsr[ 2],lfsr[ 4]),
                                           ht2bs_4a(lfsr[5],lfsr[14],lfsr[15],lfsr[17]))));
// [...] unrolled code [...]
lfsr[26] ^= lfsr[28] ^ lfsr[29] ^ lfsr[32] ^ lfsr[33] ^ lfsr[34] ^ lfsr[42] ^ lfsr[0] ^
       lfsr[1] ^ lfsr[4] ^ lfsr[8] ^ lfsr[19] ^ lfsr[20] ^ lfsr[21] ^ lfsr[24] ^ lfsr[25];
bitMask &= (~(cmpSlicedArray[7] ^ ht2bs_5c(ht2bs_4a(lfsr[28],lfsr[29],lfsr[31],lfsr[32]),
                                           ht2bs_4b(lfsr[34],lfsr[38],lfsr[40],lfsr[41]),
                                           ht2bs_4b(lfsr[43],lfsr[47],lfsr[ 1],lfsr[ 4]),
                                           ht2bs_4b(lfsr[ 6],lfsr[ 7],lfsr[ 9],lfsr[11]),
                                           ht2bs_4a(lfsr[12],lfsr[21],lfsr[22],lfsr[24]))));
/*
After computing the first 8 output bits, we check if there are any
key candidates left. If so, continue, else, terminate.
*/
if(bitMask!=0) {
    lfsr[27] ^= lfsr[29] ^ lfsr[30] ^ lfsr[33] ^ lfsr[34] ^ lfsr[35] ^ lfsr[43] ^ lfsr[1] ^
           lfsr[2] ^ lfsr[5] ^ lfsr[9] ^ lfsr[20] ^ lfsr[21] ^ lfsr[22] ^ lfsr[25] ^ lfsr[26];
    bitMask &= (~(cmpSlicedArray[ 8] ^ ht2bs_5c(ht2bs_4a(lfsr[29],lfsr[30],lfsr[32],lfsr[33]),
                                                ht2bs_4b(lfsr[35],lfsr[39],lfsr[41],lfsr[42]),
```

```
                                          ht2bs_4b(lfsr[44],lfsr[ 0],lfsr[ 2],lfsr[ 5]),
                                          ht2bs_4b(lfsr[ 7],lfsr[ 8],lfsr[10],lfsr[12]),
                                          ht2bs_4a(lfsr[13],lfsr[22],lfsr[23],lfsr[25]))));
    // [...] unrolled code [...]
}
read_mem_fence(CLK_LOCAL_MEM_FENCE);

if(bitMask!=0){ // first check, then continue computation
    // [...] unrolled code [...]
}

read_mem_fence(CLK_LOCAL_MEM_FENCE);

if(bitMask != 0) { // first check, then continue computation
    lfsr[43] ^= lfsr[45] ^ lfsr[46] ^ lfsr[1] ^ lfsr[2] ^ lfsr[3] ^ lfsr[11] ^ lfsr[17] ^
        lfsr[18] ^ lfsr[21] ^ lfsr[25] ^ lfsr[36] ^ lfsr[37] ^ lfsr[38] ^ lfsr[41] ^ lfsr[42];
    bitMask &= (~(cmpSlicedArray[24] ^ ht2bs_5c(ht2bs_4a(lfsr[45],lfsr[46],lfsr[ 0],lfsr[ 1]),
                                          ht2bs_4b(lfsr[ 3],lfsr[ 7],lfsr[ 9],lfsr[10]),
                                          ht2bs_4b(lfsr[12],lfsr[16],lfsr[18],lfsr[21]),
                                          ht2bs_4b(lfsr[23],lfsr[24],lfsr[26],lfsr[28]),
                                          ht2bs_4a(lfsr[29],lfsr[38],lfsr[39],lfsr[41]))));
    // [...] unrolled code [...]
    lfsr[2] ^= lfsr[4] ^ lfsr[5] ^ lfsr[8] ^ lfsr[9] ^ lfsr[10] ^ lfsr[18] ^ lfsr[24] ^
        lfsr[25] ^ lfsr[28] ^ lfsr[32] ^ lfsr[43] ^ lfsr[44] ^ lfsr[45] ^ lfsr[0] ^ lfsr[1];
    bitMask &= (~(cmpSlicedArray[31] ^ ht2bs_5c(ht2bs_4a(lfsr[ 4],lfsr[ 5],lfsr[ 7],lfsr[ 8]),
                                          ht2bs_4b(lfsr[10],lfsr[14],lfsr[16],lfsr[17]),
                                          ht2bs_4b(lfsr[19],lfsr[23],lfsr[25],lfsr[28]),
                                          ht2bs_4b(lfsr[30],lfsr[31],lfsr[33],lfsr[35]),
                                          ht2bs_4a(lfsr[36],lfsr[45],lfsr[46],lfsr[ 0]))));

}
read_mem_fence(CLK_LOCAL_MEM_FENCE);

/* If the bitMask is still non-zero, we have found valid key candidate(s) */
if(bitMask !=0) {
    numCollisions[0]++; //atomic_inc(&numCollisions[0]); // not necessary, see below
    numCollisions[1] = bitMask;
    numCollisions[2] = get_global_id(0);
    // Eventually, we would have to dynamically adjust the indices. However, in
    // our tests, not more than one possible key candidate per kernel run showed up.
    // As a safety measure, one can use the atomic_inc and check for a counter > 1.
    // Depending on the platform, this causes no overhead and results in same speed.
}
}
```

For the sake of completeness, we provide the two functions referenced within comments in the above source code:

```
// This function computes a complete round (output and feedback) function of the cipher
unsigned int hitag2bs_round (unsigned int * lfsr) {
    unsigned int i, y;

    y = lfsr[ 0] ^ lfsr[ 2] ^ lfsr[ 3] ^ lfsr[ 6] ^ lfsr[ 7] ^ lfsr[ 8] ^ lfsr[16] ^ lfsr[22] ^
    lfsr[23] ^ lfsr[26] ^ lfsr[30] ^ lfsr[41] ^ lfsr[42] ^ lfsr[43] ^ lfsr[46] ^ lfsr[47];

    for (i = 0; i < 47; i++) { lfsr[i] = lfsr[i+1]; } // omit if unrolled by adjusting indices

    lfsr[47] = y;
    return f20bs (lfsr);
}

// This function computes the (bit-sliced) non-linear output function of the cipher
static unsigned int f20bs (const unsigned int *x) {
return ht2bs_5c (ht2bs_4a(x[ 1],x[ 2],x[ 4],x[ 5]),
                ht2bs_4b(x[ 7],x[11],x[13],x[14]),
                ht2bs_4b(x[16],x[20],x[22],x[25]),
                ht2bs_4b(x[27],x[28],x[30],x[32]),
                ht2bs_4a(x[33],x[42],x[43],x[45]));
}
```

Reduction in Lossiness of RSA Trapdoor Permutation

Santanu Sarkar

Indian Statistical Institute, 203 B T Road, Kolkata 700 108, India
sarkar.santanu.bir@gmail.com

Abstract. We consider the lossiness of RSA trapdoor permutation studied by Kiltz, O'Neill and Smith in Crypto 2010. In Africacrypt 2011, Herrmann improved the cryptanalytic results of Kiltz et al. In this paper, we improve the bound provided by Herrmann, considering the fact that the unknown variables in the central modular equation of the problem are not balanced. We provide detailed experimental results to justify our claim. It is interesting that in many situations, our experimental results are better than our theoretical predictions. Our idea also extends the weak encryption exponents proposed by Nitaj in Africacrypt 2012.

Keywords: Multi-Prime Φ-Hiding Problem, Lattice, Modular Equation.

1 Introduction

1.1 Multi-Prime Φ-Hiding Assumption

Multi-Prime RSA is a generalization of the RSA public key cryptosystem [13] where the modulus is a product of more than two primes, i.e., $N = p_1 \cdots p_m$, with p_i (for $1 \leq i \leq m$) primes of same bitsize. Note that for a fixed bit length of Multi-Prime RSA modulus N, the number of primes m can not be very large since, in that case one may efficiently extract the smallest factor of N using the Elliptic Curve Method for factorization [10].

Φ-**Hiding Assumption** is one of the most well known assumptions in modern cryptography. It is used in various applications to produce secure primitives. For an RSA modulus $N = pq$ and a prime e, the Φ-Hiding Assumption states that

"it is hard to decide whether e divides $\Phi(N) = (p-1)(q-1)$,"

where $\Phi(\cdot)$ denotes the Euler's totient function. So the Φ-Hiding Problem is to deterministically predict whether a given prime e is a factor of $\Phi(N)$ or not, where only the knowledge of e and N is available.

It is well known that Φ-Hiding problem can be solved efficiently using the idea of Coppersmith [1] if $e \geq N^{0.25}$. In Asiacrypt 2008, Schridde and Freisleben [14] proved that the Φ-Hiding Assumption does not hold for the composite integers of the form $N = pq^{2k}$ for $k > 0$. These kind of moduli are known to be used in a variant of RSA called Takagi's RSA [15], which provides faster decryption.

A. Bogdanov and S. Sanadhya (Eds.): SPACE 2012, LNCS 7644, pp. 144–152, 2012.

Multi-Prime Φ-Hiding Assumption has been proposed by Kiltz et al [8] in Crypto 2010, where they obtained standard model instantiations of RSA-OAEP by constructing a lossy trapdoor permutation from RSA, based on the multi-prime generalization of the Φ-Hiding Assumption.

In their protocol, they considered Multi-Prime RSA with modulus $N = p_1 \cdots p_m$. The prime e is chosen such that e divides $p_1 - 1, \ldots, p_{m-1} - 1$. The lossy trapdoor permutation then relies on the Multi-Prime Φ-Hiding Assumption, which states that

"it is hard to decide whether e divides $p_i - 1$ for all but one prime factor of N".

1.2   Cryptanalysis of Multi-Prime Φ-Hiding Assumption

Kiltz et al. [8] present a cryptanalysis of the Multi-Prime Φ-Hiding Assumption using the idea of Herrmann et al. [3]. Note that if e divides all p_i-1 for $1 \leq i \leq m$, $N \equiv 1 \bmod e$. It gives a polynomial time distinguisher. To decide if e is Multi-Prime Φ-Hidden in N, consider the system of equations

$$ex_1 + 1 \equiv 0 \bmod p_1, \quad ex_2 + 1 \equiv 0 \bmod p_2, \quad \ldots, \quad ex_{m-1} + 1 \equiv 0 \bmod p_{m-1}.$$

Kiltz et al. [8] construct a polynomial equation

$$e^{m-1}\left(\prod_{i=1}^{m-1} x_i\right) + \cdots + e\left(\sum_{i=1}^{m-1} x_i\right) + 1 \equiv 0 \bmod \prod_{i=1}^{m-1} p_i \qquad (1)$$

by multiplying all given equations. Then they linearize the polynomial and solve it using a result due to Herrmann and May [3]. However, the work of [3] provides an algorithm with runtime exponential in the number of unknown variables. So for large m, the idea of [3] will not be efficient.

Note that the coefficients of the polynomial in Equation (1) are all powers of e. In Africacrypt 2011, Herrmann [4] used this fact to improved the attack of [8], by considering a different linearization to reduce the number of variables. Suppose we have $(ex_1 + 1)(ex_2 + 1)(ex_3 + 1) \equiv 0 \bmod p_1p_2p_3$. Then instead of considering the polynomial equation

$$e^3 x_1 x_2 x_3 + e^2(x_1 x_2 + x_1 x_3 + x_2 x_3) + e(x_1 + x_2 + x_3) + 1 \equiv 0 \bmod p_1 p_2 p_3, \quad (2)$$

Herrmann [4] considered the polynomial equation

$$e^2 x + ey + 1 \equiv 0 \bmod p_1 p_2 p_3, \qquad (3)$$

where $x = ex_1 x_2 x_3 + x_1 x_2 + x_1 x_3 + x_2 x_3$ and $y = x_1 + x_2 + x_3$ are the unknowns. One positive aspect of Equation (3) is that it has only two variables x, y instead of the original three x_1, x_2, x_3. On the negative side, the size of the variable x is increased by a factor of e compared to the original unknown variables x_1, x_2, x_3. However, the problem remains similar, as finding x, y allows one to factor N. In [4], it has been proved that considering Equation (3) provides an advantage in terms of better upper bounds on x_i than in the case with Equation (2).

In the general case, instead of considering the polynomial $e^{m-1}y_{m-1} + e^{m-2}y_{m-2} + \cdots + ey_1 + 1$ over the variables $y_1, \ldots, y_{m-1}$ with root

$$(y_1, \ldots, y_{m-1}) = \left(\prod_{i=1}^{m-1} x_i, \ldots, \sum_{i=1}^{m-1} x_i \right),$$

Herrmann [4] considered the polynomial $e^2x + ey + 1$ over the variables x, y with root

$$(x_0, y_0) = \left(e^{m-3} \prod_{i=1}^{m-1} x_i + \cdots + \sum_{j>i} x_i x_j, \sum_{i=1}^{m-1} x_i \right) \quad (4)$$

to obtain the improvement over the work of Kiltz et al. [8].

1.3   Our Contribution

In summary, we obtain the following attempts in analyzing the Multi-Prime Φ-Hiding problem for an RSA modulus with m factors:

- Kiltz et al. [8] used linear modular equation over $m-1$ variables. As in this case dimension of lattice will be exponential in $m-1$, method will not be efficient at all for large value of m.
- Herrmann [4] considered a bivariate modular polynomial. This makes the method efficient for larger values of m too. Also this gives better theoretical bound than the work of [8].

However, note that in Equation (4) used by Herrmann [4], the variable y_0 is much smaller than x_0. It was already indicated in [3] that one may get better bound for these unbalanced variables. However this option has not been analyzed systematically in the literature till date. In this work we analyzed this issue carefully, and use the unbalanced property of the variables x, y to get further improvement over the result of Herrmann [4].

Our improvement originates from providing extra shifts over the variable y in the same bivariate scenario as Herrmann has considered. This reduces the lossiness of the work of Kiltz et al. [8] even further. In Table 1, we present the impact of our result on the work of Kiltz et al.

Table 1. Impact of our results on the lossiness of Kiltz et al. [8] for different values of m, with 2048 bit N and for 80 bit security.

Value	Lossiness in the work of Kiltz et al. [8]		
of m	Before the work of [4]	After the work of [4]	After our work
4	806	778	**768**
5	872	822	**778**

We present the main technical result, our attack on the Multi-Prime Φ-Hiding Assumption, in Section 2, and the respective experimental results in Section 3. But before proceeding with the main content of this paper, let us state the following two existing results on lattices that will be required for our work. We first state the following due to Howgrave-Graham [5].

Lemma 1. *Let* $h(x_1, x_2) \in \mathbb{Z}[x_1, x_2]$ *be the sum of at most* ω *monomials. Suppose that* $h(x_1^{(0)}, x_2^{(0)}) \equiv 0 \pmod{N^m}$ *where* $|x_1^{(0)}| \le X_1, |x_2^{(0)}| \le X_2$ *and*

$$||h(x_1 X_1, x_2 X_2)|| < \frac{N^m}{\sqrt{\omega}}.$$

Then $h(x_1^{(0)}, x_2^{(0)}) = 0$ *over the integers.*

We also note that the basis vectors of an LLL-reduced basis fulfill the following property (as explained in [9]).

Lemma 2. *Let* L *be an integer lattice of dimension* ω. *The LLL algorithm applied to* L *outputs a reduced basis of* L *spanned by* $\{v_1, \ldots, v_\omega\}$ *with*

$$||v_1|| \le ||v_2|| \le 2^{\omega/4} \det(L)^{1/(\omega-1)}$$

in polynomial time of dimension ω *and the bit size of the entries of* L.

Now we move on to the main technical content of this paper.

2   Our Attack on the Multi-Prime Φ-Hiding Assumption

Note that from Equation (4), value of y_0 is much smaller than x_0. We use this fact to get the improvement over [4]. Our approach is exactly the same as [3] except that we use extra shifts over the variable y.

Theorem 1. *Let* $N = p_1 \cdots p_m$ *be a Multi-Prime RSA modulus where* p_i *are of same bit size for* $1 \le i \le m$. *Let* e *be a prime such that* $e > N^{\frac{1}{m}-\delta}$. *Then one can solve Multi-Prime hidden* Φ *problem in polynomial time if there exist two non-negative real numbers* τ_1, τ_2 *such that*

$$\Psi(\tau_1, \tau_2, \delta, m) = 3\tau_1\tau_2^2 m - \tau_2^3 m + 3\tau_1^2 \delta m - 6\tau_1\tau_2 m + 3\tau_2^2 m + 9\tau_1\delta m +$$
$$6\tau_1\tau_2 + 3\tau_1 m - 3\tau_2 m + 3\delta m - 9\tau_1 + 3\tau_2 + m - 3 < 0.$$

Proof. To decide if e is Multi-Prime Φ-hidden in N, consider the system of equations

$$ex_1 + 1 \equiv 0 \bmod p_1, \quad \ldots, \quad ex_{m-1} + 1 \equiv 0 \bmod p_{m-1}$$

As p_i are of same bit size and $e > N^{\frac{1}{m}-\delta}$, we have $|x_i| \le N^\delta$ for $1 \le i \le m - 1$. Denote $P = \prod_{i=1}^{m-1} p_i$. Now consider the polynomial $g(x, y) = e^2 x + ey + 1$. It is clear that $g(x_0, y_0) \equiv 0 \bmod P$ where

$$(x_0, y_0) = \left(e^{m-3} \prod_{i=1}^{m-1} x_i + \cdots + \sum_{j>i} x_i x_j, \sum_{i=1}^{m-1} x_i \right).$$

From $g(x, y)$, one can obtain a polynomial $f(x, y)$ of the form $x + a_1 y + a_2$ such that $f(x_0, y_0) \equiv 0 \bmod P$. It is clear that the size of x_0 is dominated by the term $e^{m-3} x_1 \dots x_{m-1}$. Hence we have

$$|x_0| \leq N^{(m-3)(\frac{1}{m} - \delta) + (m-1)\delta} = N^{\frac{m-3}{m} + 2\delta} \text{ and } |y_0| \leq (m-1)N^\delta.$$

As $m < \log_2 N$, we can assume $|y_0| \leq N^\delta$, neglecting $m - 1$ term.

Take two integers $X = N^{\frac{m-3}{m} + 2\delta}$ and $Y = N^\delta$. Clearly X, Y is an upper bound on x_0, y_0 respectively.

Now consider the set of polynomials

$$g_{k,i}(x, y) = y^i f^k(x, y) N^{\max\{s-k, 0\}},$$

for $k = 0, \dots, u$, $i = 0, \dots, u - k + t$ where u is a positive integer and s, t are non-negative integers. Note that $g_{k,i}(x_0, y_0) \equiv 0 \bmod P^s$.

Now we construct the lattice L spanned by the coefficient vectors of the polynomials $g_{k,i}(xX, yY)$. One can check that the dimension of the lattice L is

$$\omega = \sum_{k=0}^{u} \sum_{i=0}^{u-k+t} 1 \approx \frac{u^2}{2} + tu.$$

The determinant of L is

$$\det(L) = \prod_{k=0}^{u} \prod_{i=0}^{u-k+t} X^k \cdot Y^i \cdot N^{\max\{s-k, 0\}} = X^{s_X} Y^{s_Y} N^{s_N}, \tag{5}$$

where $s_X = \sum_{k=0}^{u} \sum_{i=0}^{u-k+t} k \approx t\frac{u^2}{2} + \frac{u^3}{6}$,

$$s_Y = \sum_{k=0}^{u} \sum_{i=0}^{u-k+t} i \approx \frac{t^2 u}{2} + \frac{tu^2}{2} + \frac{u^3}{6},$$

$$s_N = \sum_{k=0}^{u} \sum_{i=0}^{u-k+t} \max\{s - k, 0\} \approx \frac{us^2}{2} + \frac{ts^2}{2} - \frac{s^3}{6} \text{ assume } t \leq u.$$

Using Lattice reduction on L by LLL algorithm [9], one can find two non-zero vectors b_1, b_2 such that $||b_1|| \leq ||b_2|| \leq 2^{\frac{1}{4}} (\det(L))^{\frac{1}{\omega - 1}}$. The vectors b_1, b_2 are the coefficient vector of the polynomials $h_1(xX, yY), h_2(xX, yY)$ with

$$||h_1(xX, yY)|| = ||b_1|| \quad \text{and} \quad ||h_2(xX, yY)|| = ||b_2||,$$

where $h_1(x, y), h_2(x, y)$ are the integer linear combinations of the polynomials $g_{k,i}(x, y)$. Hence

$$h_1(x_0, y_0) \equiv h_2(x_0, y_0) \equiv 0 \bmod P^s.$$

To find two polynomials $h_1(x,y), h_2(x,y)$ which share the root (x_0, y_0) over integers, using Lemma 1 we get the condition

$$2^{\frac{\omega}{4}} (det(L))^{\frac{1}{\omega - 1}} < \frac{P^s}{\sqrt{\omega}}. \tag{6}$$

Note that ω is the dimension of the lattice which we may consider as small constant with respect to the size of P and the elements of L. Thus, neglecting $2^{\frac{\omega}{4}}$ and $\sqrt{\omega}$, we can rewrite (6) as $det(L) < (P^s)^{\omega - 1}$. In general [7], it is considered that the condition $det(L) < (P^s)^{\omega}$ is sufficient to find two polynomials $h_1(x,y), h_2(x,y)$ such that $h_1(x_0, y_0) = h_2(x_0, y_0) = 0$.

Under the assumption that $gcd(h_1, h_2) = 1$, we can collect the root (x_0, y_0) using resultant method. Let $t = \tau_1 u$ and $s = \tau_2 u$ where τ_1, τ_2 are non-negative reals. Now putting the value of t, s in the condition $det(L) < P^{s\omega}$, we get the required condition. $\square$

Remark 1. For fixed δ and m, we will take the partial derivative of Ψ with respect to τ_1, τ_2 and equate each of them to 0 to get non-negative solutions of τ_1, τ_2. Given any pair of such non-negative solutions, if Ψ is less than zero, then for that δ, x_0, y_0 can be obtained efficiently.

Comparison with [4] and [8]: In the work of [4], the variable τ_1 was not involved. The bound on δ in [4] is presented as

$$\delta < \frac{2}{3\sqrt{m^3}}.$$

The bound on δ in the work of [8] is

$$\delta < \frac{2\left(m^{-1/(m-1)} - m^{-m/(m-1)}\right)}{m(m-1)}.$$

In Table 2, we present a comparison of the upper bounds of δ as in our case (Theorem 1) with those in [4] and [8], for different values of m.

From Table 2, it is clear that upper bound of δ in our case is higher than that of [4]. Hence our new attack solves the Multi-Prime Φ-Hiding Problem for more values of e. Also note that when m becomes larger, difference between the upper bound of δ in Theorem 1 and the upper bound of [4] increases.

Recently Tosu and Kunihiro [16] have studied Multi-Prime Φ-Hiding Problem. In [16, Section 4.4], authors have mentioned that their bound is same as Herrmann Method for $m = 3, 4, 5$. Hence for $m = 4, 5$, our method is better than that of [16]. Also when $m = 10$ with 4096 bit modulus, attack of [16] works when size of e is more than 314. However, in our case lower bound on size of e is $(0.1 - 0.0248) \times 4096 = 308$. Hence in this situation too, our method is better.

3   Experimental Results

We have implemented the programs in SAGE 3.1.1 over Linux Ubuntu 8.04 on a laptop with Dual CORE Intel(R) Pentium(R) D CPU 1.83 GHz, 2 GB RAM and 2 MB Cache. The results are as follows.

Table 2. Comparison of upper bound on δ between our result and those of [4] and [8]

Value	Upper bound on δ		
of m	Our result (Theorem 1)	Herrmann [4]	Kiltz et al. [8]
3	0.1283	0.1283	0.1283
4	0.0835	0.0833	0.0787
5	0.0608	0.0596	0.0535
6	0.0475	0.0454	0.0388
7	0.0387	0.0360	0.0295
8	0.0327	0.0295	0.0232
9	0.0283	0.0247	0.0188
10	0.0248	0.0211	0.0154

In Table 3, we present few experimental results for different values of m.

Table 3. Experimental results for different values of m with 2048 bit N

m	δ	u	t	s	$\dim(L)$	time (sec.)
3	0.120	8	2	4	63	209.35
4	0.085	7	3	4	60	206.90
5	0.065	7	3	4	60	140.42
6	0.054	6	4	4	56	87.34
7	0.044	6	4	4	56	73.97
8	0.039	5	4	5	51	45.41
9	0.034	5	4	5	51	39.05
10	0.029	5	4	5	51	30.43

From Table 3, it may be noted that for $m \geq 4$ we get much better results in the experiments than the theoretical bounds. This is because, for the parameters we consider here, the shortest vectors may belong to some sublattice. However, the theoretical calculation in Theorem 1 cannot capture that and further, identifying such optimal sublattice seems to be difficult.

In [8, Proposition 5.3], Kiltz et al. proved that their construction provides $(m-1)(1/m - \delta - \epsilon) \log_2 N$ bits of lossiness for $\epsilon \log_2 N$ bit security. One can achieve 80 bit security by taking $\epsilon = 0.04$ for 2048 bit modulus. In this case for $m = 3, 4, 5$, Kiltz et al. showed that one can obtain 676, 778 and 822 bits lossiness respectively, considering the upper bound of δ as $\frac{2}{3\sqrt{m^3}}$. For $m = 4$, we achieve the bound of δ as 0.085. This implies that actual lossiness in this case is less than $3 \times (0.25 - 0.085 - 0.04) \times 2048 = 768$ instead of 778. Similarly for $m = 5$, actual lossiness is less than 778 instead of 822.

In many situations (like [6]), experimental results provide better bound than the theoritical prediction. Thus, any concrete parameters given in [8] for instantiating RSA-OAEP that depends on the Multi-Prime Φ-Hidding problem should need experimental verification.

3.1 Weak Encryption Exponents

Recently in Africacrypt 2012, Nitaj [12] proposed a new class of weak Encryption Exponents for RSA. The flow of the algorithm in [12] that exploits these weak keys is as follows.

- Consider that the public exponent e satisfies $ex+y \equiv 0 \bmod p$ with $|x| < N^{\gamma}$, $|y| < N^{\delta}$ and $ex + y \neq 0 \bmod N$.
- Use the idea of [3] to find x, y.
- Calculate $p = \gcd(N, ex + y)$

Nitaj [12] proved that when $\gamma + \delta \leq \frac{\sqrt{2}-1}{2} \approx 0.207$, one can find x, y in the above algorithm. He also estimated that the number of such encryption exponent is at least $N^{0.707-\epsilon}$ where $\epsilon \to 0$.

Note that when γ and δ are not same, i.e., x, y are of different bitsizes, we can improve the upper bound of $\gamma + \delta$ using our idea as in Theorem 1. In fact, when either $\gamma \to 0$ or $\delta \to 0$, it is already mentioned in [3] that the upper bound of $\gamma + \delta$ would be 0.25. Hence we have the following result, using an approach similar to that of [12, Theorem 5].

Theorem 2. *Let $N = pq$ be an RSA modulus with $q < p < 2q$. Let public exponent e satisfy $ex + y \equiv 0 \bmod p$ with $|x| < N^{\epsilon_1}$ and $|y| < N^{\delta}$. If $ex + y \neq 0 \bmod N$ and $\delta < 0.25$, one can factor N in polynomial time where $\epsilon_1 \to 0$. The number of such encryption exponents is atleast $N^{0.75-\epsilon}$, where $\epsilon \to 0$.*

4   Conclusion

In this paper we consider Multi-Prime Φ-Hidding problem and provide better theoretical results than what were obtained by Herrmann [4]. For $m \geq 4$, the experimental results are better than our theoretical prediction. In this direction, an interesting open problem would be to provide a theoretical model for constructing the sublattice.

References

1. Coppersmith, D.: Small Solutions to Polynomial Equations and Low Exponent Vulnerabilities. Journal of Cryptology 10(4), 223–260 (1997)
2. Fujioka, A., Okamoto, T., Miyaguchi, S.: ESIGN: An Efficient Digital Signature Implementation for Smart Cards. In: Davies, D.W. (ed.) EUROCRYPT 1991. LNCS, vol. 547, pp. 446–457. Springer, Heidelberg (1991)

3. Herrmann, M., May, A.: Solving Linear Equations Modulo Divisors: On Factoring Given Any Bits. In: Pieprzyk, J. (ed.) ASIACRYPT 2008. LNCS, vol. 5350, pp. 406–424. Springer, Heidelberg (2008)
4. Herrmann, M.: Improved Cryptanalysis of the Multi-Prime ϕ - Hiding Assumption. In: Nitaj, A., Pointcheval, D. (eds.) AFRICACRYPT 2011. LNCS, vol. 6737, pp. 92–99. Springer, Heidelberg (2011)
5. Howgrave-Graham, N.: Finding Small Roots of Univariate Modular Equations Revisited. In: Darnell, M.J. (ed.) Cryptography and Coding 1997. LNCS, vol. 1355, pp. 131–142. Springer, Heidelberg (1997)
6. Jochemsz, E., May, A.: A Polynomial Time Attack on RSA with Private CRT-Exponents Smaller Than $N^{0.073}$. In: Menezes, A. (ed.) CRYPTO 2007. LNCS, vol. 4622, pp. 395–411. Springer, Heidelberg (2007)
7. Jochemsz, E., May, A.: A Strategy for Finding Roots of Multivariate Polynomials with New Applications in Attacking RSA Variants. In: Lai, X., Chen, K. (eds.) ASIACRYPT 2006. LNCS, vol. 4284, pp. 267–282. Springer, Heidelberg (2006)
8. Kiltz, E., O'Neill, A., Smith, A.: Instantiability of RSA-OAEP under Chosen-Plaintext Attack. In: Rabin, T. (ed.) CRYPTO 2010. LNCS, vol. 6223, pp. 295–313. Springer, Heidelberg (2010), http://eprint.iacr.org/2011/559
9. Lenstra, A.K., Lenstra Jr., H.W., Lovász, L.: Factoring polynomials with rational coefficients. Mathematische Annalen 261, 515–534 (1982)
10. Lenstra Jr., H.W.: Factoring integers with elliptic curves. Annals of Mathematics 126, 649–673 (1987)
11. May, A.: Secret Exponent Attacks on RSA-type Schemes with Moduli $N = p^r q$. In: Bao, F., Deng, R., Zhou, J. (eds.) PKC 2004. LNCS, vol. 2947, pp. 218–230. Springer, Heidelberg (2004)
12. Nitaj, A.: A New Attack on RSA and CRT-RSA. In: Mitrokotsa, A., Vaudenay, S. (eds.) AFRICACRYPT 2012. LNCS, vol. 7374, pp. 221–233. Springer, Heidelberg (2012)
13. Rivest, R.L., Shamir, A., Adleman, L.: A Method for Obtaining Digital Signatures and Public Key Cryptosystems. Communications of ACM 21(2), 158–164 (1978)
14. Schridde, C., Freisleben, B.: On the Validity of the Φ-Hiding Assumption in Cryptographic Protocols. In: Pieprzyk, J. (ed.) ASIACRYPT 2008. LNCS, vol. 5350, pp. 344–354. Springer, Heidelberg (2008)
15. Takagi, T.: Fast RSA-type Cryptosystem Modulo $p^k q$. In: Krawczyk, H. (ed.) CRYPTO 1998. LNCS, vol. 1462, pp. 318–326. Springer, Heidelberg (1998)
16. Tosu, K., Kunihiro, N.: Optimal Bounds for Multi-Prime Φ-Hiding Assumption. In: Susilo, W., Mu, Y., Seberry, J. (eds.) ACISP 2012. LNCS, vol. 7372, pp. 1–14. Springer, Heidelberg (2012)

Adaptively Secure Efficient Lattice (H)IBE in Standard Model with Short Public Parameters

Kunwar Singh[1], C. Pandurangan[2], and A.K. Banerjee[1]

[1] Computer Science and Engineering Department
National Institute of Technology, Tiruchirappalli, India
{kunwar,banerjee}@nitt.edu
[2] Computer Science and Engineering Department
IIT Madras, Chennai, India
rangan@cse.iitm.ac.in

Abstract. Independent work by Chatterjee and Sarkar [9] and Naccache [16] provided a variant of Waters' IBE to reduce public parameters. The idea is to divide an l-bit identity into l' blocks of l/l' so that size of the vector $\overrightarrow{V}$ can be reduced from l elements of G to l' elements of G. We name this technique as blocking technique. This leads to some associated degradation in security reduction. In this paper our contribution is two fold: First we apply Waters' [21] idea to convert Agrawal et al. [1] selective-ID secure lattice HIBE to adaptive-ID secure HIBE then using blocking technique we reduce the public parameters. Second we present efficient lattice identity based encryption in standard model with smaller public key size which is variant of [1]. Using blocking technique our scheme reduces public key size by a factor of β at the cost of increasing $(\beta - lg(\beta))^2$ number of bits in q where q is size of field Z_q. There is an interesting trade-off between reducing the public parameter size and increase in the computational cost. For 160-bit identities we show that compared to scheme [1] the public parameter size can be reduced by almost 90% while increasing the computation cost by only 8.71% for appropriate choice of β.

Keywords: Lattice, Hierarchical Identity Base Encryption, Standard model, Learning with error(LWE).

1 Introduction

The concept of identity-based cryptosystem was introduced by Adi Shamir in 1984 [20]. In this new paradigm users' public key can be any string which uniquely identifies the user. For example email or phone number can be public key. As a result, it significantly reduces system complexity and cost of establishing public key infrastructure. Although Shamir constructed an identity-based signature scheme using RSA function but he could not construct an identity-based encryption and this became a long-lasting open problem. Only in 2001, Shamir's open problem was independently solved by Boneh and Franklin [6] and Cocks [11].

A. Bogdanov and S. Sanadhya (Eds.): SPACE 2012, LNCS 7644, pp. 153–172, 2012.
© Springer-Verlag Berlin Heidelberg 2012

First Canetti et al. [7] presented identity-based encryption in standard model. They proved the security of scheme in selective-ID model. In the selective-ID model the adversary must first declare which identity it wishes to be challenged before the global parameters are generated. Boneh and Boyen [4] then provided an efficient secure scheme in selective-ID model. Boneh and Boyen [5] describe a scheme that is fully secure in standard model, but their scheme is too inefficient to practical use. Finally, the first practical and fully secure IBE scheme was proposed by Waters [21] in the standard model under the Decisional Bilinear Diffie-Hellman assumption. However, one drawback was that the public parameters is very large: namely, the public parameters contain $l + 4$ group elements, where l is the size of the bit-string representing identities. In that scheme, if the identities are n-bit string then one needs $\overrightarrow{V}$ consists of n group elements. Independent work by Chatterjee and Sarkar [9] and Naccache [16] provided a variant of Waters' IBE. The idea is to divide an l-bit identity into l' blocks of l/l' so that size of the vector $\overrightarrow{V}$ can be reduced from l elements of G to l' elements of G. We name this technique as blocking technique. This leads to some associated degradation in security reduction.

The task of Public Key Generator (PKG) in IBE is to authenticate identity of the entity, generate the private key corresponding to identity of the entity and finally transmit the private key securely to the entity. In large network PKG has a burdensome job. So the notion of Hierarchical IBE (HIBE) was introduced in [13,14,5] to distribute the workload by delegating private key generation and identity authentication to lower-level PKGs. However, lower level PKGs do not have their own public parameters. Only root PKG has some set of public parameters.

Lattice based cryptogrphy have arisen in recent years. Lattice based cryptography are attractive due to their worst case hardness assumption and their potential resistance to quantum computers. Recently Regev [19] defined the learning with errors (LWE) problem and proved that it enjoys similar worst-case hardness properties, under a quantum reduction.

Based on LWE problem, Gentry et al. [18] constructed lattice based IBE scheme in random oracle model. Recently Cash et al. [8], Peikert [17], and Agarwal et al. [2] have constructed secure IBE in the standard model from LWE problem. Their construction view an identity as a sequence of bits and then assign a matrix to each bit, which resulted into less efficient scheme compared to Gentry et al.[18]. Recently Agarwal et al.[1] constructed a efficient lattice based selective-ID secure IBE scheme in standard model. They have considered identities as one chunk rather than bit-by-bit. As Water modified Boneh Boyen selective-ID secure IBE scheme (BB-IBE1)[5] to obtain an adaptive-ID (full model) secure IBE scheme [21], similarly Agarwal et al.[1] in their full version paper constructed an adaptive secure IBE using LWE problem. Similar to Waters [21], it has large public parameters of size l $n \times m$ matrices, where l is the size of the bit-string representing identities.

Recently Cash et al. [8] and Peikert [17] have constructed secure HIBE in the standard model using basis delegation technique. Their construction view an identity as a sequence of bits and then assign a matrix to each bit, which resulted into less efficient scheme. Recently Agarwal et al. [1] constructed a efficient lattice based secure HIBE scheme in standard model in weaker security notion i.e. selective-ID. They have considered identities as one chunk rather than bit-by-bit.

Our Contributions. Our contribution is two fold: First we apply Waters' [21] idea to convert Agrawal et al. [1] selective-ID secure lattice HIBE to adaptive-ID secure HIBE. Then using blocking technique we reduce the public parameters. Second one drawback of Agarwal et al. adaptive secure IBE scheme[1] was that the public parameters is very large: namely, the public parameters contain $l + 1$ $n \times m$ matrices, where l is the size of the bit-string representing identities. Using blocking technique we can reduce $n \times m$ matrices by factor β or public parameters is reduced by around factor β; encryption and decryption are almost as efficient as in [1]. This is associated with increase in size of q by 2^β where q is a prime number and size of field Z_q. We show that compared to scheme [1] the public parameter size can be reduced by almost 90% while increasing the computation cost by only 8.71% for appropriate choice of β.

2   Preliminaries

2.1   Hierarchical IBE and IBE

Here definitions and security model of HIBE and IBE are similar to [13,14,5,1]. User at depth l is defined by its tuple of ids : $(id/id_l) = (id_1, ..., id_l)$. The user's ancestors are the root PKG and the prefix of id tuples (users/lower level PKGs).

HIBE consists of four algorithms.

Setup$(d, \lambda:)$ On input a security parameter d(maximum depth of hierarchy tree) and λ, it outputs the public parameters and master key of root PKG.

Derive(PP,$(id/id_l), SK_{(id/id_l)}$): On input public parameters PP, an identity $(id/id_l) = (id_1, ..., id_l)$ at depth l and the private key $SK_{(id/id_{l-1})}$ corresponding to parent identity $(id/id_{l-1}) = (id_1, ..., id_{l-1})$ at depth $l - 1 \geq 0$ the algorithm outputs private key for the identity (id/id_l) at depth l.

If $l = 1$ then $SK_{(id/id_0)}$ is defined to be master key of root PKG.

The private key corresponding to an identity $(id/id_l) = (id_1, ..., id_l)$ at depth l can be generated by PKG or any ancestor (prefix) of an identity (id/id_l).

Encrypt(PP,(id/id_l),M): On input public parameters PP, an identity (id/id_l), and a message M outputs ciphertext C.

Decrypt(PP,$SK_{(id/id_l)}$,C): On input public parameters PP, a private key $SK_{(id/id_l)}$, and a ciphertext C outputs message M.

Identity Based Encryption. IBE is special case of HIBE when depth of hierarchy tree is one.

2.2   Adaptive-ID (Full) Security Model of HIBE and IBE

We define adaptive-ID security model using a game that the challenge ciphertext is indistinguisable from a random element in the ciphertext space. This property implies both semantic security and recipient anonymity. The game proceeds as follows.

Setup: The challenger runs Setup$(1^\lambda, 1^d)$ and gives the public parameters PP to adversary and keeps master key MK to itself.

Phase 1: The adversary issues a query for a private key for identity $(id/id_k) = (id_1, ..., id_k)$, $k \leq d$. Adversary can repeat this multiple times for different identities adaptivly.

Challenge: The adversary submits identity id^* and message M. Identity id^* and prefix of id^* should not be one of the identity query in phase 1. The challenger picks a random bit $r \in \{0, 1\}$ and a random ciphertext C. If $r = 0$ it sets the challenge ciphertext to $C^* := Encrypt(PP, id^*, M)$. If $r = 1$ it sets the challenge ciphertext to $C^* := C$. It sends C^* as challenge to the adversary.

Phase 2: Phase 1 is repeated with the restriction that the adversary can not query for id^* and prefix of id^*.

Guess: Finally, the adversary outputs a guess $r' \in \{0, 1\}$ and wins if $r = r'$.
    We refer an adversary A as an IND-ID-CPA adversary. We define the advantage of the adversary A in attacking an IBE scheme ξ as

$$Adv_{d,\xi,A}(\lambda) = |Pr[r = r'] - 1/2|$$

Definition 1. We say that depth d HIBE scheme ξ is adaptive-ID, indistinguishable from random if for all IND-ID-CPA PPT adversaries A we have $Adv_{d,\xi,A}(\lambda)$ is a negligible function.

Full Security Model of IBE. Security model of IBE is same as security model of HIBE with depth of hierarchy tree is one.

2.3   Integer Lattices

A lattice is defined as the set of all integer combinations

$$L(b_1, ..., b_n) = \left\{ \sum_{i=1}^{n} x_i b_i : x_i \in Z \text{ for } 1 \leq i \leq n \right\}$$

of n linearly independent vectors $b_1, ..., b_n \in R^n$. The set of vectors $\{b_1, ..., b_n\}$ is called a basis for the lattice. A basis can be represented by the matrix $B = [b_1, ..., b_n] \in R^{n \times n}$ having the basis vectors as columns. Using matrix notation, the lattice generated by a matrix $B \in R^{n \times n}$ can be defined as $L(B) = \{Bx : x \in Z^n\}$, where Bx is the usual matrix-vector multiplication. The determinant of a lattice is the absolute value of the determinant of the basis matrix $det(L(B)) = |det(B)|$.

Definition 2. For q prime, $A \in Z_q^{n \times m}$ and $u \in Z_q^n$, define:

$$\Lambda_q(A) := \{e \in Z^m \ s.t. \ \exists \ s \in Z_q^n \ where \ A^T s = e \ (mod \ q)\}$$

$$\Lambda_q^{\perp}(A) := \{e \in Z^m \ s.t. \ Ae = 0 \ (mod \ q)\}$$

$$\Lambda_q^u(A) := \{e \in Z^m \ s.t. \ Ae = u \ (mod \ q)\}$$

2.4 The Gram-Schmidt Norm of a Basis

Let S be a set of vectors $S = \{s_1, ..., s_k\}$ in R^m. We use the following notation:

- $|S|$ denotes the L_2 length of the longest vector in S, i.e. $\|S\| := max_i |s_i|$ for $1 \leq i \leq k$.
- $\tilde{S} := \{\tilde{s}_1, ..., \tilde{s}_k\} \subset R^m$ denotes the Gram-Schmidt orthogonalization of the vector $s_1, ..., s_k$ taken in that order.

We refer to $\|\widetilde{S}\|$ as the Gram-Schmidt norm of S.

Lemma 1([15, Lemma 7.1]). Let Λ be an m-dimensional lattice. There is a deterministic polynomial-time algorithm that, given an arbitrary basis of Λ and a full-rank set $S = \{s_1, ..., s_m\}$ in Λ, returns a basis T of Λ satisfying

$$\|\widetilde{T}\| \leq \|\widetilde{S}\| \quad and \quad \|T\| \leq \|S\| \sqrt{m}/2$$

Theorem 1([3, Theorem 3.2]). Let $q \geq 3$ be odd and $m := \lceil 6n \log q \rceil$.
  There is probabilistic polynomial-time algorithm TrapGen(q, n) that outputs a pair $(A \in Z_q^{n \times m}, S \in Z^{n \times m})$ such that A is statistically close to a uniform matrix in $Z_q^{n \times m}$ and S is a basis for $\Lambda_q^{\perp}(A)$ satisfying

$$\|\widetilde{S}\| \leq O(\sqrt{n \log q}) \quad and \quad \|S\| \leq O(n \log q)$$

with all but negligible probability in n.

Theorem 2([17]). For $i = 1, 2, 3$ let A_i be a matrix in $Z_q^{n \times m_i}$ and $A = (A_1|A_2|A_3)$. Let T_2 be a basis of $\Lambda_q^{\perp}(A_2)$. There is deterministic polynomial time algorithm ExtendBasis(A_1, A_2, A_3, T_2) that outputs a basis T for $\Lambda_q^{\perp}(A)$ such that $\|\widetilde{T}\| = \|\widetilde{T_2}\|$.

2.5 Discrete Gaussians

Let L be a subset of Z^m. For any vector $c \in R^m$ and any positive parameter $\sigma \in R > 0$, define:

$\rho_{\sigma,c}(x) = exp(-\pi \frac{\|x-c\|}{\sigma^2})$: a Gaussian-shaped function on R^m with center c and parameter σ,

$\rho_{\sigma,c}(L) = \sum_{x \in L} \rho_{\sigma,c}(x)$: the (always converging) $\rho_{\sigma,c}$ over L,

$D_{L,\sigma,c}$: the discrete Gaussian distribution over L with parameters σ and c,

$$\forall y \in L \ , \ D_{L,\sigma,c} = \frac{\rho_{\sigma,c}(y)}{\rho_{\sigma,c}(L)}$$

we abbreviate $\rho_{\sigma,0}$ and $D_{L,\sigma,c}$ will most often be defined over the Lattice $L = \Lambda_q^{\perp}$ for a matrix $A \in Z_q^{n \times m}$ or over a coset $L = t + \Lambda_q^{\perp}(A)$ where $t \in Z^m$.

Lemma 2 ([17, Lemma 2.4]). Let $q \geq 2$ and let A be a matrix in $Z_q^{n \times m}$ with $m > n$. Let T_A be a basis for $\Lambda_q^{\perp}(A)$ and $\sigma \geq \|\widetilde{T_A}\| \omega(\sqrt{(\log m)})$. Then for $c \in R^m$ and $u \in Z_q^n$:

1. There is a PPT algorithm SampleGaussian (A, T_A, σ, c) that returns $x \in \Lambda_q^{\perp}(A)$ drawn from a distribution statistically close to $D_{\Lambda,\sigma,c}$.
2. There is a PPT algorithm SamplePre (A, T_A, u, σ) that returns $x \in \Lambda_q^u(A)$ sampled from a distribution statistically close to $D_{\Lambda_q^u,\sigma}$.

2.6 The LWE Hardness Assumption

The LWE (learning with error) hardness assumption is defined by Regev[19].

Definition 3. Consider a prime q, a positive integer n, and a distibution χ over Z_q, typically taken to be normal distribution. The input is a pair (A, v) from an unspecified challenge oracle $\bigcirc$,where $A \in Z_q^{m \times n}$ is chosen uniformly. v is chosen uniformly from Z_q^m or chosen to be $As + e$ for a uniformly chosen $s \in Z_q^n$ and a vector $e \in Z_q^m$. When v is chosen to be $As + e$ for a uniformly chosen $s \in Z_q^n$ and a vector $e \in Z_q^m$ an unspecified challenge oracle $\bigcirc$ is a noisy pseudo-random sampler $\bigcirc_s$. When v is chosen uniformly an unspecified challenge oracle $\bigcirc$ is a truly random sampler $\bigcirc_\$$.

Goal of the adversary is to distinguish with some non-negligible probability between these two cases.

Or we say that an algorithm A decides the (Z_q, n, χ)-LWE problem if $|Pr[A^{\bigcirc_s} = 1] - Pr[A^{\bigcirc_\$} = 1]|$ is non-negligible for a random $s \in Z_q^n$.

Definition 4. Consider a real parameter $\alpha = \alpha(n) \in \{0, 1\}$ and a prime q. Denote by $T = R/Z$ the group of reals $[0,1)$ with addition modulo 1. Denote by ψ_α the distribution over T of a normal variable with mean 0 and standard deviation $\alpha/\sqrt{2\pi}$ then reduced modulo 1. Denote by $\lfloor x \rceil = \lfloor x + \frac{1}{2} \rfloor$ the nearest integer to the real $x \in R$. We denote by $\overline{\psi}_\alpha$ the discrete distribution over Z_q of the random variable $\lfloor qX \rceil \bmod q$ where the random variable $X \in T$ has distribution ψ_α.

Lemma 3([3]). Suppose that $m > (n + 1) \log_2 q + w(\log n)$ and that q is prime. Let A,B be matrices chosen uniformly in $Z_q^{n \times m}$ and let R be an $m \times m$ matrix chosen uniformly in $\{1, -1\}^{m \times m} \bmod q$. Then, for all vectors w in Z_q^m, the distribution $(A, AR, R^T w)$ is statistically close to the distribution $(A, B, R^T w)$.

3 Sampling Algorithms

Let A and B be matrices in $Z_q^{n \times m}$ and let R be a matix in $\{-1, 1\}^{m \times m}$. Our construction makes use of matrices of the form $F = (AR + B) \in Z_q^{n \times 2m}$ and we will need to sample short vectors in $\Lambda_q^u(F)$ for some u in Z_q^n. This can be done either a SampleLeft or SampleRight algorithm.

3.1   SampleLeft Algorithm ([1,Theorem 17])

SampleLeft Algorithm(A, M_1, T_A, u, σ):

Inputs:

a rank n matrix A in $Z_q^{n \times m}$ and a matrix M_1 in $Z_q^{n \times m_1}$.

a "short" basis T_A of $\Lambda_q^{\perp}(A)$ and a vector $u \in Z_q^n$.

a gaussian parameter $\sigma > \|\widetilde{T_A}\|\omega(\sqrt{(\log(m + m_1))})$.

Output: Let $F_1 := (A|M_1)$. The algorithm outputs a vector $e \in Z^{m+m_1}$ sampled from a distribution statistically close to $D_{\Lambda_q^u(F_1), \sigma}$.

3.2   SampleRight Algorithm ([1,Theorem 18])

SampleRight Algorithm$(A, B, R, T_B, u, \sigma)$:

Inputs:

matrices A in $Z_q^{n \times k}$ and B in $Z_q^{n \times m}$ where B is rank n,

a matrix R in $Z_q^{k \times m}$, let $s_R := \|R\|$.

a basis T_B of $\Lambda_q^{\perp}(B)$ and a vector $u \in Z_q^n$,

a gaussian parameter $\sigma > \|\widetilde{T_B}\|s_R\omega(\sqrt{\log(m)})$.

Output: Let $F_2 := (A|AR + B)$. The algorithm outputs a vector $e \in Z^{m+k}$ sampled from a distribution statistically close to $D_{\Lambda_q^u(F_2), \sigma}$.

4   Adaptively Secure HIBE Scheme in Standard Model

The new scheme is a variant of Agarwal et al. HIBE [1], but with short public parameter. In our scheme, identity id/id_l is represented as $id/id_l = (id_1, ..., id_l)$ $= ((b_{1,1}||...||b_{1,l''}), ..., (b_{l,1}||...||b_{l,l''}))$ where id_i is l' bit string and $b_{i,j}$ is $l'/l'' = \beta$ bit string. We apply Waters'[21] idea to convert Agrawal et al. [1] selective-ID secure lattice HIBE to adaptive-ID secure HIBE. Then using blocking technique we reduce the public parameters.

4.1   The HIBE Construction

Now we describe our adaptive secure HIBE scheme as follows.

Setup(d, λ). On input a security parameter λ and a maximum hierarchy depth d, set the parameters $q, n, m, \overline{\sigma}, \overline{\alpha}$ as specified in section 4.2 below. The vectors $\overline{\sigma}$ and $\overline{\alpha}$ live in R^d and we use σ_l and α_l to refer to their t-th coordinate. Next do following.

1. Use algorithm TrapGen(q, n) to generate a matrix $A_0 \in Z_q^{n \times m}$ and a short basis T_{A_0} for $\Lambda_q^{\perp}(A_0)$ such that $\|\widetilde{T_{A_0}}\| \leq O(\sqrt{n \log q})$.
2. Select $l''d + 1$ uniformly random $n \times m$ matrices $A_{1,1}, ..., A_{1,l''}, ..., A_{d,1}, ..., A_{d,l''}$ and $B \in Z_q^{n \times m}$.
3. Select a uniformly random n - vector $u \in Z_q^n$.
4. Output the public parameters and master key,
   PP $= A_{1,1}, ..., A_{1,l''}, ..., A_{d,1}, ..., A_{d,l''}$ and B, MK $= (T_{A_0})$.

Derive(PP,(id/id_l), $SK_{(id/id_{(l-1)})}$). On input public parameters PP, a private key $SK_{(id/id_{l-1})}$ corresponding to an identity (id/id_{l-1}) at depth $l-1$ the algorithm outputs a private key for the identity (id/id_l) at depth l. From equation (1),

$$F_{id/id_l} = (A_0| \sum_{i=1}^{l''} A_{1,i}b_{1,i} + B|...| \sum_{i=1}^{l''} A_{l,i}b_{l,i} + B) \tag{1}$$

Or $F_{id/id_l} = (F_{id/id_{l-1}}|\sum_{i=1}^{l''} A_{l,i}b_{l,i} + B)$ Given short basis $SK_{(id/id_{(l-1)})}$ for $\Lambda_q^{\perp}(F_{id/id_{l-1}})$ and F_{id/id_l} as defined in (1), we can construct short basis $SK_{(id/id_l)}$ for $\Lambda_q^{\perp}(F_{id/id_l})$ by invoking

$$S \longleftarrow \text{SampleLeft}(F_{id/id_{l-1}}, \sum_{i=1}^{l''} A_{l,i}b_{l,i} + B, SK_{(Id/id_{(l-1)})}, 0, \sigma_l)$$

and output $SK_{(id/id_l)} \longleftarrow S$.

The private key corresponding to an identity $(id/id_l) = (id_1,...,id_l)$ at depth l can be generated by PKG or any ancestor (prefix) of an identity (id/id_l) by repeatedly calling SampleLeft algorithm.

Encrypt(PP,Id,b). On input public parameters PP, an identity (id/id_l) of depth l and a message $b \in \{0,1\}$,do following:

1. Build encryption matrix

$$F_{id/id_l} = (A_0| \sum_{i=1}^{l''} A_{1,i}b_{1,i} + B||...|| \sum_{i=1}^{l''} A_{l,i}b_{l,i} + B) \in Z_q^{n\times(l+1)m}.$$

2. Choose a uniformly random vector $s \xleftarrow{R} Z_q^n$.
3. Choose ll'' uniformly random matrices $R_{i,j} \xleftarrow{R} \{-1,1\}^{m\times m}$ for $i = 1,...,l$ and $j = 1,...,l''$. Define $R_{id}^1 = \sum_{i=1}^{l''} b_{1,i}R_{1,i}||...||\sum_{i=1}^{l''} b_{l,i}R_{l,i} \in Z^{m\times ll''m}$
4. Choose noise vector $x \xleftarrow{\bar{\psi}_{\alpha_l}} Z_q$, $y \xleftarrow{\bar{\psi}_{\alpha_l}^m} Z_q^m$ and $z \leftarrow R_{id}^T y \in Z_q^{lm}$,
5. Output the ciphertext,

$$CT = \left(C_0 = u_0^T s + x + b\lfloor\frac{q}{2}\rfloor, C_1 = F_{id}^T s + \begin{bmatrix} y \\ z \end{bmatrix}\right) \in Z_q \times Z_q^{(l+1)m}$$

Decrypt(PP,$SK_{(id/id_l)}$,CT). On input public parameters PP, a private key SK_{id/id_l}, and a ciphertext $CT = (C_0, C_1)$, do following.

---

[1] In security proof, R_{id} is used to answer adversary's secret key query and also for valid challenge ciphertext, error vector has to be $\begin{bmatrix} y \\ R_{id}^T y \end{bmatrix}$.

1. Set $\tau_l = \sigma_l \sqrt{m(l+1)} w(\sqrt{log(lm)})$. Then $\tau_l \geq \|\widetilde{SK}\| w(\sqrt{log(lm)})$.
2. $e_{id} \longleftarrow SamplePre(F_{id/id_l}, SK_{(Id/id_l)}, u, \tau_l)$ Then $F_{id}e_{id} = u$ and $\|e_{id}\| \leq \tau_l \sqrt{m(l+1)}$
3. Compute $C_0 - e_{id}^T C_1 \in Z_q$.
4. compare w and $\lfloor \frac{q}{2} \rfloor$ treating them as integers in Z. If they are close, i.e., if $|w - \lfloor \frac{q}{2} \rfloor| < \frac{q}{4}$ in Z, output 1 otherwise output 0.

During Decryption:
$$w_0 = C_0 - e_{id}^T C_1 = b\lfloor \tfrac{q}{2} \rfloor + x - e_{id}^T \begin{bmatrix} y \\ z \end{bmatrix}.$$

4.2 Parameters and Correctness

We have during decryption, $w = C_0 - e_{id}^T c_1 = b\lfloor \frac{q}{2} \rfloor + x - e_{id}^T \begin{bmatrix} y \\ z \end{bmatrix}$.
And $x - e_{id}^T \begin{bmatrix} y \\ z \end{bmatrix}$ is called error term.

Lemma 4. Norm of the error term is bounded by $[q2^\beta l'' l^2 \sigma_l m \alpha_l w(\sqrt{\log m}) + O(2^\beta l'' l^2 \sigma_l m^{3/2})]$.

Proof: Lemma is essentially same as lemma 32 of [1] except now R_{id} is uniformly random matrix in $\{-2^\beta l'', 2^\beta l''\}^{m \times lm}$. So now $|R_{id}|$ will be equal to $2^\beta l'' R_{id}$. Hence error term will have extra factor $2^\beta l''$.

Now, for the system to work correctly we need to ensure that:

- the error term is less than $q/5$ i.e. $\alpha_l < [2^\beta l'' l^2 \sigma_l m w(\sqrt{\log m})]^{-1}$ and $q = \Omega(2^\beta l'' l^2 \sigma_l m^{3/2})$.
- that TrapGen can operate (i.e $m > 6n \log q$).
- That σ_l is sufficiently large for SimpleLeft and SimpleRight (i.e. $\sigma_l > \|\widetilde{T_B}\| s_R w(\sqrt{\log m})$) $= 2^\beta l'' \sqrt{l} m w(\sqrt{\log m})$.
- that Regev's reduction applies (i.e. $(q2^\beta)^l > 2Q$, where Q is the number of identity queries from the adversary)

To satisfy these requirements we set the parameters $(q, m, \sigma_l, \alpha_l)$ as follows, taking n to be the security parameter:

$$m = 6n^{1+\delta}, \qquad\qquad\qquad \sigma_l = l'' \sqrt{l} m w(\sqrt{\log n})$$

$$q = max((2Q/2^\beta)^{1/l}, (2^\beta l'')^2 l^{2.5} m^{2.5} w(\sqrt{\log n})), \alpha_l = [(2^\beta l'')^2 l^{2.5} m^2 w(\sqrt{\log m})]^{-1} \tag{2}$$

From above requirements, we need $q = (2^\beta l'')^2 l^{2.5} m^{2.5} w(\sqrt{\log n})$.

4.3 Security Proof

Our proof of theorem will require an abort-resistant hash functions defined as follows.

Abort-Resistant Hash Functions

Definition 5. Let $H = \{\hbar : X \longrightarrow Y\}$ be family of hash functions from X to Y where $0 \in Y$. For a set of $Q + 1$ inputs $\overline{x} = (x_0, x_1, ..., x_Q) \in X^{Q+1}$, define the non-abort probability of $\overline{x}$ as the quantity

$$\alpha(\overline{x}) = Pr\left[\hbar[x_0] = 0 \ \wedge \ \hbar[x_1] \neq 0 \ \wedge ... \wedge \ \hbar[x_Q] \neq 0\right]$$

where the probability is over the random choice of $\hbar$ in H.

We say that H is $(Q, \alpha_{min}, \alpha_{max})$ abort-resistance if for all $\overline{x} = (x_0, x_1, ..., x_Q) \in X^{Q+1}$ with $x_0 \notin \{x_1, ..., x_Q\}$ we have $\alpha(\overline{x}) \in [\alpha_{min}, \alpha_{max}]$.

we use the following abort-resistant hash family very similar to [1].
For a prime q let $(Z_q^{l''})^* = Z_q^{l''} - \{0^l\}$ and define the family

$$H : \{\hbar : ((Z_q^{l''})^*|...|(Z_q^{l''})^*) \longrightarrow (Z_q|...|Z_q)\}$$

$$\hbar(id) = \hbar(id_1|...|id_l) = (1 + \sum_{i=1}^{l''} h_{1,i}b_{1,i})|...|(1 + \sum_{i=1}^{l''} h_{l,i}b_{l,i}) \qquad (3)$$

where $h_{k,i}$ and $b_{k,i}$ are defined in section 4.1.

Lemma 5. let q be a prime and $0 < Q < q$. Then the hash family H defined in (4) is $(Q, \frac{1}{q^l}(1 - \frac{Q}{q^l}), \frac{1}{q^l})$ abort-resistant.

Proof: The proof is samilar to [1]. Consider a set of $\overline{id}$ of $Q+1$ inputs $id^0, ..., id^Q$ in $(Z_q^{l''})^*$ where $id^0 \notin \{id^1, ..., id^Q\}$ and $id^i = \{id_1, ..., id_l\}$. Since number of functions in $H = (q2^\beta)^{l''l}$ and for $i = 0, ..., Q + 1$ let S_i be the set of functions $\hbar$ in H such that $\hbar(id^i) = 0$. Hence number of such functions $= |S_i| = \frac{(q2^\beta)^{l''l}}{q^l}$.

And $\frac{|S_0 \wedge S_j|}{q^{2l}} \leq \frac{(q2^\beta)^{l''l}}{}$ for every $j > 0$. Number of functions in H such that $\hbar(id^0) = (0|...|0)$ but $\hbar(id^i) \neq 0$ for $i = 1, ..., Q. = |S|$ and

$$|S| = |S_0 - (S_1 \vee ...S_Q)| \geq |S_0| - \sum_{i=1}^{Q} |S_0 \wedge S_i|$$

$$\geq \frac{(q2^\beta)^{l''l}}{q^l} - Q\frac{(q2^\beta)^{l''l}}{q^{2l}}$$

Therefore the no-abort probability of identities is atleast equal to $\frac{\frac{(q2^\beta)^{l''l}}{q^l} - \frac{Q(q2^\beta)^{l''l}}{q^{2l}}}{(q2^\beta)^{l''l}} = \frac{1}{q^l}(1 - \frac{Q}{q^l})$ Since $|S| \leq |S_0|$, so the no-abort probability is atmost $\frac{|S_0|}{(q2^\beta)^{l''l}} = \frac{1}{q^l}$.

Now we show that our lattice-based IBE construction is indistinguishable from random under a adaptive identity attack (IND-ID-CPA).

Theorem 3. The Full-HIBE scheme with parameters$(q, n, m, \bar{\sigma}, \bar{\alpha})$ as in (3) is IND-ID-CPA secure provided that the $(Z_q, n, \bar{\psi}_{\alpha_d})$-LWE assumptions holds.

Or Suppose there exists a probabilistic algorithm A (Adversary) that wins the IND-ID-CPA game with advantage ϵ, making no more than $Q \leq q^l/2$ adaptive chosen-identity queries. Then there is a probabilistic algorithm B that solves the $(Z_q, n, \bar{\psi}_\alpha)$-LWE problem in about the same time as A and with $\epsilon' \geq \epsilon/4q^l$.

Proof. Here proof is very similar to proof of theorem 25 and theorem 33 of [1]. We assume that W_i denote the event that the adversary correctly guessed the challenge bit, namely that $r = r'$ at the end of Game i. The adversary's advantage in Game i is $|Pr[W_i] - \frac{1}{2}|$. We proceed the proof in a sequence of games.

Game 0. Game 0 is the IND-ID-CPA game between an attacker against our scheme and IND-ID-CPA challenger.

Game 1. In Game 0 the challenger generates public parameters PP by choosing $ll'' + 2$ uniformly random matrices $A_0, A_{1,1}, ..., A_{l,l''}, B$ in $Z_q^{n \times m}$. In Game 1, challenger generates uniformly random matrices A_0, B same as Game 0. But challenger generates matrices $A_{k,j}, k \in [1, l]$ and $i \in [1, l'']$ in slightly different way. The Game 1 challenger choose $R_{k,d}^*, k \in [1, l], i \in [1, l'']$ at the set up phase and chooses ll'' random scalars $h_{k,i} \in Z_q$ for $k \in [1, l], i \in [1, l'']$. Next it constructs the matrices $A_{k,i}$ as

$$A_{k,i} \longleftarrow A_0 R_{k,i} + h_{k,i} B$$

By lemma 3, the distribution $(A_0, A_0 R^*, (R^*)^T y)$ and $(A_0, (A'_{1,1}|, ..., |A'_{l,l''}),$ $(R^*)^T y)$ are statistically close, where $R^* = (R'_{1,1}|...|R'_{l,l''}) \in Z_q^{m \times lm}$ and $A'_{k,i}, i \in [1, l''], k \in [1, l]$ are uniformly independent matrices in $Z_q^{n \times m}$. It follows that with $z = (R_{id}^*)^T y$ the distributions $A_0, A_0 R_{1,1}^*, ..., A_0 R_{l,l''}^*$ and $A_0, A_{1,1}^*, ..., A_{l,l''}^*$ are statistically close. So in the attacker'view, Game 0 is same as Game 1. This shows that

$$Pr[W_0] = Pr[W_1] \tag{4}$$

Game 2. We introduce an abort event that is independent of the adversary's view and rest is same as Game 1. We will see in later part of the proof that abort event is directly related to abort-resistant family of hash functions H introduced in Lemma(6). From Lemma(6) H is a $\{Q, \alpha_{min}.\alpha_{max}\}$ abort-resistant family, where $\alpha_{min} = \frac{1}{q^l}(1 - \frac{Q}{q^l})$. For $\alpha_{min} \geq 0$ we must have $q^l > Q$. We assume $q^l \geq 2Q$ so $\alpha_{min} \geq \frac{1}{2q^l}$. For a $(Q + 1)$-tuple of identities I $= (id^*, id^1, ..., id^Q)$, Game 2 challenger behaves as follows:

- The setup phase is identical to Game 1 except that the challenger also chooses a random hash function $\hbar \in H$ and keeps it to itself.
- The challenger responds to identity queries and issues the challenge ciphertext exactly as in Game 1.

- In the final guess phase, the challenger now does following:
  1. **Abort check:** The challenger checks if $H(id^*) = 0$ and $H(id^i) \neq 0$ for $i = 1, ..., Q$, where identity id^* is the challenge identity and $id^* \notin \{id^1, ..., id^Q\}$. If not, it returns random bit from $\{0,1\}$ and game is aborted. Adversary does not know about abort condition i.e. H.
  2. **Artificial abort:** This technique was introduced by Waters [21]. Abort condition could be correlated with the adversary's query. The goal of the artificial abort step is to make the probability of abort "independent" of the adversaries queries by ensuring that in all cases its probability of abort is the maximum possible. Function $\gamma(id^*, id^1, ..., id^Q)$ or $\gamma(I)$ is defined in such a way that when there is no artificial abort $\gamma(I)$ is zero else $\gamma(I) = 1$. When $\gamma(I) = 1$, challenger returns random bit from $\{0,1\}$ and game is aborted.

  If game is not aborted, the attacker outputs its guess $r' \in \{0,1\}$ for r.

Let $\epsilon(I)$ be the probability that an abort (either real or artificial) does not happen when the adversary makes these queries. Let ϵ_{max} and ϵ_{min} be scalars such that $\epsilon(I) \in [\epsilon_{min}, \epsilon_{max}]$ for all $(Q + 1)$ tuples of identities I.

Lemma 6 (Lemma 28 of [1]). For $i = 1, 2$ let W_i be the event that $r = r'$ at the end of Game i. Then

$$\left| Pr[W_2] - \frac{1}{2} \right| \geq \epsilon_{min} \left| Pr[W_1] - \frac{1}{2} \right| - 1/2(\epsilon_{max} - \epsilon_{min}).$$

Obviously $[\epsilon_{max} - \epsilon_{min}] = [\alpha_{max} - \alpha_{min}]$, when there was no artificial abort. With artificial abort, $(\epsilon_{min} - \epsilon_{max})$ is less than $\alpha_{min} |Pr[W_1] - \frac{1}{2}|$ and therefore

$$\left| Pr[W_2] - \frac{1}{2} \right| \geq 1/2.\alpha_{min} \left| Pr[W_1] - \frac{1}{2} \right| \geq (1/4q^l) \left| Pr[W_1] - \frac{1}{2} \right|. \quad (5)$$

Game 3. Game 3 differs from Game 2 how A_0 and B are chosen. In Game 3, A_0 is generated as a random matrix in $Z_q^{n \times m}$. Matrix B is generated by using algorithm TrapGen, which returns random matrix B in $Z_q^{n \times m}$ and a Trapdoor T_B for $\Lambda_q^\perp(B)$. From adversary's point of view, Game 2 and Game 3 are identical, hence adversary's advantage against Game 2 and Game 3 will be same. So

$$Pr[W_2] = Pr[W_3] \quad (6)$$

Game 4. In Game 4 the challenge ciphertext (C_0^*, C_1^*) is always chosen as a random independent element in $Z_q \times Z_q^{2m}$. Rest is same as Game 3. Since ciphertext is random element, hence Adversary's advantage against Game 4 is zero.

Now we have to show that Game 3 and Game 4 are computationally indistinguishable. We can show it in following way.

Suppose there exist an Adversary who can distinguish Games 3 and 4 with non-negligible then simulator can construct an algorithm which can solve LWE hard problem.

Reduction from LWE. In instance of LWE a sampling oracle $\bigcirc$ is provided. Sampling oracle $\bigcirc$ can be either truly random $\bigcirc_\$$ or a noisy pseudorandom $\bigcirc_s$ for some secret random $s \in Z_q^n$.

Instance. Simulator request from $\bigcirc$ and receives a fresh pair $(u_i, v_i) \in Z_q^n \times Z_q$ for each $i = 0, ..., m$.

Setup. B constructs the system's public parameters PP as follows:

1. The random matrix $A_0 \in Z_q^{n \times m}$ is constructed by assembling LWE sample u_i for all $i = 1, ..., m$, where i^{th} column of A is u_i.
2. Public random n-vector u_0 is the zeroth LWE sample.
3. Rest of public parameters are constructed as in Game 3.

Queries. Matrices A_0 and B are generated as in Game 3. Since B was generated using KeyGen algorithm so challenger knows trapdoor T_B. Matrices $A_{k,i}$ are constructed as in Game 1.

$$A_{k,i} = A_0 R_{k,i} + h_{k,i} B \quad for \ k = 1, ..., l \ and \ i = 1, ..., l''. \tag{7}$$

where all the matrices $R_{k,i}$ are random in $\{1, -1\}^{m \times m}$ and $h_{k,i}$ is a random scalar coefficient in Z_q. Encryption matrix to encrypt to an identity $id = (id_1, ..., id_l)$ at depth $l \leq d$ is

$$F_{id/id_l} = (A_0 | \sum_{i=1}^{l''} A_{1,i} b_{1,i} + B || ... || \sum_{i=1}^{l''} A_{d,i} b_{d,i} + B) \tag{8}$$

Substituting the value of matrices $A_{k,i}$ from equation(7)

$$F_{id/id_l} = (A_0 | A_0(\sum_{i=1}^{l''} R_{1,i} b_{1,i}) + B(1 + \sum_{i=1}^{l''} h_{1,i} b_{1,i}) || ...$$

$$|| A_0(\sum_{i=1}^{l''} R_{l,i} b_{l,i}) + B(1 + \sum_{i=1}^{l''} h_{l,i} b_{l,i}))$$

Or $\quad F_{id} = (A_0 | A_0 R_{id} + B h_{id}) \quad$ where $R_{id} = \sum_{i=1}^{l''} R_{1,i} b_{1,i} || ... || \sum_{i=1}^{l''} R_{l,i} b_{l,i}$
and $B_{id} = B \hbar_{id} = (1 + \sum_{i=1}^{l''} h_{1,i} b_{1,i}) || ... || (1 + \sum_{i=1}^{l''} h_{l,i} b_{l,i})$
If h_{id} is not equal to zero then challenger responds the private key query of $id = (id^1, id^2, ..., id^l)$ by running

$$SK_{id} \longleftarrow \text{SampleRight}(A_0, B_{id}, R_{id}, T_B, 0, \sigma_l)$$

and sending SK_{id} to A. h_{id} is equal to zero will be part of abort resistant hash function.

Challenge. Adversary declares target identity $id^* = (id_1, id_2, ..., id_l)$ and message bit $b^* \in \{0, 1\}$. Simulator B creates challenge ciphertext for the target identity as follows:

1. Let $v_0, ..., v_m$ be entries from LWE instance. Set

$$v^* = \begin{pmatrix} v_0 \\ v_1 \\ \vdots \\ v_m \end{pmatrix} \in Z_q^m$$

2. Blind the message bit by letting

$$C_0^* = v_0 + b^* \lfloor \frac{q}{2} \rceil \in Z_q$$

3. Let

$$R_{id^*} = (R_1^* | ... | R_l^*)$$

where

$$R_{j^*} = \sum_{j=1}^{l''} R_{i,j} b_{i,j}$$

and set

$$C_1^* = \begin{pmatrix} v^* \\ (R_{id^*})^T v^* \end{pmatrix} \in Z_q^{m+lm}$$

4. Choose a random bit $r \leftarrow \{0,1\}$. If $r = 0$ send $CT^* = (C_0^*, C_1^*)$ to the adversary. If $r = 1$ choose a random $(C_0, C_1) \in Z_q \times Z_q^{m+lm}$ and send (C_0, C_1) to the adversary.

When the LWE oracle is pseudorandom then $F_{id^*} = (A_0 | A_0 \overline{R}_{id^*})$ since $h_{id^*} = 0$ and

$$v^* = A_0^T s + y$$

for some random noise vector $y \in Z_q^m$ distributed as $\bar{\psi}_\alpha^m$. Therefore

$$C_1^* = \begin{pmatrix} A_0^T s + y \\ (A_0 R_{id^*})^T s + (R_{id^*})^T y \end{pmatrix} = (F_{id^*})^T s + \begin{pmatrix} y \\ (R_{id^*})^T y \end{pmatrix}$$

Above C_1^* is a valid C_1 part of challenge ciphertext. Again $C_0^* = u_0^T + x + b^* \lfloor \frac{q}{2} \rceil$ is also a valid C_0 part of challenge ciphertext. Therefore (C_0^*, C_1^*) is valid challenge ciphertext as in Game 3.

When LWE oracle is random oracle, v_0 is uniform in Z_q and v^* is uniform in Z_q^m. Therefore challenge ciphertext is always uniform in $Z_q \times Z_q^{2m}$ as in Game 4.

Guess. Adversary is again allowed to make private key extraction query as in Game 3 except prefix of id^*. Then Adversary guess if it is valid ciphertext (Game 3) or random string (Game 4). Hence simulator's advantage in solving LWE hard problem is same as Adversary's advantage in distinguishing valid ciphertext (Game 3) and random string (Game 4). Since $Pr[W_4] = 1/2$, So

$$|Pr[W_3] - Pr[W_4]| = |Pr[W_3] - \frac{1}{2}| \leq \text{LWE-adv(B)} \tag{9}$$

Combining equation (4),(5),(6) and (9), we get

$$|Pr[W_0] - \frac{1}{2}| \leq 4q^l \text{ LWE-adv(B)}$$

5   New Full-IBE Scheme in Standard Model

The new scheme is a variant of Agarwal et al. IBE [1], but with short public parameter. In Agrawal et al. IBE scheme identities are represented as l-bit string. Because of this representation, scheme requires l $n \times m$ matrices. In our scheme, identity id is represented as id $= (b_1, ..., b_{l'})$, where each b_i is an $l/l' = \beta$ bit string.

5.1   The New Full-IBE Construction

Now we describe our new Full-IBE Scheme in the standard model as follows.

Setup(λ). On input a security parameter λ, set the parameters q, n, m, σ, α as specified in section 5.2 below. Next do following.

1. Use algorithm TrapGen(q, n) to generate a matrix $A_0 \in Z_q^{n \times m}$ and a short basis T_{A_0} for $\Lambda_q^\perp(A_0)$ such that $\|\widetilde{T_{A_0}}\| \leq O(\sqrt{n \log q})$.
2. Select $l' + 1$ uniformly random $n \times m$ matrices $A_1, A_2, ..., A_{l'}, B \in Z_q^{n \times m}$.
3. Select a uniformly random n - vector $u \in Z_q^n$.
4. Output the public parameters and master key,
   PP $= (A_1, A_2, ..., A_{l'}, B, u)$, MK $= (T_{A_0})$.

Extract(PP,MK,Id). On input public parameters PP, a master secret key MK, and an identity id $= (b_1, ..., b_{l'})$, where each b_i is an $l/l' = \beta$ bit string.

1. Let $A_{id} = B + \sum_{i=1}^{l'} b_i A_i \in Z_q^{n \times m}$.
2. Sample $e \in Z_q^{2m}$ as $e \longleftarrow SampleLeft(A_0, A_{id}, T_{A_0}, u, \sigma)$.
3. Output $SK_{id} = e \in Z^{2m}$.

Let $F_{id} = (A_0|A_{id})$, then $F_{id}.e = u$ in Z_q and e is distributed as $D_{\Lambda_q^u(F_{id}), \sigma}$ by lemma 2.

Encrypt(PP,Id,b). On input public parameters PP, an identity id, and a message $b \in \{0, 1\}$, do following:

1. Let $A_{id} = B + \sum_{i=1}^{l'} b_i A_i \in Z_q^{n \times m}$ and $F_{id} = (A_0|A_{id}) \in Z_q^{n \times 2m}$.
2. Choose a uniformly random $s \xleftarrow{R} Z_q^n$.
3. Choose l' uniformly random matrices $R_i \xleftarrow{R} \{-1, 1\}^{m \times m}$ for $i = 1, ..., l'$ and define $R_{id}2 = \sum_{i=1}^{l'} b_i R_i \in \{-l'(2^\beta - 1), ..., l'(2^\beta - 1)\}$.
4. Choose noise vectors $x \xleftarrow{\overline{\psi}_\alpha} Z_q$, $y \xleftarrow{\overline{\psi}_\alpha^m} Z_q^m$ and $z \longleftarrow R_{id}^T y \in Z_q^m$,
5. Set $C_0 \longleftarrow u^T s + x + b\lfloor \frac{q}{2} \rfloor \in Z_q$ and $C_1 \longleftarrow F_{id}^T s + \begin{bmatrix} y \\ z \end{bmatrix} \in Z_q^{2m}$ and .
6. Output the ciphertext CT $= (C_0, C_1) \in Z_q \times Z_q^{2m}$.

---

[2] In security proof, R_{id} is used to answer adversary's secret key query and also for valid challenge ciphertext, error vector has to be $\begin{bmatrix} y \\ R_{id}^T y \end{bmatrix}$.

Decrypt(PP,SK$_{id}$,CT). On input public parameters PP, a private key $SK_{id} = e_{id}$, and a ciphertext CT $= (C_0, C_1)$, do following.

1. Compute $w \leftarrow C_0 - e_{id}^T C_1 \in Z_q$. If they are close, i.e., if $|w - \lfloor \frac{q}{2} \rfloor| < q/4$ in Z, output 1 otherwise output 0.

During Decryption:
$$w_0 = C_0 - e_{id}^T C_1 = b\lfloor \tfrac{q}{2} \rfloor + x - e_{id}^T \begin{bmatrix} y \\ z \end{bmatrix}.$$

5.2   Parameters and Correctness

We have during decryption, $w = C_0 - e_{id}^T c_1 = b\lfloor \frac{q}{2} \rfloor + x - e_{id}^T \begin{bmatrix} y \\ z \end{bmatrix}$.
And $x - e_{id}^T \begin{bmatrix} y \\ z \end{bmatrix}$ is called error term.

Lemma 7. For an l-bit identity id $= (b_1, ..., b_{l'})$, where each b_i is an $l/l' = \beta$ bit string. Norm of the error term is bounded by $q\sigma 2^\beta l' m a\omega(\sqrt{\log m}) + O(\sigma 2^\beta l' m^{3/2})$.

Proof: The proof is identical to the proof of Lemma 22 in [1] except that matrix R is replaced by $R_{id} = \sum_{i=1}^{l'} b_i A_i$. Since $\|R_{id}\| \leq \sum_{i=1}^{l'} \|b_i\|\|A_i\|$ and by [1,theorem 15], $\|R\| \leq O(\sqrt{m})$.
So $\|R_{id}\| \leq O(2^\beta l' \sqrt{m})$. This leads to the extra factor $2^\beta l'$ in the error bound. Now, for the system to work correctly we need to ensure that:

- the error term is less than $q/5$ i.e. $\alpha < [\sigma 2^\beta l' m a\omega(\sqrt{\log m})]^{-1}$ and $q = \Omega(\sigma 2^\beta l' m^{3/2})$.
- that TrapGen can operate (i.e $m > 6n \log q$).
- That σ is sufficiently large for SimpleLeft and SimpleRight (i.e. $\sigma > \|\widetilde{T_B}\| 2^\beta l' \sqrt{m}\omega(\sqrt{\log m})) = 2^\beta l' \sqrt{m}\omega(\sqrt{\log m})$.
- that Regev's reduction applies (i.e. $q > 2Q$, where Q is the number of identity queries from the adversary)

To satisfy these requirements we set the parameters (q, m, σ, α) as follows, taking n to be the security parameter:

$$m = 6n^{1+\delta}, \qquad\qquad \sigma = 2^\beta l' \sqrt{m}\omega(\sqrt{\log n})$$

$$q = max(2Q, m^{2.5}(2^\beta l')^2 \omega(\sqrt{\log n})), \qquad \alpha = [2^\beta l' m\omega(\sqrt{\log m})]^{-1}. \qquad (10)$$

From above requirements, we need $q = m^{2.5}(2^\beta l')^2 \omega(\sqrt{\log n})$. But in [1], required value of $q = m^{2.5} l^2 \omega(\sqrt{\log n})$. In this scheme value of q is increased by $(2^\beta \frac{l'}{l})^2 = (\frac{2^\beta}{\beta})^2$. This means that when public parameters are reduced by factor β, the value of q is increased by $(\frac{2^\beta}{\beta})^2$ or number of bits in q is increased by $(\beta - lg(\beta))^2$.

5.3 Efficiency

Here efficiency analysis is similar to [9]. Difference between our scheme and scheme [1] is computation of A_{id} and R_{id}. Rest of the algorithm for key generation, encryption and decryption algorithms etc are same. Let $|Z_q|$ be the size of the representation of an element of Z_q. We assume that cost of adding two $n \times m$ matrices is approximately equal to $nm|Z_q|$. Cost of computing A_{id} is adding two $n \times m$ matrices and l' multiplication where each multiplication is multiplication of (l/l')-bit string and $n \times m$ matrix. On an average, cost of each such multiplication will be $l/2l'$ addition and $(l/l'-1)$ doubling. Hence, the total cost of computing A_{id} is l/l' addition and $(l-l')$ doubling. This cost is equal to $cnm(\frac{3l}{2} - l')|Z_q|$ for some constant c. This cost is minimum when $l' = l$ (as in [1]). Minimum value is $cnm\frac{l}{2}|Z_q|$. Maximum value is less than $cnm\frac{3l}{2}|Z_q|$. Cost of computing $F_{id}^T s$ is equal to $dnmn|Z_q|$ for some constant d. Cost of encryption is equal to $cnm(\frac{3l}{2} - l')|Z_q| + dnmn|Z_q|$. Cost of encryption in IBE [1] is equal to $cnm(\frac{l}{2})|Z_q| + dnmn|Z_q|$. Value of q is less than poly(n) assume n^5. If q is more than 512 bit then value of n is atleast 2^{100}, which is much greater than size of identity $l(160)$. So cost of encryption is $enmn|Z_q|$ for some constant e, which does not depend on l'. There is no effect of l' on computation of A_{id}. Similarly There is no effect of l' on computation of R_{id}. Hence there is no effect of l' on cost of key generation and encryption. Decryption algorithm is same in both scheme. Computational cost increases because of increase in value of q or size of $|Z_q|$.

5.4 Space/Time Trade-Off

Our scheme reduces public size by a factor β. The relative decrease in amount of space (expressed in percentage) required to store the public parameter in case of our scheme with respect to scheme [1] is equal to $\frac{l-l'}{l}$. Our scheme reduces public size by a factor of β at the cost of increasing value of q by a factor of $(\frac{2^\beta}{\beta})^2$ with same security as [1]. By making same security as [1], new q or q' is $q(\frac{2^\beta}{\beta})^2$. Size of $Z_{q'} = |Z_{q'}| = |Z_q| + (\beta - lg(\beta))^2$. Relative increase in encryption cost in case of our scheme with respect to [1] is $\frac{|Z_{q'} - Z_q|}{|Z_q|} = \frac{(\beta - lg(\beta))^2}{|Z_q|}$.

In table 1, we give the results for $l = 160$ and $|Z_q| = 512$ for different values of l' ranging from 8 to 64. Overall, we suggest $l' = 16$ to be good choice for implementing the protocol.

Table 1. Relative decrease in space and relative increase in time for different values of l'

l'	Relative decrease in space	Relative increase in time
8	95	48
16	90	8.71
32	80	1.40
64	60	0.27

5.5   Security Proof

Our proof of theorem will require an abort-resistant hash functions defined as follows.

Abort-Resistant Hash Functions([1])

Definition 6. Let $H = \{\hbar : X \longrightarrow Y\}$ be family of hash functions from X to Y where $0 \in Y$. For a set of $Q + 1$ inputs $\overline{x} = (x_0, x_1, ..., x_Q) \in X^{Q+1}$, define the non-abort probability of $\overline{x}$ as the quantity

$$\alpha(\overline{x}) = Pr\,[\hbar[x_0] = 0 \,\wedge\, \hbar[x_1] \neq 0 \,\wedge ... \wedge\, \hbar[x_Q] \neq 0]$$

where the probability is over the random choice of $\hbar$ in H.

We say that H is $(Q, \alpha_{min}, \alpha_{max})$ abort-resistance if for all $\overline{x} = (x_0, x_1, ..., x_Q) \in X^{Q+1}$ with $x_0 \notin \{x_1, ..., x_Q\}$ we have $\alpha(\overline{x}) \in [\alpha_{min}, \alpha_{max}]$.

we use the following abort-resistant hash family very similar to [1]. For a prime q let $(Z_q^{l'})^* = Z_q^{l'} - \{0^l\}$ and define the family

$$H : \{\hbar : ((Z_q^{l'})^*) \longrightarrow (Z_q)\}$$

$$\hbar(id) = (1 + \sum_{i=1}^{l'} h_i b_i) \in Z_q \tag{11}$$

where h_i and b_i are defined in section 4.1.

Lemma 8. Let q be a prime and $0 < Q < q$. Then the hash family H defined in (4) is $(Q, \frac{1}{q}(1 - \frac{Q}{q}), \frac{1}{q})$ abort-resistant.

Proof: The proof is very similar to [1]. Consider a set of $\overline{id}$ of $Q + 1$ inputs $id_0, ..., id_{\overline{Q}}$ in $(Z_q^{l'})^*$ where $id_0 \notin \{id_1, ..., id_Q\}$. For $i = 0, ..., Q + 1$ let S_i be the set of functions $\hbar$ in H such that $\hbar(id_i) = 0$. We know that number of such functions $= |S_i| = \frac{(q2^\beta)^{l'}}{q}$.

And $|S_0 \wedge S_j| \leq \frac{(q2^\beta)^{l'}}{q^2}$ for every $j > 0$. Number of functions in H such that $\hbar(id_0) = 0$ but $\hbar(id_i) \neq 0$ for $i = 1, ..., Q$. $= |S|$ and

$$|S| = |S_0 - (S_1 \vee, ..., S_Q)| \geq |S_0| - \sum_{i=1}^{Q} |S_0 \wedge S_i|$$

$$\geq \frac{(q2^\beta)^{l'}}{q} - Q\frac{(q2^\beta)^{l'}}{q^2}$$

Since number of functions in $H = (q2^\beta)^{l'}$, therefore the no-abort probability of identities is atleast equal to $\frac{\frac{(q2^\beta)^{l'}}{q} - Q\frac{(q2^\beta)^{l'}}{q^2}}{(q2^\beta)^{l'}} = \frac{1}{q}(1 - \frac{Q}{q})$ Since $|S| \leq |S_0|$, so the no-abort probability is atmost $\frac{|S_0|}{(q2^\beta)^{l'}} = \frac{1}{q}$.

Now we show that our lattice-based IBE construction is indistinguishable from random under a adaptive identity attack (IND-ID-CPA).

Theorem 4. The Full-HIBE Scheme with parameters$(q, n, m, \overline{\sigma}, \overline{\alpha})$ as in (10) is IND-ID-CPA secure provided that the $(Z_q, n, \overline{\psi}_{\alpha_d})$-LWE assumptions hold.

Or Suppose there exists a probabilistic algorithm A (Adversary) that wins the IND-ID-CPA game with advantage ϵ, making no more than $Q \leq q/2$ adaptive chosen-identity queries, then there is a probabilistic algorithm B that solves the $(Z_q, n, \overline{\psi}_\alpha)$-LWE problem in about the same time as A and with $\epsilon' \geq \epsilon/(4q)$.

Proof. Since limits of no-abort probability (Lemma 5) of identity is same as lemma 27 of [1] so security proof will be same as security proof of [1,theorem 25].

6   Conclusion

We have shown that by converting selective-ID HIBE to adaptive-ID HIBE security degradation is exponential in number of levels. In our efficient lattice based IBE scheme we have also shown that there is an interesting trade-off between reducing the public parameter size and increase in the value of q (computational cost). The main open problem in the construction of lattice based IBE protocols is to reduce the public parameter size without increasing the value of q(computational cost).

Acknowledgments. We would like to thank anonymous reviewer and PC chairs for their useful comments.

References

1. Agrawal, S., Boneh, D., Boyen, X.: Efficient Lattice (H)IBE in the Standard Model. In: Gilbert, H. (ed.) EUROCRYPT 2010. LNCS, vol. 6110, pp. 553–572. Springer, Heidelberg (2010)
2. Agrawal, S., Boyen, X.: Identity-based encryption from lattices in the standard model (2009) (manuscript), http://www.cs.stanford.edu/xb/ab09/
3. Alwen, J., Peikert, C.: Generating Shorter Bases for Hard Random Lattices. In: STACS 2009, pp. 75–86 (2009)
4. Boneh, D., Boyen, X.: Efficient Selective-ID Secure Identity-Based Encryption Without Random Oracles. In: Cachin, C., Camenisch, J.L. (eds.) EUROCRYPT 2004. LNCS, vol. 3027, pp. 223–238. Springer, Heidelberg (2004)
5. Boneh, D., Boyen, X.: Secure Identity Based Encryption Without Random Oracles. In: Franklin, M. (ed.) CRYPTO 2004. LNCS, vol. 3152, pp. 443–459. Springer, Heidelberg (2004)
6. Boneh, D., Franklin, M.: Identity-Based Encryption from the Weil Pairing. In: Kilian, J. (ed.) CRYPTO 2001. LNCS, vol. 2139, pp. 213–219. Springer, Heidelberg (2001)
7. Canetti, R., Halevi, S., Katz, J.: Chosen-Ciphertext Security from Identity-Based Encryption. In: Cachin, C., Camenisch, J.L. (eds.) EUROCRYPT 2004. LNCS, vol. 3027, pp. 207–222. Springer, Heidelberg (2004)
8. Cash, D., Hofheinz, D., Kiltz, E.: How to Delegate a Lattice Basis. IACR Cryptology ePrint Archive 2009, p. 351 (2009)

9. Chatterjee, S., Sarkar, P.: Trading Time for Space: Towards an Efficient IBE Scheme with Short(er) Public Parameters in the Standard Model. In: Won, D.H., Kim, S. (eds.) ICISC 2005. LNCS, vol. 3935, pp. 424–440. Springer, Heidelberg (2006)

10. Chatterjee, S., Sarkar, P.: HIBE With Short Public Parameters Without Random Oracle. In: Lai, X., Chen, K. (eds.) ASIACRYPT 2006. LNCS, vol. 4284, pp. 145–160. Springer, Heidelberg (2006)

11. Cocks, C.: An Identity Based Encryption Scheme Based on Quadratic Residues. In: IMA Int. Conf. 2001, pp. 360–363 (2001)

12. Dodis, Y., Ostrovsky, R., Reyzin, L., Smith, A.: Fuzzy Extractors: How to Generate Strong Keys from Biometrics and Other Noisy Data. SIAM J. Comput. 38(1), 97–139 (2008)

13. Gentry, C., Silverberg, A.: Hierarchical ID-Based Cryptography. In: Zheng, Y. (ed.) ASIACRYPT 2002. LNCS, vol. 2501, pp. 548–566. Springer, Heidelberg (2002)

14. Horwitz, J., Lynn, B.: Toward Hierarchical Identity-Based Encryption. In: Knudsen, L.R. (ed.) EUROCRYPT 2002. LNCS, vol. 2332, pp. 466–481. Springer, Heidelberg (2002)

15. Micciancio, D., Goldwasser, S.: Complexity of Lattice Problems: A Cryptographic Perspective. In: Engineering and Computer Science. The Kluwer International Series, vol. 671. Kluwer Academic Publishers, Boston (2002)

16. Naccache, D.: Secure and Practical Identity-Based Encryption. IACR Cryptology ePrint Archive 2005, p. 369 (2005)

17. Peikert, C.: Bonsai trees (or, arboriculture in lattice-based cryptography). Cryptology ePrint Archive, Report 2009/359 (2009)

18. Gentry, C., Peikert, C., Vaikuntanathan, V.: Trapdoors for hard lattices and new cryptographic constructions. In: STOC 2008, pp. 197–206 (2008)

19. Regev, O.: On lattices, learning with errors, random linear codes, and cryptography. In: STOC 2005, pp. 84–93 (2005)

20. Shamir, A.: Identity-Based Cryptosystems and Signature Schemes. In: Blakely, G.R., Chaum, D. (eds.) CRYPTO 1984. LNCS, vol. 196, pp. 47–53. Springer, Heidelberg (1985)

21. Waters, B.: Efficient Identity-Based Encryption Without Random Oracles. In: Cramer, R. (ed.) EUROCRYPT 2005. LNCS, vol. 3494, pp. 114–127. Springer, Heidelberg (2005)

Author Index